Mathematics and Reality

Mathematics and Reality

Mary Leng

OXFORD
UNIVERSITY PRESS

OXFORD

UNIVERSITY PRESS

Great Clarendon Street, Oxford OX2 6DP

Oxford University Press is a department of the University of Oxford.
It furthers the University's objective of excellence in research, scholarship,
and education by publishing worldwide. Oxford is a registered trade mark of
Oxford University Press in the UK and in certain other countries

British Library Cataloguing in Publication Data

Data available

Library of Congress Cataloging in Publication Data

Library of Congress Control Number: 2009943747

ISBN 978–0–19–928079–7 (Hbk)
ISBN 978–0–19–967468–8 (Pbk)

For my family

Acknowledgements

This book has had a long gestation period, and has benefited from discussions with a great many colleagues along the way. I cannot thank them all by name here, but will confine myself to mentioning a few whose contributions have been particularly valuable.

I started thinking seriously about this topic during my time as a postdoctoral researcher at the University of Toronto, the first half of which was spent as a visiting fellow in the Department of Logic and Philosophy of Science at the University of California at Irvine. I am grateful to Penelope Maddy, Mark Colyvan, and graduate students in our Philosophy of Applied Mathematics reading group at Irvine for setting me on this track, and to James Robert Brown, Ian Hacking, and Alasdair Urquhart at Toronto for continued intellectual support.

My thinking for the early chapters on naturalism fortuitously coincided with my visit to the University of British Columbia as a Visiting Junior Scholar at the Peter Wall Institute for Advanced Studies. During that visit I was invited to present a paper on my research to an audience of non-philosophers, and doing so helped me to step back from some of my philosophical preconceptions to think carefully about the question, 'Why naturalism?' I also benefited from discussions with Alan Richardson, at UBC, and Abraham Stone, who was also participating in the Visiting Junior Scholars programme, on the debate between Carnap and Quine.

Much of the work on this book was carried out while at Cambridge, as a research fellow, and I am grateful to the Master and Fellows of St John's College for supporting me in this research, both financially and intellectually. While at Cambridge I benefited greatly from the perceptive comments of a group of colleagues who kindly met with me to discuss my manuscript as it was being prepared. I am therefore particularly grateful to Arif Ahmed, David Liggins, Michael Potter, Peter Smith, and Florian Steinberger, as well as occasional members James Robert Brown and Cheryl Misak, for detailed comments on, and discussion of, my first draft.

The final version of this book differs quite significantly from the draft read by my Cambridge colleagues, in part due to our discussions, but also due to the generous and perceptive comments of Mark Balaguer and Mark Colyvan, who read the first version for Oxford University Press. The penultimate draft was read by my colleague at Liverpool, Stephen McLeod, and I am grateful to him for numerous suggestions which I was able to incorporate into the final version of the text.

Some of the material in this book is based on work that has appeared elsewhere in the form of articles. In particular, parts of Chapter 2 draw on my paper, 'Revolutionary fictionalism: a call to arms' (Leng 2005*c*); parts of Chapter 3 draw on my chapter, 'What's there to know? A fictionalist account of mathematical knowledge', from Leng, Paseau, and Potter (2007); and parts of Chapter 9 draw on the papers, 'Platonism and anti-platonism: why worry?' (Leng 2005*b*), and 'Mathematical explanation' (Leng 2005*a*). I am grateful to the publishers of the journals and volumes in which these appear for permitting the publication of material which overlaps with these papers.

This book is dedicated to my family, and my final thanks must go to my husband, Martin O'Neill, for support and encouragement always, and to my son, Thomas O'Neill, born during the final stages of redrafting, for sleeping enough to make the completion of this manuscript possible, and for smiling enough to make the process all the more enjoyable.

Contents

1

Introduction

A curious thing about the ontological problem is its simplicity. It can be put in three Anglo-Saxon monosyllables: 'What is there?' It can be answered, moreover, in a word—'Everything'—and everyone will accept this answer as true.

(Quine 1948: 1)

The central problem of this book is the problem of ontology, that is, the question of what there is. In particular, I am interested in the question of whether there are any mathematical objects, objects such as *numbers*, *functions*, and *sets*, to which many of our ordinary mathematical theories appear to refer. The axioms of number theory, for example, imply the existence of infinitely many mathematical objects, the natural numbers, 0, 1, 2, . . . Do we have any reason to believe those axioms, and hence to believe that the numbers apparently referred to by the numerals '0', '1', '2', . . . exist?

How on earth are we to go about answering this ontological question? What would it mean to say that we have, or lack, any *reason to believe* that numbers exist? When, indeed, does any belief (ontological or otherwise) count as being *reasonable*? A (deservedly) popular answer to this question in recent years has been that reasonable beliefs, for us, are just those beliefs that are considered warranted according to our current, best, scientific standards. On this view, if we want to know what we, as a community of inquirers, have reason to believe, we should look to our best scientific theories to answer this question. And in particular, if we want to know whether we have reason to believe that there are ϕs, we should consult our best available science, asking whether the standards of justification at work in our best scientific theorizing provide us with evidence for the claim that there are ϕs.

This approach to the question of what we have reason to believe is sometimes known as 'naturalism'. Its prominence in contemporary philosophy is largely down to W. V. Quine, who states its central tenet thus: 'What reality is like is the business of scientists, in the broadest sense, painstakingly to surmise; and what there is, what is real, is part of that question' (Quine 1960: 22). Why, one might ask, this deference to science and scientists (even in 'the broadest sense')? Simply because our current scientific theories are the result of our best efforts to understand and systematize our experience. In the words of one contemporary naturalist, 'Whatever the methods of science are, they represent the best methods known to us to work our way out of the only direct evidence we have for how things are, our empirical data, into a general understanding of how things are that explains why the empirical data is as it is' (Sklar 2003: 425). We trust our best science to tell us what we ought to believe that there is, just because that is all we have to go by.

The focus of this book will be the application of this naturalistic approach to ontology to the question of whether we have reason to believe in mathematical objects. The central question to be answered will thus be, Does our 'general understanding of how things are', as warranted according to our best scientific methods, provide us with reason to believe that there are mathematical objects such as numbers? I will answer this question in the negative: there is nothing in our current best scientific worldview that gives us reason to believe in the distinctive mathematical objects (such as numbers, functions, and sets) posited by many of our ordinary mathematical theories.

1.1. Naturalism and Mathematics

This conclusion should appear startling, for at least two reasons. First of all, given our naturalistic commitment to look to science *in the broadest sense* to tell us what there is, it might appear that this immediately requires us to believe that there are numbers. For should we not view pure mathematics as a science, indeed as one of our most successful arenas of inquiry into the nature of reality (in this case, specifically mathematical reality)? And if this is right, then surely it is obvious that we have reason to believe in very many mathematical objects. For surely the methods of pure mathematics not only give mathematicians reason *to* believe that many mathematical objects exist, but actually allow them to *prove* that this is the case. Many of our mathematical theorems concern the existence of objects: it is a theorem, for example, that there exist infinitely many prime numbers. So trusting 'science', broadly construed, to tell us what there is would appear to require us to believe that there are infinitely many prime numbers (and, indeed, to believe many further claims about the existence of mathematical objects of various sorts).

In response to this objection, I will argue that all is not as it seems with our mathematical practices. In particular, I will take issue with the view of pure mathematical inquiry as inquiry into the nature of mathematical reality. For, while mathematicians are indeed involved with proving conclusions on the basis of various axioms, this practice can be accounted for if we view it simply as inquiry into the *consequences* of various mathematical assumptions. To view mathematicians as inquiring into mathematical reality, into how things are with mathematical *objects*, we would have to show that their practice requires them to inquire into the question of the truth of their axioms. But, I will argue, nothing in our pure mathematical practices does require us to do this much. Indeed, from the perspective of pure mathematics, it would be perfectly acceptable to remain agnostic about (or even to *deny*) the truth of the axioms of the theory one is working with. And since nothing in our pure mathematical practices ever *requires* us to believe that our mathematical axioms are true, we should not view the mathematical reasons we sometimes have to speak *as if* those axioms are true (for the purposes, for example, of working out their consequences) as providing us with reasons to believe our pure mathematical theories.

In fact, although the denial that our pure mathematical practices generally provide us with reason to believe our mathematical theorems (as opposed to providing evidence that those theorems follow from our axioms) might seem jarring, it is widely (though not universally) accepted by *naturalists* that, *if* we have reasons to believe in mathematical objects, these reasons do not come from pure mathematics. So although I will have something to say about pure mathematics in this book, my main focus will actually be on the use of mathematical assumptions outside pure mathematics, in empirical applications. For it is in this context that the most prominent naturalistic argument for the existence of mathematical objects, the Quine–Putnam 'indispensability' argument, gets its bite. If I am to defend my claim that we have no reason to believe in any mathematical objects, it is this argument that I must tackle.

1.1.1. The Indispensability Argument

'Naturalism', the claim that we should look to science to discover what we have reason to believe (and, therefore, what we have reason to believe that there is), provides one premise of the 'indispensability argument' for the existence of mathematical objects. An additional premise is supplied by a further aspect of Quine's philosophy, according to which the unit of confirmation is the theory as a whole, and not individual theoretical components. In Quine's words, this premise is just that 'our statements about the external world face the tribunal of sense experience not individually but only as a corporate body' (Quine 1951: 41). Adopting this *holistic* view of confirmation means that, if we are committed, as naturalists are, to believing whatever statements are confirmed according to our best scientific standards, then this will require us to believe *all* the statements used to express our best, most successful, scientific theories. For the very fact that these theories are currently the best we have means that it is the truth of the statements that make up *those* theories that we should take to be confirmed by our best scientific standards. And if Quine is right that confirmation extends to theories as a whole, rather than to individual theoretical components, we are not at liberty to pick and choose which, amongst the statements used to express our best theories, we take to be confirmed by our theoretical successes.

Thus, the combination of naturalism with confirmational holism leads directly to scientific realism, where scientific realism is understood as the view that we ought (at least tentatively) to believe our best current scientific theories. For if confirmation in science *is* holistic, then whatever evidence we have for our scientific theories should be viewed as evidence for their truth in their entirety (and not, for example, as evidence just that they are empirically adequate: holism implies that we cannot pick off the 'confirmed' parts of our theories in this way). And if, as required by naturalism, we are committed to viewing our ordinary scientific standards of confirmation as providing us with genuine reason to believe the statements that are thereby considered to be confirmed, we will find ourselves committed to believing our current best scientific theories in their entirety (at least tentatively, until something better comes along).

Clearly, then, the combination of naturalism with confirmational holism requires us to believe in theoretical entities such as electrons. For in expressing our best confirmed empirical theories we indispensably make use of statements whose truth would require the existence of electrons. So if the confirmation our empirical theories receive extends to all the statements that are used to express those theories, then in particular that confirmation will extend to those of our theoretical statements that posit the existence of electrons. So if we undertake to believe whichever statements are confirmed by our ordinary empirical standards, we will be committed to believing that there are electrons.

Furthermore, at least if one further premise of the 'indispensability' argument is correct, the combination of naturalism with confirmational holism will likewise require us to believe in mathematical entities such as numbers, functions, and sets. For, this further premise hypothesizes, in expressing our best confirmed empirical theories we make indispensable use of statements whose truth would require the existence of numbers, functions, and sets. So if the confirmation our empirical theories receive extends to all the statements used to express those theories, then likewise that confirmation will extend to those of our theoretical statements that posit the existence of numbers, functions, and sets. Hence, if we undertake to believe whichever statements are confirmed by our ordinary empirical standards, we will find ourselves committed to believing that there are mathematical objects such as numbers.

Is this further premise correct? Are statements whose truth would require the existence of numbers, functions, and sets indispensable in formulating our best confirmed empirical theories? Setting aside the word 'indispensable', for the time being, it is certainly the case that in formulating ordinary empirical laws we do regularly make use of statements that are not just about electrons and other physical objects, but also about *sets* of those objects, and *functions* from them to mathematical objects such as real numbers. Thus, Hilary Putnam suggests that anyone who is tempted to assume that statements hypothesizing the existence of mathematical objects are inessential in empirical science should take a close look at Newton's law of universal gravitation. This law tells us that,

There is a force f_{ab} exerted by any body a on any other body b. The direction of the force f_{ab} is towards a, and its magnitude F is given by:

$$F = \frac{gM_aM_b}{d^2}$$

where g is a universal constant, M_a is the mass of a, M_b is the mass of b, and d is the distance which separates a and b.   (Putnam 1971: 338)

With its use of real numbers to represent forces and masses, the law of universal gravitation seems mathematical through and through.

One might of course object that the ultimate subject matter of this law is surely *non-mathematical*: it concerns the force exerted by any body a on any other body b. But as soon as we consider what the law says about this force and these bodies, we must concede that, read literally, the law posits the existence of numbers and functions as well as bodies and forces. For what does the law *say* about the force between the two bodies, exactly? Just that *there is a real number* F representing its magnitude as a multiple of some basic unit of force, and that this real number F is related (in the way the equation states) to the *real numbers* M_a and M_b representing the masses of a and b respectively, the *real number* d representing the distance between them, and the *real number* g representing the universal gravitational constant. Claiming that this law is true while simultaneously denying that there are any numbers would, as Putnam puts it, be like

trying to maintain that God does not exist and angels do not exist while maintaining at the very same time that it is an objective fact that God has put an angel in charge of each star and the angels in charge of each of a pair of binary stars were always created at the same time!   (Putnam 1975: 74)

Just as the truth of the claim 'God has put an angel in charge of each star' would require the existence of God and angels (as well as stars), the truth of the claim that, for example, 'there is a function M which represents the mass of any object a as a real number M_a' would requires the existence of functions and real numbers (as well as massive objects).

If, then, one wished to claim that statements whose truth would require the existence of mathematical objects are not essential in formulating our best empirical theories, then one would have to show that laws such as this one, which hypothesizes *real numbers* associated (by means of functions) with the objects *a* and *b* and representing properties such as their masses and the distance between them, can ultimately be dispensed with in favour of non-mathematical alternatives. In the absence of such an argument for the ultimate dispensability of mathematics in empirical science, our ordinary uses of mathematics in empirical science provide us with prima facie evidence for the third premise required for the argument from the naturalist's trust of empirical science to the conclusion of mathematical realism. Unless we can find a compelling argument to the contrary, we can assume that mathematics is indeed indispensable in formulating our best empirical theories.

Putting together these various ingredients, then, we have the following indispensability argument for believing in mathematical objects:

> P1 (Naturalism): We should look to science, and in particular to the statements that are considered best confirmed according to our ordinary scientific standards, to discover what we ought to believe.
>
> P2 (Confirmational Holism): The confirmation our theories receive extends to all their statements equally.
>
> P3 (Indispensability): Statements whose truth would require the existence of mathematical objects are indispensable in formulating our best confirmed scientific theories.
>
> ∴
>
> C (Mathematical Realism): We ought to believe that there are mathematical objects.

Since I will be arguing in this book that there is nothing in our scientific worldview that requires us to believe in mathematical objects, I will in the process of this be finding fault with this argument.

1.1.2. Rejecting Holism

I have said that the focus of this book is on the naturalistic approach to ontology: I am interested in what follows if we accept the naturalist's commitment to look to science to discover what we ought to believe and what, therefore, we ought to believe that there is. So rejecting the indispensability argument will, for me, require rejecting one of its other two premises, confirmational holism, or the indispensability of mathematics.[1]

While I am committed to the naturalistic first premise of the argument, I am less sure of the truth of the *indispensability* claim. In the most well-known response to the indispensability argument, Hartry Field (1980) has gone some way towards showing how we might find ways of stating the empirical laws of our theories without positing the existence of any mathematical objects. To the extent that this can be done, and to the extent that these *nominalistically acceptable* versions of our scientific theories can be viewed as expressions of our *best* scientific theories, we can view the confirmation our best scientific theories receive as extending to these non-mathematical formulations, and not the mathematical alternatives that we find it convenient to use.

Whether Field's proposed nominalistic theories are genuinely nominalistic, or indeed whether it is even plausible that their could be nominalistically acceptable alternatives to some of our best mathematically stated scientific theories, is controversial. I do not wish to defend a Field-style dispensability claim in this book, not because I think that such a defence cannot be given (I am happy simply to remain open-minded about the possibility of providing non-mathematical alternatives to our ordinary mathematically stated scientific theories), but rather, because I think the question of whether we can dispense with mathematics in formulating our best scientific theories is ultimately besides the point. For, if *confirmational holism* is incorrect, then even the *indispensable* use of a mathematically stated hypothesis in formulating our best theoretical picture of the world might not be enough to give us reason to believe that hypothesis. We will have to look more closely at the question of the relation between theory and evidence in order to discover whether our use of a mathematical hypothesis gives us reason to believe it to be true.

My first aim in this book, is, then, to throw doubt on the holistic view of confirmation. In particular, I aim to disentangle this view of confirmation from the broadly naturalistic approach to philosophy with

---

[1] A further option would be to question the argument's *validity*: perhaps the terminology in which I have expressed the premises is loose enough to allow for some slippage that could destroy its apparent validity. I will not, however, pursue this option here, since I think that we can more reasonably accept its validity and yet reject one of its premises.

which it has come to be associated, arguing that naturalism actually speaks *against* the assumption that confirmation extends to all our theoretical hypotheses equally. Naturalism requires us to look to science to discover what we have reason to believe that there is, accepting as confirmed those statements that are considered confirmed according to our best scientific standards. But taking a closer look at the kind of theoretical statements that are generally considered as receiving confirmation from our theoretical successes, it appears that scientists do not in general take all the hypotheses of their best empirical theories to be equally confirmed by their theoretical successes.

Of course, scientists could simply be *wrong* about this: as I will argue, 'naturalism' does not require us to endorse everything said by scientists. Importantly, then, I will argue that we can uncover a *rationale* for this rejection of the holistic view of confirmation in our ordinary scientific practices, which makes sense of the practice of withholding belief from some of the statements used in formulating our best scientific theories. A reflective understanding of the *value* of including a given theoretical hypothesis in one's theory might be such as to take away from our confidence in the truth of that hypothesis, or might even contradict any straightforward belief that that hypothesis is true. Scientists, I will argue, rightly recognize many practical purposes for adopting a given theoretical hypothesis in the context of their theorizing, not all of which are best served by adopting hypotheses that are thought to be literally true. If this is the case even in our best empirical theories, then the mere presence of a hypothesis amongst the statements used to formulate a successful scientific theory ought not automatically to count as evidence for its truth.

Shaking the automatic assumption of confirmational holism allows us to consider whether we ought to view the *mathematical* statements used in expressing our empirical theories as being confirmed by our theoretical successes. In order to answer this question, we will need to look to our best reflective understanding of the value of adopting mathematically stated hypotheses in formulating our empirical theories. As regards this question, I will argue that it is reasonable to view the assumption that there are mathematical objects that are related to non-mathematical objects in various ways as generative of a *fiction*, which provides us with a means, indirectly, to represent non-mathematical objects and their relations. Merely *pretending* that there are mathematical objects satisfying the axioms of a given mathematical theory provides us with a means to represent non-mathematical objects (as being related to these mathematical objects in certain ways). In particular, if we adopt the pretence that the axioms of our favourite version of set theory with urelements are true, then if we take the urelements to be just whatever non-mathematical objects there are, hypotheses about non-mathematical objects can be represented as hypotheses about sets of non-mathematical urelements and functions relating the members of these sets to further sets. Nothing, I will argue, in our scientific practices requires us to view the *truth* of our mathematically stated empirical hypotheses as confirmed by our empirical successes. We can be content instead with holding that *all* that is confirmed by our empirical successes is that these hypotheses are indeed *fictional* (in a technical sense of the term to be explained), that is, that they are correct in their representation of the non-mathematical objects they concern.

1.1.3. Rejecting 'Scientific Realism'

It is worth noting that my rejection of confirmational holism amounts to a rejection of scientific realism, on at least one characterization of the view. For, in rejecting holism, my claim will be that it is sometimes reasonable to make use of a scientific theory without believing all the statements that are used to express that theory to be true. Scientific realists find this claim acceptable for *some* theories (for example, for some literally false theories that nevertheless approximate those more complex theories that best express our theoretical beliefs). However, I will argue that the same goes even for our *best* scientific theories: our best understanding of the contribution of various hypotheses to the success of such theories might speak against the assumption that such hypotheses are true. So if by 'scientific realism' we mean the view that we ought to believe that our best scientific theories, taken at face value, are true or approximately true, then this amounts to a rejection of scientific realism.

Indeed, since scientific realism so understood by itself implies that we ought to believe in all the objects indispensably posited to exist by the statements that we use to express our best scientific theories, scientific realism combined with the indispensability of mathematics automatically implies mathematical realism. (Scientific realists, then, should already be compelled, on recognizing the indispensability of mathematics in science, to accept the existence of mathematical objects, even if they do not accept the further (naturalist and holist) premises of the 'indispensability argument' as I have presented it.) So the *only* way of rejecting the existence of mathematical objects while remaining a scientific realist in this sense would be to carry out Field's project of dispensing with mathematics. Since my own project is not to dispense with mathematics in the expression of our best scientific theories, I cannot claim to be a scientific realist in this sense.

This might make the central thesis of the book, that the use we make of mathematically stated empirical theories gives us no reason to believe in the mathematical objects posited by those theories, seem rather less interesting. For there are already anti-realist views of science that reject the assumption that the existence of mathematical objects receives empirical confirmation. In particular, one major alternative to scientific realism is constructive empiricism, according to which the use we make of our scientific theories at best confirms our belief that they are empirically adequate, not that they are true. Since the claim that a given theory is *empirically adequate* amounts to the claim that it is correct in its picture of *observables*, and since mathematical objects are surely unobservable if anything is, one who was already convinced of constructive empiricism should find no problem in accepting that we have no reason to believe in mathematical objects.[2] So an account of empirical science that combines a general antirealism about the statements of our scientific theories with an antirealism about the mathematical objects posited by those theories should not be thought of as big news. Constructive empiricism is (or at least ought to be) just such a combination.

What makes my own combination of scientific antirealism with antirealism about mathematical objects importantly different, though, is that I wish to argue that we *do* have reason to believe in many of the unobservable physical objects posited by our best scientific theories. Although I will be arguing that theoretical confirmation does not extend to all the assumptions that make up our best scientific theories, I will argue that the use we make of those theories *does* generally give us reason to believe in the unobservable physical objects posited by those theories. So although I am defending an anti-realist view of science in rejecting the claim that we

---

[2] Actually, Bas van Fraassen's mathematical presentation of empirical adequacy means that the natural combination of constructive empiricism with agnosticism about mathematical objects is more problematic to maintain than at first appears, as we will see in Ch. 8.

ought to believe that our best scientific theories are true or approximately true, the view I will be defending is realist in a different sense of scientific realism: it amounts to realism about (many of) the unobservable *physical* entities posited by our theories. And since many self-professed 'scientific realists' are most concerned with the claim that we have reason to believe in the unobservable physical objects posited by our theories, I hope that my defence of a limited anti-realism, according to which we have no reason to believe in the *mathematical* objects posited in the context of our best scientific theories, should appeal to those whose main motivation for 'scientific realism' is the rejection of constructive empiricism.

This, then, is the main project of the book: to defend, from a broadly naturalistic starting point, a view of the use of mathematics in science that does not see the mathematical assumptions that we make use of in our successful theories as being confirmed by our theoretical successes. Chapters 2 and 3 focus on the premises of the indispensability argument that I accept: P1 (Naturalism), and P3 (Indispensability). Chapter 2 sets out, and defends, a naturalistic approach to ontology, while Chapter 3 considers Hartry Field's attempt to dispense with mathematics, and the difficulties Field's programme faces. In Chapter 4, I consider the question whether our successful pure mathematical practices give us reason to believe in the existence of mathematical objects, arguing that a naturalistic respect for pure mathematics does not establish platonism. But if our successful pure mathematical practices do not give us reason to believe in any mathematical objects, then the question of whether we ought to believe in such things becomes, for the naturalist, the question of whether their existence is confirmed by their presence in our successful empirical theories. In Chapter 5, I argue that, despite Quine's assumption to the contrary, naturalism actually speaks against Quine's holistic view of confirmation (P2 of the Indispensability argument). Indeed, I claim, our best expressions of our best scientific theories may indispensably include many statements whose theoretical value is not best accounted for by means of the hypothesis that those statements are true. In the light of this, the naturalist approach to ontology, presented in Chapter 6, therefore requires a more careful look at the role of theoretical posits in our scientific theorizing, considering whether our best reflective understanding of the role of, for example, mathematical posits in our theories requires us to accept the existence of the objects posited.

Chapter 7 attempts such a reflective understanding of the role of mathematics in empirical science, borrowing from Kendall Walton's (1990) account of fiction to provide an understanding of our mathematically stated scientific theories as developed against the backdrop of a 'fiction' according to which non-mathematical objects can be collected into sets. It is argued that indulging in this fiction provides us with a rich means of representing how things are taken to be with the non-mathematical objects posited by our theories, by presenting them as the way they would have to be in order for our theoretical utterances to be appropriate. In holding that the appropriate attitude to our scientific theories falls short of belief, the fictionalist understanding of the role of mathematics in science presented in Chapter 7 is in many respects analogous to Bas van Fraassen's constructive empiricism. In Chapter 8, I discuss the extent of this analogy, before going on, in Chapter 9, to defend fictionalism, as against the alternatives of scientific realism and constructive empiricism, by showing that the hypothesis of fictionalism, unlike constructive empiricism, can account for the predictive successes and explanatory value of our mathematically stated empirical theories. It is concluded (in Ch. 10) that, since we can account for the uses we make of mathematically stated scientific theories on the assumption that the mathematical objects posited by those theories are merely useful fictions, the use we make of mathematics in science provides us with no reason to believe that there are any mathematical objects. And since we ought not to believe in entities beyond those whose existence is confirmed according to our best scientific theories, it follows (I argue) that we ought to deny that there are any mathematical objects.

Before proceeding with this argument, though, I would like to note, to forestall misunderstanding, a couple of background assumptions that stand behind my discussion. I will not be providing any complete defence of these background assumptions, but instead offer the following short remarks as some justification for my adopting them in what follows.

1.2. A Note on Existence and Quantification

One might wonder whether my claim that our ordinary scientific theories include statements whose truth would require the existence of mathematical objects was too quick. Certainly, our ordinary scientific theories include statements such as

> (M) There is a real number M_a which represents the mass of the object a as a multiple of some unit mass.

But perhaps the truth of M does not *really* require the existence of a real number. One way of defending this claim would be to provide an alternative semantics for the mathematical claims of our scientific theories. For example, one might argue that when one utters the sentence M, what one means to *assert* is just something like,

> (M′) *According to our mathematical theory of real numbers*, there is a real number M_a which represents the mass of the object a as a multiple of some unit mass.

Whether or not some such alternative non-standard semantics is possible,[3] the possibility of providing such an alternative semantics for the mathematical claims of our scientific theories does not conflict with the claim that our ordinary scientific theories include statements whose *literal* (face-value) truth would require the existence of mathematical objects. In simultaneously claiming that it is *true* that there is a real number M_a which represents the mass of the object a as a multiple of some unit mass, and yet that there are not (really) any real numbers, any anti-realist about mathematical objects who wished to take this route of providing a non-standard semantics for our theoretical claims would surely be accepting that there is a *literal* reading of our use of the mathematical 'there is' in the sentence M, as well as the alternative reading provided in their proposed non-standard semantics. For it is only on the assumption that 'there is a real number' can have a literal, face-value interpretation, as well as a nominalistically acceptable reinterpretation, that we can make sense of the anti-realist's denial that there are any numbers.

The claim I wish to make is just that the *literal* or *face-value* truth of some of the statements that are used to express our best scientific theories

---

[3] In the example I have given, it is rather tricky to see how such a reinterpretation might be made to work for mixed mathematical/empirical statements such as these. For if by 'our mathematical theory of real numbers' we just mean an axiomatic theory of a complete ordered field $\langle \mathbb{R}, +, \times \rangle$, then this theory does not tell us anything about any physical objects such as a, so it is hard to see how it could be true that, according to *this* theory, there is a real number M_a which represents the mass of the object a as a multiple of some unit mass.

requires the existence of mathematical objects. My aim is just to show that confirmation does not extend to the literal truth of these statements, not that there is not some further interpretation of these statements according to which they *can* be viewed as truths. Since what is at issue in the indispensability argument for mathematical objects is whether science gives us reason to believe in the *literal* truth of statements that posit the existence of such objects, I will for now set aside the question of whether there is *some* alternative semantics for such statements according to which we can view those statements as true.

Alternative semantics aside, then, what of the claim that the *literal* truth of many of the statements that are used to express our ordinary scientific theories would require the existence of mathematical objects? One might think that *this* claim at least should be controversial. For denying it would amount to saying that it can be *literally true* that there is a real number M_a that represents the mass of the object a as a multiple of some unit mass, and also *literally true* that no real numbers exist. And this surely looks like an out-and-out contradiction: it is just the claim that

$(\exists x)(Rx \ \& \ Axa) \ \& \ \neg(\exists x)Rx$, from which it follows that
$(\exists x)Rx \ \& \ \neg(\exists x)Rx$.

There is, though, one way of avoiding this apparent contradiction, which involves recognizing a difference between the 'there is' as used in the claim 'there is a real number M_a . . .', and the 'exists' in the claim 'no real numbers exist'. According to this route, only *some* of our 'existence' claims amount to genuine *ontological* claims about what (really) *exists*. In particular, we should distinguish between the 'there is' of existential quantification (correctly formalized by the quantifier '$(\exists x)$'), and the ontologically weighty 'there exists' of metaphysics (correctly formalized by an existence *predicate* 'Ex'). The claim that there is a real number (M_a) and yet that no real numbers *exist* is, on this view, correctly formalized as the consistent claim $(\exists x)Rx \ \& \ \neg(\exists x)(Rx \ \& \ Ex)$ (there is a real number but there are no *existent* real numbers). If we allow for *non-existent objects* in our domain of quantification, or alternatively reject the view of quantifiers as ranging over a domain of objects, then the truth of claims such as M might not require the *existence* of any mathematical objects (despite asserting that *there are* such things).

Thus, in the context of the debate over the indispensability argument for the existence of mathematical objects, Jody Azzouni (2004) has adopted such an approach to argue that the indispensable use of quantification over mathematical objects in empirical science implies nothing about the *existence* of those objects. On Azzouni's (2004: 67) view, 'there is' generally functions in English as an 'ontologically neutral anaphora', carrying with it no commitment to any ontology. Azzouni's view is motivated by the thought that such an account provides the best way of preserving some apparently conflicting intuitions we have about, for example, fictional characters. We might think that it is both *true* that there is a fictional detective (Sherlock Holmes) who is admired by all real detectives, and also *true* that Sherlock Holmes does not exist. One option to remove the apparent conflict between these two claims while preserving the intuition that both are true is to reject, as Azzouni does, the ontological implications of the idiom 'there is'. Alternatively, one might follow neo-Meinongians such as Terence Parsons (1979–80), in accepting that the existential quantifier commits us to an ontology of sorts, but allow that ontology to include some *non-existent* objects. In either case, the truth of sentences such as *M* can be maintained even if we go on to insist that nominalism is correct in denying the reality of mathematical objects.

Although I wish to deny the existence of mathematical objects, I do not wish to take either of these routes. For I for one find it hard to see what we do mean when we say that an existentially quantified claim $(\exists x)\phi(x)$ is literally true if not that *there exists* an object satisfying the condition ϕ. But aside from the apparent jarringness of its denial, it is hard to see what considerations could be used to *establish* the univocality of 'there is' against the likes of Azzouni and Parsons who wish to deny it. Indeed, Azzouni himself has argued that any attempt to provide considerations in favour or against taking an ontologically weighty reading of the existential quantifier will be question-begging against someone who doesn't already accept such a reading. One's criterion for reading off 'ontological commitments' from the statements whose truth one accepts is, Azzouni (1998: 10) argues, 'so fundamental that there's no hope of slipping a rationale under it'. At best, we can simply advance an empirical hypothesis about how we in fact use language to express ontological claims.

In plumping for an ontologically neutral reading of the existential quantifier in his more recent work, though, Azzouni does take a stand on the question of how we in fact express beliefs concerning objects, holding that such a reading provides the best interpretation of the way we actually use the words 'there is' and 'exists'. But if ordinary usage is all we have to go by, then we might also consider the following story[4] of van Inwagen's as a prima facie consideration against allowing two-senses of 'exist':

One day my friend Wyman told me that there was a passage on page 253 of Volume IV of Meinong's *Collected Works* in which Meinong admitted that his theory of objects was inconsistent. Four hours later, after considerable fruitless searching, I stamped into Wyman's study and informed him with some heat that there was no such passage. 'Ah', said Wyman, 'you're wrong. There is such a passage. After all, you were looking for it: there is something you were looking for. I think I can explain your error; although there *is* such a passage, it doesn't *exist*. Your error lay in your failure to appreciate this distinction.' I was indignant. (van Inwagen 1998: 236)

Although I suspect that Azzouni might be right that there is no compelling *argument* for the univocality of 'there is', I take the moral of this story to be that an answer to the indispensability argument of the form, 'Of course science gives us reason to believe that there are numbers, it just doesn't give us reason to believe that these objects really *exist*', would be liable to obscure rather than to illuminate matters.[5] In my own denial of the existence of mathematical objects, then, I prefer to assume just one ontologically committing literal meaning of 'exists' and 'there is' when used quantificationally, and to argue more straightforwardly against the assumption that we have reason to accept the literal truth of those statements used to express our scientific theories that posit the existence of mathematical objects.

---

[4] Van Inwagen calls it a funny story. 'At least,' he qualifies, 'I think it's funny. But I expect that if you think that there is an important difference between 'there is' and 'exists', you will find the story more annoying than funny. (This expectation is grounded on a certain amount of empirical evidence: W. V. Quine thinks the story is funny and Terence Parsons thinks it is annoying)' (van Inwagen 1998: 235).

[5] This is not to denigrate Azzouni's own (2004) development of a rather more sophisticated response along these lines. Indeed, despite our differences regarding the interpretation of existential quantification, I find much to agree with in Azzouni's discussions of the question of precisely which ontological claims are justified by our ordinary empirical evidence.

1.3. A Note on 'Abstract'

I have presented the conclusion of the indispensability argument as the claim that we ought to believe that there are mathematical objects. Thus the indispensability argument is a defence of mathematical 'realism' understood as 'realism in ontology': the view that (we ought to believe that) there are mathematical objects such as numbers, functions and sets.[6] But being a realist in this sense tells us nothing about the *nature* of the mathematical objects that one is required to believe to exist. Yet in this book I will use the label mathematical realism interchangeably with the label 'platonism', where platonism is the view that we ought to believe in mathematical objects understood as *abstracta*. Furthermore, my main argument against adopting mathematical realism will be an argument that empirical science provides us with no reason to believe in *abstract* mathematical objects. But is it fair, in the context of an argument against mathematical realism in ontology, to assume that mathematical realism in this sense must amount to *platonism*, according to which the mathematical objects realists claim that we are committed to believing in are *abstract*?

To answer this question, we should consider what it might mean to claim of an object that it is abstract. Here, as John P. Burgess and Gideon Rosen (1997) have stressed, aside from providing examples of purported *concrete* and *abstract* objects, our best way of characterizing what it would mean for an object to be abstract appears to be the 'Way of Negation', 'since the features most often cited are negative ones: (i) lack of spatial location; (ii) lack of temporal location; (iii) causal impassivity; (iv) causal inactivity' (Burgess and Rosen 1997: 20). If we take this entirely negative characterization of abstracta, then any version of mathematical realism that denied the abstractness of mathematical objects would have to argue that mathematical objects are spatially or temporally located, or that they are causally efficacious. And while it is not *inconceivable* that a plausible

---

[6] This contrasts with Michael Dummett's characterization of 'realism' as 'realism in truth-value', according to which mathematical realism is the view that mathematical statements have objective truth values, or that 'they are true or false in virtue of a reality existing independently of us' (Dummett 1963: 146), whereas 'anti-realism' about mathematics is the view the truth or falsity of mathematical statements is tied to the evidence we have for them. The labels 'realism in ontology' and 'realism in truth-value' are borrowed from Stewart Shapiro (1997: 37). Since the indispensability argument is an argument about realism in ontology, I will in this book use the label 'realism' to stand for realism in ontology, rather than realism in truth-value.

account of mathematical objects that, for example, viewed them to be causally efficacious or spatiotemporally located may be defensible,[7] my own assessment of the prospects for such a proposal is that they are slim: is it really plausible that the number 2 could exist in space or time? At any rate, at least until a plausible defence of mathematical objects as spatiotemporally located or causally efficacious has been given, I take it to be safe to assume that belief in mathematical objects amounts to belief in abstracta negatively characterized in this way.

With these qualifications aside, we can now turn to the task at hand: of arguing that adopting a broadly naturalistic approach to ontology, looking to science to discover what we have reason to believe that there is, provides us with no reason for believing in (abstract) mathematical objects such as numbers, functions, and sets.

---

[7] Indeed, Penelope Maddy (1990) defends a position according to which at least some *sets* are spatiotemporally located.

2

Naturalism and Ontology

The argument of this book takes place against the backdrop of a broadly naturalistic approach to ontological questions. My main aim is to show that merely adopting such an approach does not, as defenders of the indispensability argument have supposed, imply that we ought to be realists about all of the objects indispensably posited by our best scientific theories. But since 'naturalism', as a philosophical term of art, has been used to describe a variety of positions, my own claim that one can adopt a broadly naturalistic approach to ontological questions and yet remain sceptical about the existence of mathematical objects will probably not be defensible on *some* understandings of the requirements of naturalism. So it will be important at this stage to get a little clearer on just what my understanding of the requirements of naturalism involves. My aim in this chapter is to lay out an approach to ontology that is recognizably naturalistic. In the process, I hope to make clear why one *ought* to adopt such an approach to ontological questions.

The version of naturalism I wish to defend is Quinean naturalism, defined by Quine (1981b: 21) as, 'the recognition that it is within science itself, and not in some prior philosophy, that reality is to be identified and described'. According to Quinean naturalism, if we have reason to believe anything, we have reason to believe what our current scientific worldview requires us to believe. Thus, once we have worked out which beliefs are justified according to our current best scientific worldview, there is no room for the further question, 'But are these beliefs *really* justified?' As regards ontological questions, then, the question of what we have reason to believe that there is is to be understood as the question of precisely which existentially quantified claims are currently considered to be justified according to our best scientific standards.

The immediate question that arises is, *why* privilege science rather than, for example, some 'prior philosophy', in answering the question of what ought we to believe? Naturalists have offered a variety of answers to this question, some more compelling than others. I will start by considering a motivation for this attitude that I take to be mistaken, before presenting the Quinean motivation, which I accept. But Quine's motivation in rejecting the use of a 'prior philosophy' to answer ultimate metaphysical questions is also shared by Rudolf Carnap, who uses this starting point to argue, not that ontological questions are to be answered by scientific means, but rather that there is *no* meaningful philosophical project of ontology. It will be necessary, then, to show that the naturalistic rejection of 'first philosophy' need not force us into Carnapian ontological scepticism, in order to make a case for our following Quine in assuming that our ordinary scientific methods of inquiry are properly viewed as providing us with the means to answer the question of what there is.

Having accepted the naturalistic project of looking to science to discover what we ought to believe that there is, I will turn finally to the question of why Quine assumes that his naturalistic project of ontology implies that we ought to consider the truth of *all* of the statements used to express our best scientific theories to be equally confirmed by our ordinary scientific standards. Since my own aim is to separate naturalism from confirmational holism, I hope that my discussion will make plausible the claim that this holistic view of confirmation does not automatically follow from Quine's recasting of ontological questions as scientific.

2.1. Rejecting 'First Philosophy'

The characteristic mark of Quinean naturalism is the rejection of the idea of a distinctively *philosophical* inquiry into the nature of reality. According to Quine, naturalism requires the 'abandonment of the goal of a first philosophy. It sees natural science as an inquiry into reality, fallible and corrigible but not answerable to any supra-scientific tribunal, and not in need of any justification beyond observation and the hypothetico–deductive method' (Quine 1975: 72). Naturalists thus reject the Cartesian view of philosophy according to which the role of the philosopher is to question the rationality of our ordinary methods of inquiry, and to answer the question of which beliefs, amongst those that are held justified according to those methods, really *are* justified. Rather, in so far as a role for philosophy remains, on the naturalistic view philosophical inquiry should be viewed as *continuous* with ordinary empirical inquiry, and not ultimately distinct in its nature. This strand of naturalism is central also to logical positivism, and indeed to earlier positivist philosophies as developed in the second half of the nineteenth century. Thus, Quine's insistence that naturalistic philosophy, in contrast with traditional metaphysics, is just the result of the systematic extension of our common-sense methods of reasoning to their natural conclusion, can already be found in Auguste Comte's (1953: 512) description of positivist philosophy: 'the positive philosopher takes the spontaneous wisdom of mankind for his radical type, and generalizes and systematizes it, by extending it to abstract speculations'. Indeed, Quine (1975: 72) himself recognizes the positivist roots of naturalism when he notes that naturalism 'had a representative already in 1830 in the antimetaphysician Auguste Comte, who declared that "positive philosophy" does not differ in method from the special sciences'.

But why on earth *should* we privilege our ordinary scientific methods, taking such methods as the proper methods of inquiry? What is wrong with taking an approach to philosophical inquiry that asks, 'I know which of my customary beliefs are justified according to our ordinary scientific standards of evidence, but are these beliefs *really* justified? Can I really trust my *observations* as a route to reasonable belief? Am I right in relying on enumerative *induction* as a means of justifying universal generalizations? Is it rational to assume that the future will be like the past in making predictions? . . . ' Many would think that the role of the philosopher is *precisely* to answer questions such as these. And if so, it would at least appear that the philosophical method cannot be continuous with that of the special sciences, but rather, must involve some more stringent methods of inquiry from which the rationality of our ordinary scientific methods can be established.

I will present Quine's route to the rejection of this view of philosophy in sections 2.1.2 and 2.1.3. First, though, I would like to consider an alternative route to the rejection of first philosophy that is often presented in the context of the defence of a 'naturalistic' doctrine of sorts. This kind of naturalism appears to imply as an immediate conclusion that we ought simply to accept the face-value truth of all utterances that are held to be 'justified' according to the internal standards of any successful discipline. I do not think that this route to (a version of) naturalism is compelling, and I do not think that the 'naturalism' that is argued for by means of this route is an attractive position. It will be important, then, to distinguish the motivation given for this form of naturalism from the proper motivation for Quinean naturalism.

2.1.1. Philosophical Modesty

The bad argument for naturalism comes from simply noting the many successes of our scientific theories, as against the many failures, wrong turns, and inconclusive results of philosophy. According to this view, when it comes to deciding what we ought to believe, we should have more faith in the claims of practitioners working in successful scientific theories than we have in the conclusions of philosophical inquiry. After all, the track record of these successful disciplines is just so much better than that of philosophy. The naturalism that results appears to require the *abandonment* of philosophical inquiry, as opposed to the acceptance of such inquiry when properly construed as continuous with our best scientific theorizing. And unlike Quinean naturalism, the motivation for this version of naturalism stems more from the worry of being laughed at or ignored than from any principled consideration of the limitations of philosophical inquiry. According to such naturalistic philosophers, while as philosophers we *might* use our independent philosophical standards to test which of our beliefs are rationally justified, we're better off not bothering. At best, our efforts will be ignored as practitioners in more productive areas of inquiry continue their theorizing, for the most part successfully, in blissful ignorance of our philosophical scruples. At worst, given our past record of spectacular failures, we run the risk of being laughed out of town.

David Lewis has provided one such argument for privileging science over philosophy, holding that we should shelve any ontological scruples we may have as philosophers regarding the existence of mathematical objects:

I am moved to laughter at the thought of how *presumptuous* it would be to reject mathematics for philosophical reasons. How would *you* like the job of telling the mathematicians that they must change their ways, and abjure countless errors, now that *philosophy* has discovered that there are no classes? Can you tell them, with a straight face, to follow philosophical argument wherever it may lead? If they challenge your credentials, will you boast of philosophy's other great discoveries: that motion is impossible, that Being than which no greater can be conceived cannot be conceived not to exist, that it is unthinkable that anything exists outside the mind, that time is unreal, that no theory has ever been made at all probable by evidence (but on the other hand that an empirically ideal theory cannot possibly be false), that it is a wide-open scientific question whether anyone has ever believed anything, and so on, and on, *ad nauseam*?

Not me!   (Lewis 1991: 59)

Rather less dramatically, Penelope Maddy presents the motivation for naturalism as arising out of an appropriate level of 'philosophical modesty' in the light of the acknowledged successes of other disciplines. Thus Maddy (1997: 184) feels free to extend Quine's respect for the methods of natural science to other successful disciplines, on the grounds that 'the fundamental spirit that underlies all naturalism' is just 'the conviction that a successful enterprise, be it science or mathematics, should be understood and evaluated on its own terms, that such an enterprise should not be subject to criticism from, and does not stand in need of support from, some external, supposedly higher point of view'. Indeed, Maddy (ibid.: 161) herself suggests the label 'philosophical modesty' as an alternative to 'naturalism' when describing her own naturalistic position.

If we did adopt such a 'modest' position, accepting that utterances that are justified (as appropriate) according to the internal standards of successful disciplines really are justified (as true), then as regards the question of whether we have reason to believe that there are mathematical objects, it would appear that the case would be closed very quickly. For, according to the internal standards of 'justifiability' for statements made in the context of number theory, for example, we certainly are justified in assuming that there are natural numbers satisfying the Dedekind-Peano axioms. And according to the internal standards of 'justifiability' at work in ZFC set theory, we are justified in assuming that there are sets satisfying the ZFC axioms (that is, the Zermelo-Fraenkel axioms for set theory together with the axiom of choice). If we modestly commit to accepting the truth of claims that are justified according to the internal standards of our best mathematical theories, it would appear that we are immediately committed to accepting the existence of mathematical objects such as numbers and sets.[1]

---

[1] The qualifying 'it would appear' is important here, because there is a more quietist reading of the requirements of modesty, according to which we should not always accept the truth of utterances made in the context of our successful disciplines, on the grounds that to do so would also be to impose an external, philosophical reading onto utterances made by practitioners of those disciplines. Thus, Penelope Maddy has suggested that internal mathematical standards of justification do not answer the

Two questions arise regarding the rationale for this form of philosophical modesty. First, to what extent, if at all, does the acknowledged success of a discipline require philosophers to be 'modest' in passing judgement concerning what is to count as a good or bad move within the context of that discipline? Should we accept the internal standards of a successful discipline as determining how that discipline ought to be practised, or is there a role for philosophical criticism of how practitioners of successful disciplines proceed? Secondly, if considerations of modesty *do* require us to hold back from criticizing the internal standards that determine what is to count as good practice in the context of a successful discipline, do such considerations also require us to abandon the philosophical question of whether claims that are held to be 'justified' according to the internal standards of such disciplines *really are* justified *as true*? That is, does philosophical modesty in the face of a successful practice require us to accept the truth of theoretical utterances that are accepted as justified according to the internal standards of that practice?

As regards the first question, there is certainly something to be said for a degree of modesty in providing philosophical accounts of successful enterprises. If our philosophical inquiry leads us to conclude that mathematicians should *give up* on doing number theory or set theory because we are not sure that numbers or sets exist, or that empirical scientists should *give up* on doing calculations with real numbers in deriving empirical predictions, since we are not sure whether there are any such numbers, then we might well wonder, as Lewis does, whether it is not philosophical inquiry, rather than mathematics or science, that has gone awry. Weighing up philosophical scruples about the lack of an ultimate justification for the truth of our theoretical hypotheses against the immense advantages that accrue if we do adopt those hypotheses in our theorizing, most of us would willingly trade in the philosophical high ground for the ability to build bridges or prove theorems.

---

question of whether statements justified as 'good' according to these standards should also be thought of as justified as 'true' ('the methodological debates have been settled, but the philosophical debates [concerning the truth of utterances justified according to our chosen mathematical methods] have not' (Maddy 1997: 191)). If mathematicians' internal agreement over which methods to adopt is not best viewed as agreement over whether their methods justify the *truth* of conclusions reached by means of these methods, then if we also abandon the prospects of providing an *external* justification for the truth of mathematical utterances, it looks as though the modest approach places the question of whether we ought to believe mathematical utterances forever beyond our reach.

But even if we agree to be modest to the extent that we do not advocate the *revision* of successful disciplines, and commit to allowing practitioners of those disciplines to carry on as they always did, this is a far cry from the abandonment of the philosophical question of whether we have reason to *believe* all that's said by practitioners in the context of carrying out their successful theoretical practices. For it is plausible that the acknowledged successes of a given practice might be down to something other than the truth of utterances made in the context of that practice. This would leave open the possibility of questioning, perhaps from the perspective of a prior philosophy, whether the internal justificatory standards of a successful discipline really provide us with reason to *believe* the statements that are considered to be 'justified' according to these standards, without advocating any *revision* of these internal standards. For it is plausible that these internal standards of 'justification' are well suited to the development of *successful* theories, even if the hypotheses considered to be 'justified' according to these standards are not in fact justified as *true*. If the success of a given practice does not depend on the truth of utterances made in the context of that practice, then questioning whether statements justified as *good* or *appropriate* according to the internal standards of a given discipline are also justified as being *true* need not lead one to advocate abandoning that discipline as it is currently practised.

We may, then, willingly adopt a degree of modesty, holding back from advocating the *revision* of successful practices, without committing ourselves to abandoning our philosophical attempts to understand and describe those successful practices 'from the outside'. We may even, as a result of our examination of these practices, come to hold that most or even all practitioners are *mistaken* in some aspect of their own conceptualization of their practices, for example, in believing that utterances justified as 'good' or 'appropriate' according to the internal standards of their disciplines are also justified as true.[2] Such a philosophical stance would be defensible provided that we *also* give some account of why the discipline in question should be expected to be successful, to the

---

[2] Recognizing that standards of justification can serve norms other than truth, though, opens up the possibility that practitioners may themselves consider their utterances as justified only in serving these other norms. In fact, in the case of mathematics, in so far as they consider the question, many mathematicians themselves would explicitly reject the idea that it is truth (rather than, for example, mathematical interest or beauty) at which they aim.

extent that it is acknowledged to be so, even though it is held to be mistaken or perhaps just misleading in some respects. It is, we will agree, a mistake to advocate the *abandonment* of a successful discipline on the basis of philosophical scruples about, for example, the ontological assumptions of that discipline. To this extent, we may be modest. However, so long as we can explain why a practice that is in some respects misguided is nevertheless successful, we need not advocate the abandonment of that practice just because it falls short of some of our expectations. Since questioning the *truth* of utterances made in the context of our successful theoretical practices need not imply the immodest conclusion that we should revise those practices in any way, Lewis's and Maddy's rejection of the philosophical question of whether we have reason to believe those utterances that are justified according to the internal standards of successful disciplines takes the requirements of a reasonable degree of modesty too far.

In fact, not only is the abandonment of the question of whether utterances that are 'justified' according to the internal standards of a given discipline really are justified *unnecessary* on grounds of modesty, it is also potentially extremely dangerous. For consider what it means to say that any successful enterprise should be evaluated only on its own terms, and not held to any external standards. What do we mean by successful enterprise here? If we accept the modest philosopher's worries about external appraisal, then surely we cannot use external standards to identify successful practices. Rather, taking Maddy's plea for evaluation of enterprises on their own terms more seriously, an excessively modest philosopher might consider that it is the place of the disciplines themselves to evaluate their own success. For isn't it overly chauvinistic, and against Maddy's 'fundamental spirit that underlies all naturalism', to define success in narrowly scientific, or purely philosophical, terms?

But in this case, we have a real problem, since, *by their own lights*, very many disciplines are extremely successful. Who are we, then, to cast judgement on the enterprise of fortune-telling when, after all, many of those involved in this discipline are evangelical about its success? Shouldn't we just examine what it is that astrologers claim to be true, abandoning the further question of whether their claims really are true? How about the claims of creationists regarding the origins of humanity? Should we confine ourselves to considering how these claims are warranted according to the internal standards of their particular brand of theology?[3] Of course not—we evaluate them, and we do so using the best philosophical and scientific methods available to us, which after all are the result of our best attempts at systematically discovering how things are.[4]

2.1.2. Quietism and Carnap

Quine's own motivation for the rejection of 'first philosophy' results, not from mere modesty, but from a more principled scepticism about the *possibility* of such a discipline. This principled scepticism has its roots in Carnap's worries about the possibility of a distinctively *philosophical* inquiry into the ultimate justification for utterances 'justified' according to the internal standards of a given theoretical framework. Unlike Quine, though, Carnap does not see these worries as implying that we should accept as *really* justified those utterances that are considered justified according to the internal standards of our best scientific practices. Instead, Carnap's quietist conclusion is that we should abandon completely the *philosophical* question of whether we have any reason to believe those utterances that are 'justified' according to the internal standards of our best theories. Rather than converting ontological questions, as Quine does, into questions about what it is that our ordinary scientific standards give us reason to believe, Carnap holds that the abandonment of 'first philosophy' also requires the abandonment of the philosophical question of 'what there is' as ultimately unscientific. It is worth, then, considering Carnap's

---

[3] Several critiques of Maddy's mathematical naturalism have focused on precisely this kind of issue. See e.g. Dieterle (1999), and Rosen's (1999) review of Maddy (1997), where he labels the problem, of distinguishing between those disciplines we ought to defer to concerning the truth of their assertions and those whose assertions are open to criticism, the 'Authority Problem for Naturalized Epistemology' (p. 471).

[4] It is easy to overstate the degree of Maddy's own 'modesty'. Although it often sounds as if she accepts quietism regarding the issue of whether successful theories are really true, at places she too has made clear that there is a role for evaluative philosophy. Thus, in a paper that presents a case for philosophical modesty in evaluating mathematical methodology, Maddy (1995: 268) explicitly leaves the possibility of an extra-theoretical critique open: 'I would like to emphasize, to forestall misunderstanding, that nothing I have said rules out consideration of ontology or extra-theoretic truth or any such philosophical matters; if such studies were conducted within natural science, I see no reason they shouldn't be fully acceptable, even welcome, to the neo-naturalist. What I have suggested is merely that these matters are irrelevant to methodological issues within mathematics, that these studies would be descriptive rather than prescriptive.' I have used some of Maddy's more quietist characterizations of naturalism in order to illustrate the difficulties that arise from taking this approach too far. However, I suspect that in her more careful moments Maddy would continue to qualify her quietism, as she does here.

argument for philosophical quietism regarding the question of what we are (really) justified in believing, before considering Quine's own conversion of Carnap's *negative* motivation for the rejection of first philosophy into a *positive* motivation for the recasting of ontological questions as answerable by recourse to our ordinary scientific methods of inquiry.

The problem that Carnap and Quine alike find with the Cartesian project of 'first philosophy' is that this project requires us to *abandon* all our former beliefs and start again from scratch, considering one by one whether each of them is *really* justified. The difficulty with this project is actually rather a simple one: if we set out to doubt *all* our former beliefs, on the grounds that the standards of inquiry by which we reached those beliefs may not have been stringent enough, then what tools remain for us in putting those beliefs to the test? The ordinary methods of inquiry that we have previously relied on are themselves under scrutiny, so we will need some distinctive *philosophical* method that allows us to build up from scratch a system of beliefs that is set on solid ground, without presupposing that any of our former hypotheses about the relations between our various beliefs are correct. Thus it is Descartes' hope that we can start with a foundation of indubitable beliefs and consider, one by one, whether each of our former beliefs can be justified on the basis of this foundation.

Carnap and Quine's shared starting point is a scepticism about the possibility of a foundationalist philosophical inquiry of this sort, on the grounds that individual hypotheses simply cannot be tested in this way in isolation from one another. The foundationalist project would require that each individual theoretical hypothesis by itself can be tested by consideration of its relation to our foundational beliefs, so that, for example, if such a hypothesis conflicts with some of our foundational beliefs we can reject it. But both Carnap and Quine find this picture of theoretical inquiry implausible. Set adrift from the meaning-giving rules of a general theoretical framework, individual theoretical hypotheses lack any discernible content. It is only when placed in the context of a general theoretical framework that a theoretical hypothesis may be said to have testable consequences, and only then if we take for granted the framework in which it occurs. Thus Carnap and Quine alike adopt a *holistic* view of theories, according to which we have to *presuppose* a framework of inferential connections between our theoretical hypotheses before we can put our theoretical hypotheses to the test. Hence Quine (1951: 41) cites Carnap's *Aufbau* in supporting his holistic countersuggestion to Cartesian foundationalism, announcing 'that our statements about the external world face the tribunal of sense experience not individually but only as a corporate body'.

Where Carnap differs from Quine is in his understanding of what it is that is tested when a given theoretical framework faces the tribunal of sense experience. Carnap notes that it is the *conventions* that we adopt regarding the relations between the hypotheses of a theoretical framework that give meaning to those hypotheses, and, indeed, it is these conventions that allow us to test theoretical hypotheses against experience. So when it turns out that a theoretical framework survives the test of experience, the best that is confirmed is that our theoretical hypotheses are good ones *given our meaning-giving conventions*. The tribunal of sense experience tests our practical decision to adopt a given theoretical framework in describing and organizing our experience. So in particular, if a theoretical framework within which the utterance 'There are ϕs' is considered to be justified has continued success in describing and organizing our experience, the best that we can say about what is *really* confirmed by the success of this framework is just that adopting a framework which allows us to speak as if there are ϕs is practically useful. But, on Carnap's (1950: 208) view, practical reasons to speak as if there are ϕs do not count as reasons to believe in the *reality* of ϕs, for 'there is no such belief or assertion or assumption'. As a result, on Carnap's view we cannot hope to answer the philosophical question of what (we ought to believe that) there is, for there is no meaningful question for us to answer.

Carnap presents this worry in his (1950) paper 'Empiricism, semantics, and ontology', where he puts forward his famous distinction between internal and external questions regarding the existence claims of a given discourse, or linguistic framework. According to Carnap, if we ask the question 'Do ϕs exist?', we may mean to ask the question from a perspective internal or external to a given framework. As an internal question, 'Do ϕs exist?' amounts to the question, 'Is the utterance "There are ϕs" justified according to the internal rules of the framework?' And although this might sometimes be a very difficult question to answer for some frameworks and some values of ϕ, there are many cases where the answers to such questions will be trivial. Thus, if the framework in question is the framework of arithmetic, it will be trivial that numbers exist according to the internal rules of that framework. But similarly, if the framework in question is the framework of a theological discourse, it may likewise be trivial that God exists according to the internal rules of that framework.

What worries *philosophers*, Carnap thinks, is not these internal, often trivial, existence questions, but rather, the question 'Do φs exist?' understood when asked from a perspective that is external to the framework in question. But the holistic realization that it is only *within* the context of a theoretical framework that as sentence such as 'There are φs' is given meaning precludes the possibility of there being any meaningful external philosophical question of this sort. The philosopher aims to set aside the presuppositions of a given linguistic framework to ask whether the objects said to exist in the context of that framework *really do* exist. But in doing so they divorce the question 'Do φs exist?' of any discernible meaning. Thus philosophers who insist on asking an external *metaphysical* question regarding the real existence of objects said to exist in the context of a given framework have failed to give 'a formulation of their question in terms of the common scientific language' (ibid.: 209). Rather, the only external question that Carnap thinks *can* be asked about a given theoretical framework is the *practical* one, of whether adopting the framework is convenient for the purposes of theoretical investigation. Our adoption of the 'linguistic forms which constitute the framework of numbers', as opposed to the linguistic forms which constitute the framework of (for example) astrology in our empirical scientific theorizing should not be thought of as indicative that we have reason to believe in the reality of numbers, but rather, as indicative only that we have found that form of speaking convenient. Thus Carnap stresses that the question, 'Shall we introduce such and such forms into our language?' is 'not a theoretical but a practical question, *a matter of decision rather than assertion*' (ibid.: 213, my italics).

2.1.3. Quine's Revival of Ontology

Quine agrees with Carnap on many of these points. In particular, Quine agrees that it is only in the context of a background theoretical framework that theoretical hypotheses can be given meaning. And Quine agrees, therefore, that aside from the *practical* decision of whether to adopt a framework according to which it is acceptable to utter the sentence 'There are φs', there is no further external *philosophical* or metaphysical question of whether there (really) are φs. Yet, Quine thinks, we can still draw genuine *ontological* conclusions from our practical decisions to speak as if there are φs.

For, on Quine's view, any reason we may have to offer a positive answer the question, 'Shall we introduce such and such forms into our language?' simply *is* a reason to believe whichever theoretical utterances that follow from the introduction of such linguistic forms. So while Quine thinks that Carnap is right in rejecting the external *metaphysical* question of whether (divorced from any of our usual theoretical standards of justification) we have reason to believe that there are ϕs, he does not follow Carnap in concluding that we should *abandon* ontological questions and remain forever quiet on the question of what there is. Rather, Quine (1951: 127) hopes to resurrect the 'crusty old word' ontology to apply to the internal question of what there is according to whatever theoretical frameworks we have found it most convenient to adopt in describing and organizing our experience. So while Carnap holds that the successful adoption of a theoretical framework can only establish that we have found a practically useful way of organizing our experience, Quine thinks that the fact that a given framework has proved to be *practically* useful should itself be viewed as *evidential*, as confirmation of the truth of utterances justified according to the internal standards of that framework.

Why is there this disagreement between Carnap and Quine on the question of whether *practical* reasons to speak as if there are ϕs in the context of empirical inquiry can be viewed as *evidence* for the existence of ϕs? According to Carnap, there is a strong distinction to be drawn between the conventionally adopted rules that set up what it means for a statement to be justified according to the internal standards of justification for a given framework, and the theoretical statements that are justified in the light of these conventionally adopted rules, together with empirical evidence. Thus there is a clear distinction to be drawn between answering the *theoretical* question of whether an utterance *S* is indeed justified (in the light of empirical evidence and the rules that tell us what justification *is* for our theoretical framework), and deciding on the *practical* question of whether to adopt the rules of a given framework. And realizing that questions of the justification of one's theoretical utterances can only be given meaning once one has made a conventional decision to adopt a given linguistic framework, Carnap's thought is that this element of convention should undercut the idea that utterances that are considered justified in the light of our conventionally adopted framework rules should be viewed as *really* justified. At best we can say that *given these conventional decisions about which linguistic framework to utilize*, we are justified in speaking as if S is true. But the realization that we could just as easily have adopted an alternative linguistic framework should undercut the idea that there is anything philosophically significant in our speaking as if there are φs.

Quine's response to Carnap is simply to blur the distinction between theoretical questions concerning what is justified according to the internal rules of justification for a given theoretical framework and practical/conventional questions concerning whether to adopt a framework with such rules. Carnap calls our attention to a distinction between accepting a theoretical claim made within a framework as internally warranted (given our experience together with the meaning-fixing rules of that framework), and accepting a meaning-fixing rule for a framework as a prudent choice of convention (given that it allows for a framework within which our experiences can be conveniently organized). Quine's response is just to note that, if there is a difference here, it is a difference in degree rather than character. In each case, we are putting theoretical claims to empirical test, and adopting them to the extent that they contribute, within the context of a theoretical framework, to the efficient organization of our experience. Thus, 'Carnap maintains that ontological questions, and likewise questions of logical or mathematical principle, are questions not of fact but of choosing a convenient conceptual scheme or framework for science; and with this I agree only if the same be conceded for every scientific hypothesis' (ibid.: 134).

On Quine's view, then, in our ordinary scientific theorizing, 'external' practical reasons to adopt a particular language form in describing, explaining, and predicting our experience are not to be distinguished from 'internal' reasons to accept particular statements expressed within our chosen language as *warranted* in the light of experience and the meaning-giving rules of the linguistic framework. But if this is right, then the claim that a particular way of organizing our experience is 'merely conventional' (along with the implication that we could, if we so decided, drop that way of doing things and help ourselves to a radically different way of describing reality) cannot be used to detract from the claim that we have reason to believe utterances warranted according to our usual theoretical standards. If *all* questions concerning the evidential support there is for a hypothesis involve an element of practicality or convention, then, Quine thinks, the fact that a hypothesis is adopted on practical grounds in no way speaks against our assumption that we have evidence for its truth.

What, though, of the realization that we could have adopted other conventions, that is, that we could have found alternative theoretical frameworks practically useful in organizing our experience? Shouldn't this take away from our willingness to assign a special, ontologically significant status to the existentially quantified utterances that are warranted according to our conventionally adopted theoretical worldview? Indeed, one might expect that Quine's claim that *all* questions concerning the 'evidence' for a theoretical hypothesis involve some element of convention or practicality should make us less, not more, ready to view the existentially quantified utterances warranted according to our own standards of evidence as indicative of ultimate ontological 'matters of fact'.

On this point, Quine's response is simply to accept that there might well be other ways of going about things, which would make the question of what one ought to believe that there is ultimately relative to the community of inquirers that one finds oneself in. Although this may well be true, it is on Quine's view an idle worry: the best we can ever do is to inquire, with whatever resources are available to *us*, into what it is that *we* have reason to believe. 'I philosophize from the vantage point only of our own provincial conceptual scheme and scientific epoch, true; but I know no better' (Quine 1969c: 25). Our predicament as theorists trying to understand the world around us thus requires us to adopt, at least for the time being, the theoretical framework we find ourselves with. No wonder, then, that in presenting this predicament Quine is so taken by Neurath's image of the sailor who has to fix his boat while out at sea: 'The naturalistic philosopher begins his reasoning within the inherited world theory as a going concern. He tentatively believes all of it, but believes also that some unidentified portions are wrong. He tries to improve, clarify, and understand the system from within. He is the busy sailor adrift on Neurath's boat' (Quine 1975: 72).

When Quine (1969a: 26) says '[t]here is no place for a prior philosophy', then, he is not led to that view by considerations of philosophical modesty. Such considerations would acknowledge that there is such a thing as a distinctive 'philosophical method', but would simply refrain from applying that method in evaluating successful disciplines. Rather, following Carnap, Quine's claim is that there is no such thing as a distinctive philosophical method aside from the methods of ordinary inquiry, for there is no such thing as the possibility of setting aside our provincial conceptual scheme so as to criticize that scheme 'from the outside'. The rejection of a prior philosophy is just a reflection of the predicament we find ourselves in: we are condemned to take for granted an entire theoretical framework in putting new theoretical hypotheses to the test. So, far from *privileging* 'science' as having some special methods that are better than those of philosophy, Quine's hope is to recognize a place for a non-sceptical, naturalized philosophy *alongside* science (and, indeed, alongside common sense).

There are, though, many competing theoretical frameworks for understanding the world around us. Why, then, look to 'science', however broadly construed, rather than, for example, the framework provided by a particular theological worldview? Quine's reason for looking to science, in particular, to discover what we ought to believe that there is is just that it is our current best science that is the result of our most concerted efforts at refining and improving our conceptual scheme in describing and systematizing our experience. If, as naturalized philosophers, we take our cue from our scientific theories and methods, rather than seeking to abandon them, we can hope to contribute to this internal refinement of our current state of reasonable belief rather than seek to undermine it (as, for example, not *really* reasonable). Thus, according to Quine (1957: 216–17), the process of replacing our ordinary commonsense beliefs with those beliefs warranted by our scientific theories is 'one of growth and gradual change':

we do not break with the past, nor do we attain to standards of evidence and reality different in kind from the vague standards of children and laymen. Science is not a substitute for common sense, but an extension of it. The quest for knowledge is properly an effort simply to broaden and deepen the knowledge which the man in the street already enjoys, in moderation, in relation to the commonplace things around him.

We are left, then, in a position whereby wholesale scepticism regarding the question of whether we have reason to believe those utterances that are warranted according to our usual standards of evidence is set aside. This is not, though, to suggest that we cannot worry about the justifiability of *any* of the utterances made within the context of best theories. On the contrary, empirical inquiry *requires* us constantly to adapt our beliefs to experience, and this will involve us in questioning whether hypotheses we have adopted in our theorizing really should be considered as justified according to our own internal standards of evidence. Part of the job of examining our theories in this way will naturally fall to philosophers. But, as Quine (1960: 3) tells us, '[t]he philosopher and the scientist are in the same boat'. Sharing the concerns of scientists to provide a coherent theoretical systematization of our experiences, philosophers should approach the question of the justifiability of our theoretical claims using the same kinds of concepts, methods, and styles of reasoning as are accepted by scientists. The proper position of philosophy is, on this view, not above ordinary scientific theorizing, but not (as the more modest position suggests) below it either. Philosophical concerns regarding the justification for claims made within the context of our ordinary theorizing may still be raised, but only as concerns regarding the warrant these claims receive from our usual standards of evidence.

2.2. Naturalized Ontology

According to Quinean naturalism, then, the impossibility of stepping outside our current theoretical framework does not yield the negative, Carnapian, conclusion that we have no reason to accept the reality of the objects posited by utterances considered justified according to the internal perspective of that framework. Rather, Quine offers a positive spin on the rejection of 'external' philosophical questions about the ultimate nature of reality: the question of what there is, or of what *we ought to believe* that there is, is just the internal question of which existentially quantified utterances are justified according to the internal standards of justification for the theoretical framework we have in fact found it convenient to adopt. The question of what there is is to be answered in the same way we hope to answer any empirical question, by recourse to our current best science.

Having argued that practical reasons to speak as if there are ϕs *can* be viewed as evidence for the existence of ϕs, Quine (ibid.) thinks that the naturalistic project of ontology becomes a relatively simple matter. We just look to the existentially quantified sentences that are used to express our *best* scientific theories, since it is such theories that represent the results of our best efforts to 'get clearer on things'. And, on Quine's view, this ultimately amounts to looking to the existentially quantified utterances used to express our best *physical* theories, for he thinks that there is a presumption in science of supervenience, such that, although the concepts of ordinary language and of special sciences other than physics may also allow for useful ways of describing and understanding the world, the truth of utterances within those theories should ultimately supervene on matters of physical fact. Thus, in answering the question of why 'this special deference to physical theory?' Quine (1978: 98) responds:

The answer is not that everything worth saying can be translated into the technical vocabulary of physics; not even all good science can be translated into that vocabulary. The answer is rather this: nothing happens in the world, not the flutter of an eyelid, not the flicker of a thought, without some redistribution of microphysical states. It is usually hopeless and pointless to determine just what microphysical states lapsed and what ones supervened in the event, but some reshuffling at that level there had to be; physics can settle for no less. If the physicist suspected there was any event that did not consist in a redistribution of the elementary states allowed for by his physical theory, he would seek a way of supplementing his theory. Full coverage in this sense is the very business of physics, and only of physics.

Whether or not Quine is right about this presumption of supervenience is not particularly important as regards our own application of the naturalistic approach to answer ontological questions about whether there are mathematical objects. Since, as we have already noted, existentially quantified claims whose truth would require the existence of mathematical objects already appear in our current best *physical* theories, whether we follow Quine in focusing on the existentially quantified claims of our best physics, or go further to allow existentially quantified claims made in the context of other theories also to be ontologically significant, either way we will find ourselves faced with statements whose truth would require the existence of mathematical objects.

The only situation in which a focus on physics might be thought to cause special problems is if we thought that the existentially quantified utterances of *pure mathematics* should be viewed as ontologically significant. For in that case, even if we found a way of rejecting the Quinean conclusion that our best *physical* theories give us reason to believe in mathematical objects, the presence of utterances whose truth would require the existence of mathematical objects in our best expressions of our pure mathematical theories would mean that we would still find ourselves committed to believing in mathematical objects. Pure mathematics thus deserves special consideration, if we are to justify our focus on the role of mathematics in empirical science and particular in physics. But, as I will argue in Chapter 4, our best understanding of our pure mathematical practices does not in fact give us reason to view the existentially quantified utterances made in the context of our mathematical theorizing as ontologically significant. So the focus on empirical science (and particularly on physics) in the debate over the 'indispensability argument' is justifiable.

What *is* interesting about Quine's willingness to defer to the existentially quantified utterances of our best *physical* theories in considering the question of what we (ultimately) have reason to believe is that it is just one example of many cases where, despite his blurring of the practical/theoretical distinction, Quine allows that 'practical' reasons to speak as if there are ϕs and 'theoretical' reasons to *believe* that there are ϕs *can* come apart. In thinking that we can focus on our best *physics* in answering the ultimate questions of what it is we (really) have reason to believe, Quine appears to be acknowledging that the practical advantages of adopting the vocabulary of the various special sciences, or indeed of common sense, need not be viewed as *evidence* for the ontologies of theories expressed using this vocabulary. And here is just one of many cases where Quine thinks that we *can* distinguish between a practical reason to speak as if there are ϕs and a theoretical reason to believe in ϕs, for he thinks that the hypothesis of supervenience can be used to explain why it may be convenient for us to speak as if there are ϕs even if ϕs are not amongst the objects ultimately posited by our best physical theory.

Indeed, as we shall see in what follows, despite his initial insistence against Carnap that, when it comes to our best scientific theories, there is no distinction to be drawn between merely practical and properly evidential reasons to speak as if there are ϕs, Quine's focus on our best, ideally regimented physical theories as the ultimate arbiter of questions of truth and existence shows that he certainly does recognize plenty of room for *merely* practical ways of speaking in our ordinary theorizing. The fact that many of our ordinary ways of speaking are practically useful is *not* to be considered as confirmation of the existence of objects apparently quantified over in these contexts. In holistically viewing all the utterances used to express our *best* physical theories (when properly regimented) as equally confirmed by our theoretical successes, Quine's claim is that in our *ultimate*, cleaned up, and carefully regimented best theoretical efforts to describe and organize our experience, the distinction between *merely* practical and genuinely evidential reasons to speak as if there are ϕs cannot be made. It is only against the backdrop of this assumption that Quine's response to Carnap (that practical reasons *can* also be evidential) allows him to hold that, in our best science, practical reasons are *always* evidential, such that a reason to utter a sentence 'there are ϕs' in the context of the theoretical framework of our best science is automatically viewed as a reason to *believe* that there are ϕs. Even for Quine, then, the project of uncovering our 'ontological commitments' from our theoretical utterances is rather less straightforward than it might at first seem.

2.2.1. *Uncovering our Ontological Commitments*

We have seen that, according to Quine's naturalistic approach to ontological questions, the previously 'metaphysical' ontological question of what there is becomes recast as an internal scientific question, concerning which existentially quantified claims should be considered to be justified according to our best scientific theories and standards of justification. And Quine's short answer to this question is 'all of them'. That is, on Quine's view, if an existentially quantified statement is amongst the statements used in expressing our best theory of the world around us, we are committed to believing that that statement is literally true, and hence to believing in the objects that the statement posits to exist.

In Chapter 1, I accepted an 'ontologically committing' reading of the 'there is' of existential quantification, holding that the literal truth of a statement of the form '$(\exists x)\phi(x)$' requires the existence of an object x satisfying the condition ϕ. I will therefore follow Quine in talking about the *ontological commitments* of a theory as the objects whose existence is required by the truth of the statements used to express that theory. The ontological commitments of a theory thus line up with the *existential commitments* of those statements used to express that theory: 'a theory is committed to those and only those entities to which the bound variables of the theory must be capable of referring in order that the affirmations made in the theory must be true' (Quine 1948: 13–14), or, to use Quine's slogan, 'To be is to be the value of a variable' (ibid.: 15).

But in claiming that our *use* of a given scientific theory requires us to *believe* that the statements that are used to express that theory are literally true, Quine allows for the label 'ontological commitment' to be used in a second sense. For he can be viewed as claiming that *our* ontological commitments, the objects that our successful use of a given theory *commits us to believing in*, are, in the case of our best scientific theories, precisely the ontological commitments of the theory (the objects that would have to exist in order for the utterances of the theory to be literally true).[5]

As we have noted, Quine's reference to our 'best' theories is important here, for there are cases where even Quine does not think that *our* ontological commitments in using a theory line up with the ontological commitments of the utterances used to express that theory (in other words, with those existentially quantified statements we use in formulating the theory). That is, there are cases where even Quine does not think that our successful use of a theory counts as confirmation for the literal truth of all of the utterances used to express that theory. We have said that Quine's attitude to the special sciences aside from physics provides one example of this, since he thinks that our ultimate commitments are to the ontological claims made in expressing our more fundamental physical theories. But even amongst the utterances standardly used in expressing our *fundamental* theories, there are various cases where Quine thinks that we should not read *our* ontological commitments directly from the quantifier commitments of those utterances. For even amongst our fundamental theories, Quine thinks that there are cases where the literal truth of our theoretical utterances should not be thought of as confirmed by our theoretical successes, for a variety of reasons.

---

[5] Indeed, in some presentations of the indispensability argument, it is precisely this second sense of 'ontological commitment' that is emphasized. Thus, Mark Colyvan (2001: 11) presents the Quine–Putnam indispensability argument thus: '1. We ought to have ontological commitment to all and only those entities that are indispensable to our best scientific theories; 2. Mathematical entities are indispensable to our best scientific theories. Therefore: 3. We ought to have ontological commitment to mathematical entities.' The first premise of the argument as presented here combines the *normative* aspect of naturalism (that we ought to believe whatever is confirmed according to our best science), with the assumption of *confirmational holism* (that it is the truth of all of the utterances used to express our best theories, and hence the existence of all the objects posited by those utterances, that is confirmed by our successful use of those theories). Since I am aiming to separate naturalism from holism, I have opted to keep the premises separate in my own presentation of the indispensability argument.

For example, we may notice that many of our usual ways of speaking are often uneconomical. Existential quantifications are introduced in places where they are *unnecessary*, and in these cases, the mere use of an idiom involving quantification might not be thought to commit us to genuinely believing in the existence of the kind of object apparently quantified over. A loose use of language may license certain transformations that *appear* to introduce ontological commitments that are not really present in our theoretical assumptions. Thus, Quine (1939: 65) considers the transition from 'Pebbles have roundness' to 'Pebbles have something' (i.e. $(\exists x)$(Pebbles have x)). This inference is, Quine tells us, only valid if 'roundness' is a genuine name, rather than a syncategorematic expression that gets its meaning only through its presence as a component in a wider context (for example, the predicate 'has roundness'). If we *do* view this inferential step as valid, then it appears that we will be committed to the existence of 'roundness' when we utter the sentence 'Pebbles have roundness'. And indeed, in general, one way of discovering whether an expression such as 'roundness' should be thought of as naming something is by considering whether such quantifier-introducing inferences are valid. However, Quine notes, there are cases where we may find it useful to allow some such inferences, treating expressions *as if* they were names, even when in fact their function is *not* really to name things. Thus, we might find it useful to introduce new variables into our language by explicit definitions, which show them ultimately to be *eliminable* in favour of syncategorematic expressions. If our acceptance of the new kinds of 'objects' in the range of our quantifiers is conditional on quantifications over such objects ultimately being eliminable, then we may think that our use of these existentially quantified utterances does not require us to believe their literal truth (that is, to believe that there are indeed objects of the sort apparently quantified over), but only requires us to believe the unquantified claims that they are eliminable in favour of. 'Eliminable' existential quantifications of this sort may just be read as a convenient shorthand for the unquantified claims they replace.

As an example of this, Quine considers the introduction, into a language that did not previously allow quantification over arbitrary propositions, of variables standing for propositions. In such cases, the *eliminability* of the quantified claims would be enough, Quine (ibid.: 67) thinks, to show that the quantified forms of expression are introduced *merely* for reasons of practical convenience, and may reasonably be treated as theoretical fictions:

Statements now become names; propositions—designata of statements—become recognized as entities. But this is only a manner of speaking, resting on abbreviations; so we rate the statements as fake names, and the alleged propositions as fictions. The difference between fiction and reality may be regarded thus as reducing to the difference between defined quantification and quantification belonging to the primitive notation.

If we can eliminate our existential quantifications, then our successful use of existentially quantified claims in our theories does not commit us to belief in the literal truth of such quantified claims (and hence the existence of objects in the range of the quantifiers), but only in the truth of the utterances with which our existentially quantified claims can be replaced. Even on Quine's view, then, *our* commitments in using a theory are not simply to be identified with that theory's quantifier commitments as it is currently stated. In order to uncover the genuine ontological commitments incurred in making use of a theory, we need to consider which quantified claims will remain once we have eliminated these defined quantifications.

A further case where a theory's quantifier commitments should not, according to Quine, be taken to signify our ontological commitments in using that theory appears when we use explicit idealizations in our theorizing. Thus, there are many cases where, in order to give a tractable theoretical account of a particular process, we choose to ignore details that would complicate the picture we provide. For example, we may treat spatially extended objects as point masses; treat a section of the earth's surface as flat rather than curved; ignore air resistance and consider objects as falling in a vacuum; ignore friction and consider the motion of balls rolling down frictionless planes.... If such idealizations are present amongst the quantifier commitments of our theories, then we would not want to consider our use of theories that posit such objects as implying a genuine commitment on our part to the existence of such objects.

Again, Quine appeals to the possibility of elimination to deal with these cases. When we speak *as if* there are frictionless planes, we do not commit ourselves to accepting the existence of such objects, since such theoretical utterances are, Quine thinks, eliminable in favour of literally believed claims regarding what happens to ordinary planes as friction approaches a limit. Thus, our use of a theory that is quantifier-committed to frictionless planes does not indicate *our* ontological commitments in using such theories, because such quantifier commitments are theoretically eliminable, and therefore, Quine thinks, *merely* practical. We can explain our successful use of utterances whose truth would require the existence of frictionless planes by showing that it is the relation of these utterances to literally believed claims about *actual* planes that accounts for their theoretical successes. So we should not consider our theoretical utterances that posit the existence of frictionless planes to be confirmed by our theoretical successes, but rather, should consider the claims about actual planes that those utterances abbreviate to receive theoretical confirmation.

Quine's naturalistic ontological project therefore requires a little more sophistication than simply looking to the existentially quantified statements used in expressing our ordinary scientific theories. The mere presence of an existentially quantified statement amongst the statements used in formulating a successful theory does not automatically commit us to believing the literal truth of that statement (and hence to accepting the existence of the objects apparently quantified over). Rather, on Quine's view, we may discharge our commitment to the truth of such a theoretical statement if we can show it to be a merely convenient form of expression, ultimately eliminable in favour of some literally believed alternative. Here, then, Quine has resurrected something of the distinction between language forms that are adopted simply on grounds of practical convenience and language forms that are epistemically justified. However, *on Quine's view*, the distinction can only be made by showing exactly what this practical convenience amounts to—that is, by stating precisely which genuinely believed claims are conveniently glossed by the fictional alternatives. Thus, for Quine, existentially quantified utterances in our theories are guilty until proven innocent—we are committed to the literal truth of existentially quantified utterances used in expressing our theories unless we can show how they are eliminable in favour of other claims, which express more carefully what we 'really' wanted to say all along.

2.3. Naturalism and the Indispensability Argument

Returning to the indispensability argument as characterized in Chapter 1, I have presented in this chapter a defence and clarification of P1 (Ontological Naturalism). I will, then, follow Quine in trusting science to tell us what there is, noting that 'science' here is broadly construed to cover the combined results of our systematic attempts to organize, explain, and predict our experience.[6] My discussion of examples where the supposition that there are ϕs may be shown to be *merely* practical shows that P2 (Confirmational Holism) is only plausible for theories from which *merely* practical uses of the existential quantifier have been eliminated. Quine's assumption, that our *best* scientific theories will be such that we *can* eliminate all merely practical uses of existentially quantified claims, makes the holistic premise plausible. This assumption (which I will question in what follows) also explains the presence of the word 'indispensable' in P3 (Indispensability). For if we could *dispense* with mathematics in expressing our best scientific theories, then our use of mathematically stated versions of those theories could be viewed as *merely* practical, and not confirmed by the success of those theories. Having accepted Quine's naturalism, then, the question remains as to what attitude naturalists should take to the other two premises of the argument. We will consider the indispensability premise (P3) in the following chapter, and return to holism (P2) in Chapter 5.

---

[6] It is, then, an empirical question whether this will amount, as Quine supposes, to looking to our best *physics* to answer ultimate questions concerning what there is. We will largely set this question to one side for the purposes of this discussion.

3

The Indispensability of Mathematics

According to Quine, then, we ought to believe those statements used to express our best, most carefully formulated, scientific theories, at least until something better comes along. While he accepts that there are sometimes *merely* practical reasons for speaking as if there are ϕs, which provide us with no reason to believe that there are ϕs, he thinks that in the context of our *best* theories such merely practical forms of speaking must be eliminated. It is ultimately on this point that I will challenge Quine, and will, as a consequence, find fault with premise P2 (Confirmational Holism) of the indispensability argument. However, before developing this response, it is worth pausing to consider the prospects for challenging P3, the claim that mathematics is indispensable in our best scientific theories.

3.1. Is Mathematics Dispensable?

If we were to accept confirmational holism for our best, most carefully expressed scientific theories, then the only option for naturalists who wish to reject the existence of mathematical objects would be to reject P3 of the indispensability argument, showing that quantification over mathematical objects can be *dispensed with* in expressing the assumptions of our best scientific theories. This is the approach of Hartry Field, who in *Science without Numbers* (1980) argues that we can account for the role of mathematics in our scientific theories as a useful, but ultimately eliminable, fiction. Field's project involves arguing that our usual mathematically stated scientific theories can be replaced by nominalistically stated counterparts in such a way that our use of the mathematical versions of these theories can be justified on the grounds of mere practical utility.

3.1.1. Nominalistically Acceptable Theories and their Platonistic Counterparts

A nominalistic theory is one whose quantifiers need not be interpreted as ranging over abstract objects. On the assumption that the quantifiers of our usual mathematical theories must range over abstracta in order for those theories to assert truths, for a theory to be nominalistically stated, at the very least, its quantifiers cannot range over mathematical objects. Whether other quantifier-commitments of a theory are nominalistically acceptable can be decided on a case-by-case basis. For example, Field's non-mathematical version of Newtonian gravitational theory quantifies over space-time points, and Field argues that these are 'nominalistically acceptable' since they pass the test (which standard abstracta fail) of being spatiotemporal. But for our purposes, since we are interested in the question of whether we ought to believe in mathematical objects rather than the more general question of whether we ought to believe in any objects that might be thought of as abstracta, the most important thing to note about Field's 'nominalistically stated' theories is that they aim to avoid quantification over mathematical objects.

Field hopes, then, to show that quantification over mathematical objects is eliminable from empirical science, at least in our *best* expressions of our empirical theories. This does not, however, mean that he wishes scientists to stop using their ordinary mathematically stated ('platonistic') scientific theories, any more than Quine wishes scientists always to abandon convenient idealizations in favour of literally true alternatives. Rather, Field hopes to *explain* the successful use of our ordinary mathematically stated theories by showing them to be *conservative extensions* (in a sense to be defined) of nominalistic theories which state their true empirical content. If a platonistic theory is a conservative extension of a non-mathematical theory, then the truth of that *non-mathematical* theory is sufficient to account for the predictive success of its platonistic counterpart, even if we do not believe that that the platonistic theory that has been used to derive accurate predictions is itself true. Thus, although we may well make extensive use of the platonistic counterparts of our nominalistic theories, we are not committed to accepting the truth of *those* theories, since we can explain the successful use of the mathematized versions without the assumption of their truth, simply in terms of the relation of those theories to the nominalistic theories that we do believe.

Field's project is thus twofold. He must first find nominalistically acceptable versions of our ordinary platonistic scientific theories, which plausibly express the true non-mathematical content of those theories. And second, he must show that our ordinary platonistic theories are 'conservative extensions' of their nominalistic counterparts, in a sense which is sufficient to explain why it might be reasonable to expect the platonistic versions of our theories to be extremely practically useful even if one does not believe them to be literally true.

3.1.2. Field's Dispensability Claim

Field's 'dispensability' claim is defended in *Science without Numbers* by example. Field hopes to show how we might go about finding nominalistically acceptable versions of our ordinary scientific theories by sketching a nominalistically acceptable version of Newtonian gravitational theory, which expresses the laws of that theory without quantifying over any mathematical objects. Field then argues that our use of the usual *platonistic* version of Newtonian science can be justified, without assuming its truth, on the grounds that this mathematically stated physical theory is a conservative extension of the alternative nominalistically acceptable theory that we believe to be true. As such, Field's nominalization programme is a direct response to Hilary Putnam's (1975: 74) challenge to explain what one takes the 'objective content' of Newton's law of universal gravitation to be if one does not believe in real numbers and functions. The 'objective content' of Newton's law is just what's said by its counterpart in the nominalistic version of the theory.

The equations of Newtonian gravitational theory relate properties of points in space-time (their mass, their distance from each other, etc.). Field's strategy is to find a nominalistic theory of this subject matter (replacing properties defined in the Newtonian theory in terms of real-valued functions of space-time coordinates with intrinsic non-mathematical properties of space-time points defined in terms of comparative predicates).[1] For

---

[1] One might worry, from this presentation of Field's strategy, that this involves Field in a nominalistically unacceptable commitment to *properties*. It would perhaps be more accurate to characterize Field as replacing platonistically characterized predicates with nominalistically characterized predicates in his

example, in place of a distance metric defined as a function over pairs of 4-dimensional vectors (coordinates representing space-time points), in Field's nominalistic theory distance claims are expressed in terms of a betweenness relation, a simultaneity relation, and a spatial congruence relation on space-time points ('y Bet xz', 'x Simul y', and 'xy S-Cong zw'). Similarly, rather than representing mass as a function from (coordinates of) space-time points to real numbers, claims about mass are expressed in terms of comparative relations of mass-betweenness and mass-congruence. The mathematical machinery of functions from n-tuples of four-dimensional vector coordinates to real numbers makes for a neat way of representing that these intrinsic relations hold between space-time points, but ultimately, Field argues, this machinery can be dispensed with in favour of a direct representation in terms of nominalistically acceptable relations between space-time points.

Field's account of the use of mathematics in Newtonian science is meant to serve as a template for further nominalizations of other scientific theories. For this reason, the fact that we do not really *believe* the Newtonian theory is not of any great importance here—Field hopes that the template he has provided for nominalizing this theory will show us how to go about the perhaps more complicated process of nominalizing our current best theories. For Field's dispensability claim to be plausible, then, there would have to be reasonable prospects for extending his strategy to theories other than Newtonian gravitational theory.

3.1.3. Field's Conservativeness Claim

A theory T' is a conservative extension of a theory T if all consequences of T' expressible in the language of the theory T are also consequences of T. It is important to note that a *semantic* notion of consequence is intended here (such that S is a semantic consequence of the theory T if and only if it is not logically possible for the axioms of T to be true and S to be false).[2] If we opted instead for a syntactic (deductive) notion of

theory, avoiding any talk of *properties*. Given that Field accepts Quine's identification of ontological commitments with quantifier commitments, the use of predicate and relation symbols in his theories does not commit Field to an ontology of properties if those predicates and relation symbols are not quantified over. And as we will see, where second-order quantification is used in Field's 'nominalistic' theories, Field interprets this quantification as quantification over arbitrary mereological sums of space-time points.

  [2] Field is sometimes, unfortunately, unclear on this in *Science without Numbers*: some of his claims suggest that he has a deductive notion of conservativeness in mind (as when, for example, he claims

'consequence', such that S is a deductive consequence of T if and only if S is provable (in some suitable derivation system) from the axioms of T, then our mathematically stated theories would *not* in general be conservative extensions of nominalistically statable alternatives.

If we do adopt a semantic notion of consequence, then Field has a set theoretic *proof* of the conservativeness of a theory he calls 'ZFU$_{V(T)}$' over any other theory T, so long as T is itself 'agnostic' about the question of whether there are any mathematical objects.[3] ZFU$_{V(T)}$ is ZF set theory with urelements, where the only non-set-theoretic vocabulary allowed to appear in the comprehension axioms is the vocabulary $V(T)$ of theory T. Since ZFU$_{V(T)}$ allows for us to combine non-mathematical objects with mathematical ones (by forming them, as urelements, into sets), it is a natural setting for mathematically stated empirical theories (which require us, for example, to speak of functions relating physical objects to numbers). So long as Field can show that our ordinary platonistic theories can be viewed as the result of combining our nominalistic theories with set theory with urelements, then this proof provides a mathematically rigorous defence of Field's conservativeness claim for these theories.[4] The link between platonistic theories and their nominalistic counterparts is given by *representation theorems*.

3.1.4. *Representation Theorems and the Juice Extractor*

In order to tie up platonistic theories with their nominalistic counterparts, and indeed in order to see how platonistic theories are in general going to be useful in drawing out the consequences of nominalistic theories, we need to be in possession of a representation theorem. Representation theorems allow us to link nominalistically stated sentences with their 'abstract counterparts': sentences which, according to our 'platonistic'

that 'any inference from nominalistic premises to a nominalistic conclusion that can be made with the help of mathematics could be made (usually more long-windedly) without it' (Field 1980. p. x).) This claim is in fact *false* if our nominalistic theories make use of second-order logic. But Field is careful at points to emphasize that his considered conservativeness claim involves the *semantic* conservativeness of mathematics (see ibid.: 115 n. 30), and in his writing since *Science without Numbers* he has consistently stressed that his conservativeness claim is a semantic one (see e.g. Field 1985).

[3] Making use of the axiom of inaccessible cardinals, Field (1980: 16–19) shows how to extend a model of $T + \neg S$, where the theory T and the statement S are nominalistic and mathematically agnostic, to a model of ZFU$_{V(T)} + T + \neg S$. From this it can be concluded that if S follows from ZFU$_{V(T)} + T$ then S also follows from T.

[4] There remains, of course, the question of what a mathematical fictionalist such as Field can make of a *mathematical* defence of the conservativeness of mathematics. This is a special case of a general worry about the nominalistic acceptability of uses of mathematics in metalogic, discussed below in sect. 3.2.1.

(mathematically stated) scientific theories, are materially equivalent to the nominalistically acceptable sentences whose truth we are (really) interested in. If we have such a theorem, then in considering the question of whether a given nominalistically stated sentence S is a consequence of our nominalistically stated theory T, we can, if we wish, move instead to the question of whether the abstract counterpart of S, S', is a consequence of our platonistic theory T' (a question which might be much easier for us to answer). If S' follows from T', then by our representation theorem, S must also follow from T'. But then, so long as T' is a conservative extension of T, we can conclude from the fact that S follows from T' that S follows from T, even if we don't believe the truth of the mathematized theory T'.

Thus, with all of these ingredients in place, the applicability of mathematics can explained as *merely practical* in that, as in Carl G. Hempel's (1945: 391) image of mathematics as a 'theoretical juice extractor', it allows us to extract nothing non-mathematical out of our non-mathematical assumptions that did not already follow from those assumptions:

> Thus, in the establishment of empirical knowledge, mathematics (as well as logic) has, so to speak, the function of a theoretical juice extractor: the techniques of mathematical and logical theory can produce no more juice of factual information than is contained in the assumptions to which they are applied; but they may produce a great deal more juice of this kind than might have been anticipated upon a first intuitive inspection of those assumptions which form the raw material for the extractor.

Given a nominalistically stated scientific theory whose assumptions we believe, we may wish to extract factual information in the form of concrete predictions. Applying the machinery of our theoretical juice extractor, we may ascend to a mathematically stated counterpart of our initial theory to draw out this factual information, safe in the knowledge that, so long as our mathematical theory is a conservative extension of the theory we started with, we will extract no non-mathematical claims that were not already implied by the non-mathematical theory we began with.

3.2. Problems for Field's Programme

Whether Field's programme of dispensing with mathematics in favour of nominalistically acceptable theories of non-mathematical objects can ultimately be carried out has been the subject of much debate. One group of worries comes from the powerful *logical* apparatus that Field's programme would appear to require, in defending his claim that mathematics is conservative over non-mathematical theories. It has been argued that these logical assumptions are themselves really at root *mathematical*, or at least that our justification for believing these assumptions requires us to accept the existence of mathematical objects. Another group of worries concerns Field's confidence that nominalistically acceptable versions of our ordinary platonistic theories can be found. These include questions concerning the nominalistic acceptability of Field's own 'nominalistic' version of Newtonian gravitational theory, as well as questions concerning the plausibility of extending this style of nominalization to our current best physical theories. We will start by considering worries concerning Field's logical assumptions.

3.2.1. *Problems with Conservativeness*

The 'juice extractor' view of the application of mathematics that Field offers aims to show that we can account for our successful use of mathematically stated theories without believing those theories to be true, on the grounds that such theories are bound to be predictively successful just so long as the non-mathematical theories that they *conservatively extend* are true. Several worries arise regarding the logical apparatus required by this account.

A first worry concerns the precise notion of 'conservativeness' that Field appeals to. Conservativeness is defined in terms of the notion of logical consequence, such that T' is a conservative extension of T if and only if any consequence of T' that is expressed in the language of T is also a consequence of T. And, as we have noted, Field has to appeal to a *semantic* notion of consequence in his account of conservativeness, according to which S is a semantic consequence of T if and only if it is not logically possible for the axioms of T to be true and S false. Mathematical theories are not in general deductively conservative over nominalistic theories (see Shapiro 1983).

But one might think that our use of the notion of *logical possibility* in the definition of semantic consequence is itself in need of elaboration. Indeed, when we consider what we mean by logical possibility, it is arguable that the claim that a theory is logically possible should be simply reduced to the claim that it has a set theoretic *model* (i.e. that it is satisfiable). Certainly, if one accepts that there are sets, then at least for first-order theories, one will accept that such a theory is logically possible if and only if it is satisfiable: against a platonistic backdrop, the notions of logical possibility and satisfiability are coextensional for first-order theories. But the proposal under consideration requires more than this. The claim is that *what it means* for a theory to be logically possible just is for it to be satisfiable. If logical possibility *just is* satisfiability, then Field's account of the applicability of mathematics in terms of its conservativeness over non-mathematical theories must itself appeal to the existence of mathematical objects (set theoretic models of these theories).

To avoid this conclusion, Field adopts a primitive, modal notion of logical possibility, not reducible to the model-theoretic notion of satisfiability. Field defends this reading of logical possibility in various papers in his (1989) (see also Field 1991), where he argues (adapting a discussion of Georg Kreisel's (1967)) that even *platonists* should not accept satisfiability as anything more than coextensional with an independently given notion of logical possibility. Aside from the reasons Field gives there (which include the conceivable existence of consistent second-order theories which lack set-theoretic models, a situation that is avoided in the first-order case merely due to the the Löwenheim–Skolem theorem, a rather lucky 'accident of first order logic' (Field 1989: 31)), one consideration in favour of accepting the existence of irreducible modal facts is that the alternative, according to which modal facts simply are facts about what sets there are, seems to have the order of explanation precisely wrong. Surely the set-theoretic realm, if it exists, fails to contain certain sets (such as, for example, a set of all sets), simply because it is not logically possible for it to contain such a thing? But if modal facts just are facts about what sets there are, then it follows from this that, for example, it is *because* there is no set of all sets that the existence of such a set is logically impossible.[5]

For Field, then, the claim that a theory is consistent (logically possible) is not reducible to the claim that that theory has a model (although, of course, if there *are* sets, then at least for first-order theories a theory will be consistent precisely when it has a model). But one might still object that to claim, *of a theory*, that it is consistent will embroil Field in some

---

[5] This argument adapts an objection of Scott Shalkowski's (1994) to David Lewis's possible worlds theory as a reductive account of metaphysical possibility. I develop this point in my (2007).

nominalistically unacceptable machinery however he proposes to interpret this claim, even if it is not interpreted as a claim about set-theoretic models. For, however we choose to understand the notion of logical possibility, surely the mere assertion *of a theory* that it is consistent (logically possible) involves us in a claim about at least one abstract object—a *theory*? Thus, Gideon Rosen (1994: 169) objects to Field's fictionalist programme that,

> When Field says that set theory is false but useful, and useful because conservative, what precisely does he mean by 'set theory'? A scattered mass of ink and chalk? A theory shaped region of spacetime? The general worry is that on a wide range of restrictive ontological views, theories turn out to be among the entities the theorist professes not to believe in. And whenever this is the case, the fictionalist way out is simply not available.

If Field's conservativeness claim is as it appears—a claim about the relation of one theory to another, then Rosen's worry is that he will have to find a nominalistically hygienic account of *theories* that does not interpret theories as abstracta.

Field's response to this second worry is to adopt a deflationist strategy analogous to deflationism about the concept of truth. According to deflationism about truth, to claim *of a proposition* that one expresses by means of the sentence *S* that that proposition is *true* is not (despite appearances) to assert that a substantial property (truth) holds of a kind of abstract object (a proposition). Rather, such a claim is just an inflated and indirect way of saying something that one says directly when one utters the sentence *S*. Similarly, according to deflationism, to claim *of the axioms* of a theory that those axioms are true is simply an inflated and indirect way of saying something that one says directly when one utters the sentences that are used to express those axioms. In semantically ascending to a metalanguage to assert *of a theory* that it is true (that is, to assert that its axioms, and therefore all their consequences, are true), we really do no more than asserting, in our object language, the axioms of the theory.

Of course, our ability to make such an assertion will depend on the complexity of the theory and on the resources of our object language. For theories without finite axiomatizations, if our language lacks a device for infinite conjunction, such as a substitutional quantifier, which would allow us to assert in a single sentence all the allowed instances of an axiom schema, we cannot directly assert the axioms all at once. But if we augment our object language with such a device, then we can assert the truth of a theory in a deflationary way without committing ourselves to the existence of *theories* as objects to which the substantial property *truth* applies.[6] If AX_T is the (perhaps infinite) conjunction of the axioms of the theory T, the metalevel assertion of the truth of the theory T is interpreted by the deflationist as the assertion of AX_T.

Turning to logical possibility, Field's deflationist strategy is to do for possible truth what the standard deflationist does for truth. That is, inflated talk of the (logically) possible truth of theories is to be replaced by object-level assertions of logical possibility. To do this, Field needs to augment his object language further with a unary sentential operator, '$\diamondsuit$' (to be read as 'it is logically possible that . . .', and grasped, like the other logical constants, by means of its inferential role). The apparently inflationary assertion of the consistency of a theory T then becomes the object-level assertion of the sentence $\diamondsuit AX_T$. Similarly, the assertion that $\text{ZFU}_{V(T)}$ is conservative over a theory T can be expressed as the object level assertion that, for any sentence S in the language of T, $\diamondsuit(AX_T \,\&\, \neg S) \supset \diamondsuit(AX_{\text{ZFU}_{V(T)}} \,\&\, (AX_T \,\&\, \neg S))$. Talk of 'theories' and of 'logical possibility' as a substantial property of theories is thus avoided.

But even if Field can avoid problems with *stating* beliefs about logical possibility (and related notions such as logical consequence and conservativeness) by means of this account, there remains a final worry for nominalists about the use of mathematics in *justifying* such beliefs. For example, if our nominalistically stated theories are second order, there will be *more* semantic consequences of those theories than can be deduced from the assumptions of those theories taken on their own. And, in general, 'ascending' to the mathematically stated counterparts of these theories will allow us to deduce *more* nominalistically acceptable consequences than could be deduced, even in principle, from just the nominalistic assumptions on their own. So on the 'juice extractor' view of applications, mathematics is an *indispensable* juice extractor: in practice, there are consequences of our non-mathematical theories that we cannot squeeze out without the help

---

[6] Is it really possible for us finitary creatures to speak a language with such 'infinitary' resources? Well, one way of understanding the (essentially infinitary) assertion of all instances of an axiom schema is via its inferential role: those who utter such a sentence thereby commit themselves to accepting anything that can be shown to be an instance of the schema. Since we clearly can recognize instances of axiom schema, there seems to be nothing especially problematic with adopting a language that allows us to express such commitments.

of their mathematical counterparts. Thus, as Alasdair Urquhart (1990: 151) has objected, 'mathematics remains indispensable in drawing out the consequences of our theories, if not in expressing our theoretical assumptions'. The natural question to ask is, does this indispensable use of mathematics in *reasoning* require us to believe the mathematical theories utilized, and hence to believe in mathematical objects?

On this point, Field can respond simply that his dispensability claim does not require him to dispense with *all* uses of mathematics. Recall that the purpose of Field's dispensability claim is to respond to P3 of the indispensability argument—a premise that claims that mathematics is indispensable *in formulating our best scientific theories*. The indispensability of mathematics in drawing out the consequences of our nominalistically stated scientific theories is simply irrelevant to this project—so long as mathematics can be dispensed with in expressing our theoretical assumptions, then the indispensability argument is blocked.

But although this response shows how Field's specific aim of responding to the Quine–Putnam indispensability argument can survive the indispensability of mathematics in drawing out the consequences of our theories, it does not answer a wider objection that, plausibly, stands behind Urquhart's comment. Our use of mathematics as a theoretical juice extractor requires us to have confidence in this tool. In particular, we must be confident that the nominalistic consequences of our platonistic scientific theories really are already consequences of the theories they extend (that is, that our platonistic theories really are conservative extensions of their nominalistic counterparts). And, we might wonder, if we do not believe the mathematics used to prove Field's conservativeness claim, what reason have we for having confidence in the mathematical machinery we utilize in empirical science?

The essence of this objection is that our apparently indispensable use of mathematics in *metalogic*, in justifying claims about logical possibility and logical consequence (such as the conservativeness claim) requires us to believe the truth of the mathematics utilized. Two strategies of response suggest themselves: one might either attempt to dispense with uses of mathematics in metalogic or, alternatively, argue that such uses of mathematics, though indispensable, do not require belief in the truth of the mathematics used. Field opts for the second strategy. This strategy requires us to find some other virtue of the mathematics that is utilized in model-theoretic proofs that accounts for its trustworthiness. And for this, we can plump for the consistency of that mathematics.

Suppose, for example, we make use of a model-theoretic argument to justify the claim that a sentence S does not follow from AX_T, the axioms of a theory T. To do this, we will construct a set theoretic model of AX_T & $\neg S$, to show that $\neg S$ is consistent with the theory T. The objector complains that a fictionalist cannot conclude, from the purported existence of this set theoretic model, that $\Diamond (AX_T$ & $\neg S)$, since a fictionalist does not believe in sets. Field's fictionalist response is essentially that, in model-theoretic proofs of consistency, we do not prove the actual existence of any set-theoretic models, but rather, show that the existence of a model of the theory in question follows from the axioms of our preferred set theory (say ZFC). Such a proof will show that AX_T & $\neg S$ is consistent *if ZFC is* (since, if AX_T & $\neg S$ implied a contradiction, the fact that ZFC implies the existence of a model of AX_T & $\neg S$ could be used to infer that ZFC is also contradictory). So, we can be confident in model-theoretic justifications of consistency claims just so long as we are confident in the consistency of the background set theory against which we provide these justifications. Since Field believes that ZFC *is* consistent,[7] he therefore feels justified as a fictionalist in using ZFC to justify claims about the consistency of other theories.[8]

I think that Field's deflationist account of logical possibility as a primitive modal notion is essentially correct, and has the resources to respond to these objections concerning the strong *logical* assumptions required by his 'juice extractor' account of applications. Indeed, it will turn out that precisely the same assumptions about the nature of logical concepts (such as *logical possibility*), and about our ability to make use of mathematical justifications of our logical knowledge, are required at various points in my own account, both of pure mathematics and its applications. In what follows, then, I will adopt Field's deflationary, non-reductive understanding of consistency claims, and his defence of the fictionalist's use of mathematics

---

[7] Field (1984: 88–9) cites inductive reasons for this belief; to this we may add the conceivable existence of objects satisfying the ZFC axioms, as elaborated in the iterative conception (see Leng 2007: 104–7).

[8] This brief discussion hides several of the complexities of Field's own argument (which also considers the question, ignored here, of how a fictionalist can make use of proof-theory in drawing modal conclusions). See sect. 2 of Field (1991) for details of his position, and Leng (2007) for a more detailed presentation of my own reading of the essentials of Field's account.

in justifying such claims. My own concerns with Field's programme pertain not to his logical assumptions, but to the dispensability claim itself.

3.2.2. Problems with 'Nominalizing' Physical Theories

A second group of concerns about the viability of Field's nominalization programme relates to the possibility of finding genuinely nominalistic theories of which our usual mathematical theories are conservative extensions. These concerns arise both for the 'nominalistic' version of Newtonian gravitational theory that Field sketches and for the prospects of providing nominalistically acceptable alternatives to further empirical theories. On Field's account of applications, it is only by finding non-mathematical counterparts of our platonistic (mathematically stated) scientific theories that we can account for the successful use of those platonistic theories without assuming their truth. For if we can find such theories, then we can argue that the success of our usual platonistic theories is due entirely to the truth of the nominalistic theories that they conservatively extend. But one might well wonder about the prospects of finding genuinely *non-mathematical* theories whose truth we can consider to be confirmed by our theoretical successes. And if our worry is with *abstract* objects in general, one might worry about the prospects of finding genuinely *nominalistic* theories to play this role.

Take Field's own proposed nominalization of Newtonian gravitational theory. The basic objects quantified over in Field's 'nominalistic' version of that theory are space-time points and arbitrary regions of such points (thus committing Field to a *substantivalist* view of space-time). But talk of such objects as space-time points and regions might be thought to be at least as problematic for a nominalist as talk of points and arbitrary sets of points in $\mathbb{R}^4$. For one thing, in Field's nominalistic theory space-time points are held to have precisely the same structure as $\mathbb{R}^4$. If Field's nominalization simply builds all the structure of the mathematical theory of $\mathbb{R}^4$ into physical space, can he really be said to have dispensed with mathematics?

In part, this objection is wrong-headed since it assumes erroneously that Field's nominalistic theories must have nothing that looks remotely mathematical in them. What makes a theory nominalistic is that it posits the existence of no abstract objects (and in particular, no abstract mathematical objects). If a theory posits only the existence of concrete, *non-mathematical* objects, then even if some or all of those objects happen to satisfy the axioms of some mathematical theory, that theory will still count as nominalistic, in that its truth does not require the existence of any abstracta. So it is no objection to a nominalistic theory that it posits the existence of concrete objects about which the axioms of some mathematical theory can be interpreted as asserting truths.

If there is a genuine objection here, then, the objection must be to the status of space-time points and regions as nominalistically acceptable objects. Field (1980: 31) has defended his commitment to space-time points as being less problematic than a commitment to the existence of points in $\mathbb{R}^4$, by stressing the disanalogy between space-time points and more usual examples of abstract objects: 'space-time points are not abstract entities in any normal sense. After all, from a typical platonist perspective, our knowledge of mathematical structures of abstract entities (e.g. the mathematical structure of real numbers) is *a priori*; but the structure of physical space is an empirical matter.' The nature of space-time does seem to be a more clear-cut case of an empirical question than does the question of the nature of $\mathbb{R}^4$, and there are defences of substantivalism regarding space-time that proceed largely independently of attempts to dispense with $\mathbb{R}^4$.

The question of whether it is nominalistically acceptable to quantify over arbitrary *regions* of space-time, as well as over individual space-time points, is potentially more problematic for a nominalist, as it amounts to the question of whether a nominalist can make use of the full resources of a version of second-order logic (which Field calls 'the complete logic of Goodmanian sums'). Our usual semantics for second-order logic takes second-order quantifiers to range over arbitrary *sets* of objects in the domain of our first-order quantifiers. In helping himself to second-order logic (in the guise of quantification over arbitrary regions of space-time points), isn't Field effectively helping himself to 'set theory in sheep's clothing' (Quine 1970: 66)?

Field (1985) *has* considered making do with a first-order nominalization of Newtonian gravitational theory (with first-order quantifiers ranging only over regions of space-time, and with a subregion relation in the language). But, as Shapiro (1983) stresses, and Field acknowledges, if we aim to apply mathematics to first-order non-mathematical theories we will in general lack the means to prove suitable *representation theorems*, which allow us to match up non-mathematical statements with equivalent (in the mathematical theory) abstract counterparts. Since such representation theorems are essential to the claim that our ordinary platonistic theories are conservative extensions of their nominalistic counterparts (which replace their mathematically stated laws with equivalent nominalistic claims), rejecting second-order logic in formulating the nominalistic counterparts to our mathematical theories would seriously weaken Field's project.

In fact, though, Field's original reasons for thinking his use of second-order logic to be nominalistically acceptable hold water, despite Quine's charge. Although second-order quantification *can* be interpreted as quantification over arbitrary sets of those objects in the domain of first-order quantification, the fact is that we *can* do the work Field needs in his theories by allowing quantification over arbitrary regions (arbitrary mereological sums of space-time points). And the notion of an arbitrary mereological sum contains nothing that should worry the nominalist whose gripe is with non-spatiotemporal abstracta—such things are spatiotemporally located where their parts are located. Indeed, Quine's charge dangerously overstates the relation between second-order logic and full set theory: even if we thought that second-order quantification was quantification over set-like *collections* of objects, this would still be a far cry from accepting the existence of the full iterative hierarchy of sets.[9] And if one does not wish to allow mereological sums *or* set-like collections of space-time points into one's ontology, George Boolos (1984) has argued that second-order quantification can be interpreted as plural quantification over the objects in the domain of one's first-order quantifiers. As such, he thinks, second-order quantification involves us in no further ontological commitments than to the objects our first-order quantifiers range over. There are thus numerous interpretations of second-order quantification that avoid the identification of second-order logic with set theory.[10]

---

[9] Stewart Shapiro (1991) has thus argued that we should separate the 'logical' notion of set, as an arbitrary collection of objects from some base domain, from the 'iterative' notion of set, taken as a member of the iterative hierarchy. If second-order quantification over a given base domain of objects commits us to set-like things at all, it will at most commit us to belief in the 'logical' sets of objects in that domain, and not the full iterative hierarchy.

[10] Field's own concerns about his use of second-order quantification really come down to his concerns about the strength of the second-order consequence relation, which is non-axiomatizable. ('I share the feeling that the invocation of anything like a second-order consequence relation is distasteful' (Field 1980: 38)) One worry about this relation is that we often need to make use of set-theoretic arguments to discover the consequences of our second-order theories. However, as we saw in the previous section, the use of set theory in metalogic, in discovering the consequences of theories, is defensible from a nominalistic perspective.

Finally, Field's project would give us reason to think that we are not committed to the truth of the mathematics that we use in expressing our usual scientific theories only if it was clear that the nominalizing strategy Field uses for Newtonian science is extendable to other empirical theories. The nominalization of Newtonian gravitational theory is achieved by taking space–time points and regions as the basic objects, and rewriting claims that are usually made in terms of mathematical quantities in terms of properties of these objects. So long as we assume that space–time has the same structure as $\mathbb{R}^4$, or some other standard geometrical space, it is plausible that such rewritings can be found. However, as Alasdair Urquhart (1990: 151) has pointed out, in our current theories where space–time is assumed to have non-constant curvature, the prospects for finding appropriate representation theorems are less clear.

But perhaps the biggest hurdle for the completion of Field's project is that many current scientific theories are not relevantly like Newtonian gravitational theory in consisting of abstract mathematical representations of a straightforwardly nominalistically acceptable subject matter. The equations of Newtonian gravitational theory relate points in space–time (and their properties such as mass, distance from each other, etc.). Field's strategy is to find a nominalistic theory of this subject matter (replacing 'mathematically' defined properties of space–time points with intrinsic non-mathematical properties defined in terms of comparative predicates), so that our usual mathematical statements about functions acting on vectors of $\mathbb{R}^4$ can be interpreted as *really* just providing convenient representations of facts about space–time points and their relations. But for many of our scientific theories, although they are similarly formulated as claims about functions acting on vectors, the vectors do not represent straightforwardly nominalistic objects.

Thus, David Malament has pointed out that Field's programme will have difficulties with *phase space* theories, such as classical Hamiltonian mechanics and ordinary (non-relativistic) quantum mechanics. As with Newtonian gravitational theory, these theories use vectors in their representations of their subject matter. But rather than representing actual space–time points, vectors are used in these theories to represent *possible states* of a physical system. So if we had to take seriously all the non-mathematical objects represented by our mathematical theories, it looks as though this would require us to be committed to possibilia, which are potentially at least as problematic as abstract mathematical objects. Here is Malament's (1982: 533–4) presentation of the objection:

The point here is very simple. Suppose Field wants to give some physical theory a nominalist reformulation. Further suppose the theory determines a class of mathematical models, each of which consists of a set of 'points' together with certain mathematical structures defined on them. Field's nominalization strategy cannot be successful unless the objects represented by the points are appropriately physical (or non-abstract). In the case of classical field theories the represented objects are space-time points or regions. So, Field can argue, there is no problem. But in lots of cases the represented objects *are* abstract. In particular this is true in all 'phase space' theories.

   Quantum mechanics is even a more recalcitrant example than Hamiltonian mechanics. Here I do not really see how Field can get started at all. I suppose one can think of the theory as determining a set of models—each a Hilbert space. But what form would the recovery (i.e. representation) theorem take? The only possibility that comes to mind is a theorem of the sort sought by Jauch, Piron, *et al.* They start with 'propositions' (or 'eventualities') and lattice-theoretic relations as primitive, and then seek to prove that the lattice of propositions is necessarily isomorphic to the lattice of subspaces of some Hilbert space. But of course no theorem of this sort would be of any use to Field. What could we worse than *propositions* (or *eventualities*)?

The success of Field's dispensability programme depends on viewing our mathematically stated scientific theories as convenient representations of an ultimately non-mathematical subject matter. But if it turns out that the subject matter represented is itself abstract, then Field's nominalistic cause gains nothing from attempts to dispense with mathematics.

   In assessing the prospects for Field's dispensability programme, it is worth getting quite clear on the nature of this objection, and in particular its generality. One could be forgiven for thinking that, if Field's problem is simply that it's not clear what he should say about *quantum mechanics*, one should not hold that against him. For, although in quantum mechanics we have a mathematical theory that does as a matter of fact allow for very good experimental predictions, even our best physicists are unsure about what we should conclude about the underlying non-mathematical world that this theory represents. Thus, Richard Feynman advises, 'Do not keep saying to yourself, if you can possibly avoid it, "But how can it be like that?" because you will get "down the drain," into a blind alley from

which nobody has yet escaped. Nobody knows how it can be like that'
(Feynman 1965: 129). If the precise interpretation of quantum mechanics
provided the only stumbling block for Field's programme, perhaps we
could allow him the benefit of the doubt, at least until physicists have
worked out what they want to say about this notoriously paradoxical
subject matter. But the fact that Malament's objection applies not just to
quantum mechanics but to any phase space theory shows that this charitable
attitude to Field's dispensability programme is unwarranted. To get clear
on Malament's objection, then, let us first consider his concern as it applies
to classical mechanics, before considering what further worries arise when
we turn to the special case of the applicability of mathematics in quantum
mechanics.[11]

3.2.3. *The Trouble with Phase Space Theories*

Suppose we have a closed system of n particles, and wish to provide a
theory of the dynamic behaviour of these particles over time. Classical
mechanics hypothesizes that the behaviour of these particles is determined
by the position and momentum of each at a given point in time. For
a given system of n particles at time t, we can represent the position of
each particle by three position coordinates, and its momentum by three
momentum coordinates. So the state at a point in time of a system of
n particles can be represented by $6n$ real numbers (the 6 position and
momentum coordinates of each of the n particles). It is convenient to
represent this state as an ordered $6n$-tuple of real numbers: a vector ω in
the 'phase space' $\Omega = \mathbb{R}^{6n}$ of possible states of the system of n particles.
This particular use of mathematics to represent the actual state of a physical
system at a given point of time should not cause any difficulties for a
Field-style nominalization: the coordinates of ω are being used to represent
intrinsic properties of an actual system of objects.[12]

Having represented the state of the system in this manner as a vector
$\omega \in \Omega$, it is hypothesized that further observable properties of the system

---

[11] To help with the transfer from representations of the state of a system in classical mechanics
to representations of the state in quantum mechanics, I borrow heavily in what follows from R. I.
G. Hughes's (1989) discussion of both, which is formulated in such a way as to make clear the analogies
between the two approaches.

[12] Where numerical representations of position and momentum can be replaced, as in the nominalization of Newtonian gravitational theory, with appropriate intrinsic relations.

(such as the mass and kinetic energy of each particle) are determined by its state, such that for any observable A there will be a *function* $f_A : \Omega \to \mathbb{R}$, which outputs the value of that observable for any state specification ω as input. Since the specification of the state of the system determines the values of all observables, the state specification will provide a yes or no answer to any question we may care to ask about where the value of a given observable lies. That is, to any question (A, Δ) of the form 'Does observable A have a value within Δ?' (for Δ any subset of the reals), the state will provide a determinate answer. As a result, we can if we wish view the *state* of the system as itself defining a function on the set of experimental questions of the form (A, Δ), such that $\omega(A, \Delta) = 1$ if and only if $f_A(\omega) \in \Delta$ (and 0 otherwise). And again, to the extent that we are happy that the various quantitative properties of the system can be nominalized (for example, by introducing for any real-valued property A a collection of nominalistically acceptable relational properties 'A-Less', 'A-Cong', 'A-Bet' for which a representation theorem can be given), we need not be overly worried about this mathematical representation of the state as answering experimental questions of this sort: having a value of the observable A lying between r_1 and r_2, for example, will correspond to some more complex, but more fundamental relation expressed in terms of 'A-Bet', 'A-Cong', and 'A-Less'.

Finally, in classical mechanics, it is hypothesized that the state of a system after an elapse of time t will be fully determined by the state of the system at time 0, according to differential equations governing the rate of change in the *Hamiltonian* of the system (the function $H(q, p)$ representing the total energy in the system with position coordinates q and momentum coordinates p) with respect to time. Thus the equations of motion

$$\frac{dq_i}{dt} = \frac{\delta H}{\delta p_i}, \frac{dp_i}{dt} = -\frac{\delta H}{\delta q_i}$$

determine the values of the position and momentum coordinates p_i and q_i at any point in time given an initial specification of these coordinates. To sum up, then, in order to provide a general theory of the time evolution of a system of n particles, we need to give (*a*) various functions that allow us to recover observable properties of the system when given a specification of its state, and (*b*) dynamic equations that allow us to determine the evolution of the state over time.

Note, though, that these functions and these equations apply to *any* state specification as input. What makes our theory a *general* one is that it allows us to represent *all possible* states of a system as vectors $\omega \in \Omega$, and tells us how any possible state determines the value of observables and evolves with time. Indeed, we represent the *actual* time evolution of an actual closed system by means of the trajectory of a point over time through this phase space of all possible states. So the time evolution of the state is represented in the theory in terms of a *relation* holding between points in the state space (where one point may be related to another by being in the trajectory of that original point as the state evolves with time). It appears, then, that the basic objects represented in our classical mechanics are not just *actual* systems of particles and the actual relations between particles within a system (as represented by their position and momentum coordinates, and the observables defined on the individual system), but rather, all *possible* states of a system of particles (represented by all of the vectors in the phase space) related by dynamic equations that govern the transition from one state to another.

The difficulty, then, for an adherent of Field's nominalization programme is simply that if we wish to hold that our mathematical theory is good because it respects fundamental relations that do indeed hold between the non-mathematical objects it represents, it appears that we will ultimately find ourselves committed to believing in all the *possible* states of a system represented by the vectors in our mathematical theory. So, as Malament (1982: 533) says, even if we do manage to trade in the mathematically defined *properties* our theory utilizes for 'qualitative relations' on the objects in the phase space, this will only get us so far. In particular, the best this will allow us to do is just to 'reformulate the theory so that its subject matter is the set of "possible dynamical states" (of particular physical systems) and various relations into which they enter. But this is no victory at all! Even a generous nominalist like Field cannot feel entitled to quantify over *possible dynamical states'*. If, as Field thinks, quantification over ϕs in our best theories commits us to belief in ϕs, it looks as though any attempt to dispense with the mathematical terminology of classical mechanics in favour of the underlying objects that that mathematics is being used to represent will lead one to commitment to the existence of possible dynamical states.

3.2.3.1. The Application of Mathematics in Quantum Mechanics   In so far as quantum mechanics is also a phase space theory (with Schrödinger's equation $i\hbar\frac{\delta v}{\delta t} = \mathbf{H}\mathbf{v}$ governing the evolution of states through the phase space), exactly the same objection applies here: even if we dispense with the mathematics used in quantum mechanics, it looks as if we will remain committed to the existence of possible states of a quantum mechanical system. But aside from this general problem, there are some further difficulties specific to quantum mechanics in providing an interpretation of quantum mechanical states, which lead Malament to suggest that the case of quantum mechanics is even more recalcitrant.

We saw that the mathematical representation of the classical state of a system could be viewed in two ways, neither of which appeared particularly problematic for a nominalist such as Field who aims ultimately to replace mathematical representations with fundamental nominalistically acceptable descriptions. On the one hand, the state can be represented as a vector ω in the phase space Ω. But the numbers that define this vector can fairly easily be given a physical interpretation: they are coordinates of position and momentum, where the position and momentum of a particle are at least plausibly reducible to nominalistically stable facts in the way Field suggests. On the other hand, given that the value of any observable is hypothesized to be determined by the state of the system in classical mechanics, we saw that the state could also be viewed as a *function* over the set of empirical questions, defining a 'yes' or 'no' answer to each question of the form 'Does observable A have value within Δ?' Again, this view of the state did not appear particularly problematic, since if Field is right that claims about the quantitative values of observables can always be replaced with alternative qualitative claims, a yes or no answer to such a question would correspond to a yes or no answer to a related qualitative claim. And viewing the state of a system as a convenient way of representing a list of answers to merely *qualitative* questions should be acceptable to a nominalist: a system's state will correspond to a list of nominalistically stable *truths*.

The state of a quantum mechanical system is a rather different matter. In the mathematical representation, a pure quantum mechanical state is represented as a normalized vector $\mathbf{v}$ in a Hilbert space $\mathcal{H}$, while an observable is represented as a Hermitian operator $A : \mathcal{H} \rightarrow \mathcal{H}$, the eigenvalues of the operator (which, since A is Hermitian, will all be real numbers) being the possible values of the observable. Why, one

might ask, use vectors in a Hilbert space and operators acting on a
Hilbert space to represent states and observables? Well, this form of
representation is well suited to representing a probabilistic theory according
to which the state of a system assigns probabilities to various mutually
exclusive and exhaustive experimental outcomes (for example, to the
various values a_i, for $i = 1 \ldots n$, of an observable A).[13] We can represent
these various experimental outcomes as mutually orthogonal subspaces L_i^A,
which together span a Hilbert space $\mathcal{H}$.[14] Since these subspaces span $\mathcal{H}$,
each vector $\mathbf{v}$ in $\mathcal{H}$ can be decomposed into a sum $\Sigma_i \mathbf{P}_i^A \mathbf{v}$, where $\mathbf{P}_i^A$ is the
projection operator into the subspace L_i^A.

We wish to view a specification of a pure state of a system as an
assignment of *probabilities* to events defined in terms of observables such as
A (for example, to the event of a measurement of A yielding the value a_i),
such that the state specification can be viewed as answering the question
'What is the probability of a measurement of A yielding a_i?' But if we
choose *normalized* vectors, then there is a natural way of associating these
vectors with probability assignments. For, such a vector can be decomposed
into the sum $\Sigma_i \mathbf{P}_i^A \mathbf{v}$, with $\Sigma_i |\mathbf{P}_i^A \mathbf{v}|^2 = 1$. So if we view the values $|\mathbf{P}_i^A \mathbf{v}|^2$
as the *probabilities* the state assigns to the experimental questions 'What is
the probability of a measurement of A yielding a_i?', we know that our
probability distribution will add to 1, as required. In general, then, we
can define $p_\mathbf{v}(A, a_i)$, the probability that the state represented by $\mathbf{v}$ assigns
to the event of a measurement of A yielding the value a_i, to be $|\mathbf{P}_i^A \mathbf{v}|^2$
(or $\langle \mathbf{v}|\mathbf{P}_i^A \mathbf{v}\rangle$). And the state can likewise be used to assign probabilities
to further experimental questions of the form 'What is the probability of
a measurement of A being in the set Δ?': we simply find a projection
operator $\mathbf{P}_\Delta^A$ onto the subspace of $\mathcal{H}$ spanned by the L_i^As which correspond
to values of A that fall in Δ. Then $p_\mathbf{v}(A, \Delta) = \langle \mathbf{v}|\mathbf{P}_\Delta^A \mathbf{v}\rangle$.

---

[13] For simplicity of presentation, I am assuming in what follows that A can take only finitely many
distinct values. If we allow the observable to take countably many values or even continuously many
values (for example, ranging over all of $\mathbb{R}$), then our mathematical presentation will be rather more
complex, as we will have to move to infinite dimensional vector spaces and allow for operators with a
continuous spectrum. But in so far as the quantum mechanical state yields conceptual difficulties that
we must wrangle with, it does so even in the finite, discrete case.

[14] A Hilbert space is just a vector space on which an inner product $\langle v, w \rangle$ has been defined, which is
complete (i.e. converging sequences of vectors in the space converge to vectors in the space). We need
an inner product to define the notion of orthogonality. Since we are restricting our discussion to the
finite case, and since all finitely dimensional vector spaces are complete, this second restriction need
not concern us.

How about the representation of observables as Hermitian operators on the state space? Well, having represented the various values a_i of the observable A by mutually orthogonal subspaces L_i^A, we can define a linear operator $\mathbf{A}$ on $\mathcal{H}$ in terms of the projection operators onto these subspaces by $\mathbf{A}\mathbf{v} = \Sigma_i a_i \mathbf{P}_i \mathbf{v}$. The eigenvectors of this operator will be vectors lying in the subspaces L_i^A (for which $\Sigma_i \mathbf{P}_i^A \mathbf{v} = a_i \mathbf{v}$), and so the corresponding eigenvalues will be the real numbers a_i. On the other hand, if we start with a specification of a finite dimensional Hilbert space $\mathcal{H}$, then the spectral decomposition theorem tells us that, for any Hermitian operator $\mathbf{A}$, there are distinct real numbers $a_1, \ldots a_m$ and projectors $\mathbf{P}_1, \ldots, \mathbf{P}_m$ projecting onto mutually orthogonal subspaces of $\mathcal{H}$ such that $\mathbf{A} = \Sigma_{i=1}^m a_i \mathbf{P}_i$. (Furthermore, this decomposition is unique given that the a_i are assumed to be distinct.) Given the natural association of mutually orthogonal subspaces with mutually exclusive and exhaustive experimental outcomes, we can view any Hermitian operator $\mathbf{A}$ as representing an observable taking m distinct values a_i.[15]

The formalism of Hilbert spaces provides, in this way, for a convenient way of representing the quantum mechanical state of a system as an assignment of *probabilities* to measurement events (A, Δ) (the event of a measurement of A yielding a value within the set Δ).[16] So just as the classical state can be viewed as a two-valued function defined on the set of experimental *questions* (A, Δ) (yielding the value 1 just in case the value of observable A is in the set Δ), the quantum mechanical state can be viewed as a real-valued function defined on the set of experimental questions of the form (A, Δ), yielding a value in $[0, 1]$ for each such question. Indeed, to any question of the form (A, Δ), there corresponds a subspace L_Δ^A of $\mathcal{H}$ such that the probability of a measurement of A yielding a value in Δ is given by $\langle \mathbf{v} | \mathbf{P}_\Delta^A \mathbf{v} \rangle$. Thus the subspaces of a Hilbert space can be viewed as representing experimental questions (A, Δ) via an isomorphism: 'The partially ordered set of all questions in quantum mechanics is isomorphic to the partially ordered set of all closed subspaces of a separable, infinite

---

[15] If we move to the infinite dimensional case, and allow operators with a continuous spectrum, things are complicated somewhat. In particular, we need a generalized version of the spectral decomposition theorem which says that, for any Hermitian operator $\mathbf{A}$ there is a *spectral measure* $\{\mathbf{P}(x)\}$ such that, for any vector $\mathbf{v}$, $\langle \mathbf{v} | \mathbf{A} \mathbf{v} \rangle = \int_{-\infty}^{+\infty} x \, d\langle \mathbf{v} | \mathbf{P}(x) \mathbf{v} \rangle$.

[16] Actually, we have just dealt here with *pure* states. Quantum mechanics also allows for mixed states, weighted sums of pure states, represented by weighted sums of projection operators.

dimensional Hilbert space (Mackey (1963), 71)' (Scheibe 1994: 197). The state then represents a probability measure on this set.

Despite the sophisticated mathematical setting in which the theory of quantum mechanics is presented, the real question that concerns nominalists who wish to view our standard mathematical theory of quantum mechanics as an ultimately dispensable representation of non-mathematical matters of fact can be put relatively simply. It is the question of just what ultimate *non-mathematical* properties of the system correspond to the mathematically stated property of 'yielding a value of A in the set Δ with probability p'. For answering this question will be essential if we wish, as Field does, to *dispense* with the mathematical machinery of Hilbert spaces in favour of a direct non-mathematical characterization of a quantum mechanical state. In the classical case, the various 'yes/no' answers to the experimental questions (A, Δ) given by the classical state could be viewed as a long list of nominalistically acceptable statements ultimately expressible just in terms of the predicates A-Bet, A-Less, and A-Cong. So the representation of the state as a function on experimental questions could be viewed as a merely useful way of representing these ultimately non-mathematical facts. But in the case of quantum mechanics, we replace these 'yes/no' answers to experimental questions with assignments of probabilities. So if Field wishes to do away with the set of experimental questions (or, equivalently, with the set of quantum 'events' or propositions of the form (A, Δ)),[17] as well as the view of the state as defining a probability measure on this set, he will need to answer the question of what fundamental non-mathematical facts about a quantum mechanical system are being represented by our mathematical assignment of probabilities to experimental questions/events.

But although this *question* is relatively simple to put, its answer certainly is not an easy one. For the question of precisely what the non-mathematical world must be *like* in order to be describable by the probabilistic representation as provided by our theory is surely just the problem of providing an interpretation of quantum mechanics. And here it is tempting, in the light of Feynman's scepticism about the prospects for making sense of the

---

[17] As surely he must if he wishes to provide a nominalistically acceptable interpretation of quantum mechanics in terms of a theory that he can believe. To reiterate Malament's objection, 'What could be worse than *propositions* or *eventualities*' as the basic objects whose properties are conveniently represented by our mathematical theory?

underlying reality described by the formalism of quantum mechanics, to give up on looking for an answer, at least against the backdrop of contemporary physics. But although Feynman's scepticism is reasonable in relation to the *ultimate* question of what makes the probabilistic description of the quantum mechanical world appropriate, perhaps this scepticism can be bypassed, at least when it comes to the interpretative question that matters for providing a nominalization of quantum mechanics. For all we would need to provide is nominalistically acceptable counterparts of statements assigning probabilities to quantum events (A, Δ). And so long as we can do this, perhaps we can leave unanswered the question of what the world must be like for these nominalistically acceptable statements to be true of it.

This aspect of the nominalization programme has been attempted by Mark Balaguer (1996), who has argued that we can dispense with the assignment of probabilities to quantum events just so long as we assume that there are physically real *propensity* properties of physical systems. And the assumption that physical systems have such propensity properties is, Balaguer (ibid.: 217) thinks, 'compatible with all interpretations of QM except for hidden variables interpretations'. So perhaps we can be content with providing an interpretation of the *non-mathematical* properties represented by our mathematical theory of quantum mechanics while setting aside the further interpretative question of how it is that quantum mechanical systems could have such properties. On this assumption, Balaguer sketches a representation theorem for quantum mechanics which aims to show, for each Hilbert space $\mathcal{H}$ that we use in quantum mechanics, the set $S(\mathcal{H})$ of closed subspaces of $\mathcal{H}$ can be used to represent truths concerning physically real propensities (of the form 'the system has an r-strengthed propensity to yield a value in Δ for a measurement of A').[18] Furthermore, Balaguer suggests that we can give a nominalistic theory of these propensities that will allow us to prove that our mathematical representation is a good one, as Field's project would require.

If Balaguer is right that a propensity interpretation of the probabilities present in our mathematical theory of quantum mechanics can be

---

[18] If one is concerned about hypothesizing the existence of continuum many propensity properties for each strength of propensity, we may follow Field's strategy in introducing qualitative 'Prop-Less', 'Prop-Cong', and 'Prop-Bet' relations to dispense with this use of real number indexes. Similarly, the description of a measurement of A yielding a value in Δ will likewise correspond to a long list of nominalistically acceptable statements expressed in terms of the qualitative relations A-Less, A-Cong, and A-Bet.

nominalistically acceptable, then it seems that quantum mechanics provides no special problem for Field's nominalization programme. But this does nothing to alleviate Malament's original worry, concerning the nature of quantum mechanics and classical mechanics as *phase space* theories. To reiterate, such theories consist of mathematical representations of the possible states of a physical system. Applying the strategy of *Science without Numbers* would dispense with the mathematics but leave behind a theory about the qualitative relations holding between these possibilia. This leaves just three options for a nominalist such as Field who wishes to accept premises P1 and P3 of the indispensability argument: argue that commitment to possibilia is nominalistically acceptable; find an alternative strategy for dispensing with mathematics in phase space theories; or abandon nominalism.[19]

3.3. Accepting Indispensability

None of these worries about Field's programme are conclusive, but they do show that Field's approach to 'explaining away' the presence of mathematics in our scientific theories requires a lot of hard work. I will reserve judgement on whether Field's programme can in fact be completed: the central claim of this book is that the indispensability argument can be shown to fail even if mathematics *is* indispensable in formulating our scientific theories.

The details of this argument are to come, but the beginnings of an objection can be seen by focusing on the scientific realism that stands behind Field's acceptance of Quine's challenge to dispense with mathematics. Note that Field needs to argue that mathematics is dispensable in our best scientific theories because he thinks that the truth (or approximate truth) of such theories is confirmed by our theoretical successes. So once we remove the mathematics from such a scientific theory to come up with its nominalistic counterpart, Field (and Quine) think we ought to believe the claims made by that counterpart theory. But for the theories we actually have, this claim

---

[19] Even if a strategy can be found for dispensing with phase space theories, that might not be enough to save Field's nominalism. Aidan Lyon and Mark Colyvan (2008) have recently argued that phase space theories have explanatory power that would be lost in nominalist reformulations that do without phase spaces. Given that Field's project is to show that nominalistically unacceptable objects are dispensable from our *best* scientific theories, this loss of explanatory power is potentially fatal.

is surely implausible: even nominalistic versions of our best *actual* theories will contain elements whose truth we ought not to accept.

Consider Field's nominalization of Newtonian gravitational theory (ignoring for now the fact that this is not our best current theory—similar considerations will apply to nominalized versions of those theories if they are found). The basic objects of this theory are space-time points and regions of such points, configured in such a way that our usual mathematical version of Newtonian gravitational theory, with its $\mathbb{R}^4$ representations of these points, preserves the nominalistically stable facts about these objects. One implication of this is that, for example, straight lines in physical space (at a given time) must be thought to be isomorphic to segments of the real line, so that space (and indeed time) must be assumed to be continuous in this theory. So if we were to *believe* Field's nominalistic version of Newtonian gravitational theory, we would have to believe that space-time is continuous.[20]

As well as requiring us to make strong assumptions about the structure of physical space, believing Field's nominalistic alternative to Newtonian gravitational theory would likewise require us to make rather strong assumptions about the qualitative relations holding between space-time points, in order to claim that the quantitative mathematical correlates of these relations preserve these mathematical relations. Thus, for example, in mathematically representing *temperature* as a continuous function $t(x)$ on $\mathbb{R}^4$, our mathematical theory represents there to be a fact of the matter about the numerical temperature at each given point of space-time. And according to Field, this mathematical representation is a good one just because it preserves fundamental relational facts regarding the nominalistically acceptable relations 'y Temp-Bet xz', 'xy Temp-Cong zw', and 'x Temp-Less y' that do indeed hold between space-time points. But this means that, if we were to believe Field's nominalistic versions of Newtonian gravitational theory, we would have to believe that there are facts of the matter regarding whether any given *space-time point x* bears the relation of 'Temp-Less' to any other space-time point y.

But neither of these assumptions (that space and time are continuous, and that temperature is defined at the level of space-time points such that

---

[20] Note that the fact that Newton has been usurped by Einstein does not matter here: real number coordinates are still used to represent space-time points, and the assumption of continuity remains, even on the assumption of a more complicated curved space-time structure.

there is always a fact of the matter regarding whether x Temp-Less y or y Temp-Less x) are uncontroversially true. Indeed, the latter claim seems fairly uncontroversially *false*, given that 'temperature' is best understood as a macroscopic property of macroscopic regions. We might try to define 'x Temp-Less y' as 'x is a part of a region A and y is a part of a region B such that the region B is hotter than region A', but then depending on the size and shape of regions taken, both x Temp-Less y and y Temp-Less x might turn out to be true, contradicting our theory. And since we cannot take our regions to be arbitrarily small without losing the ability to define temperature for a region, we cannot rectify this problem by taking limits of the temperature at regions centred on x and y. So the assumption that there really are fundamental facts about the relative temperatures of pairs of individual space-time points seems overly strong. And while the assumption that space-time is continuous is not out-and-out *contradicted* by empirical evidence, it is nevertheless something that we might not consider to be supported by our current scientific worldview.

Thus, for example, in questioning the holist assumptions of the indispensability argument, Penelope Maddy (1997) has gathered evidence to suggest that, while scientists regularly make used of continuum mathematics in their theories of space-time, the jury is out as to whether space-time really is continuous. Maddy quotes the physicist Chris Isham's (1989: 72) concerns about the assumption of continuity:

It must be admitted that, at both the epistemological and ontological levels, our current understanding of space and time leaves much to be desired. In a gross extrapolation from daily experience, both special and general relativity use a model for spacetime that is based on the idea of a continuum, i.e. the position of a spacetime point is uniquely specified by the values of four real numbers (the three space, and one time, coordinates in some convenient coordinate system). But the construction of a 'real' number from integers and fractions is a very abstract mathematical procedure, and there is no *a priori* reason why it should be reflected in the empirical world. Indeed, from the viewpoint of quantum theory, the idea of a spacetime point seems singularly inappropriate: by virtue of the Heisenberg uncertainty principle, an *infinite* amount of energy would be required to localise a particle at a true point; and it is therefore more than a little odd that modern quantum field theory still employs fields that are functions of such points. It has often been conjectured that the almost unavoidable mathematical problems rising in such theories (the prediction of infinite values for the probabilities of physical processes occurring, and the associated need to 'renormalise' the theory . . .) are a direct result of ignoring this internal inconsistency. Be that as it may, it is clear that quantum gravity, with its natural Planck length, raises the possibility that the continuum nature of spacetime may not hold below this length, and that a quite different model is needed.

Richard Feynman (1965: 166–7) is even more committal, stating his conviction that 'the theory that space is continuous is wrong . . . I rather suspect that the simple ideas of geometry, extended down into infinitely small space, are wrong.'

If we are genuinely required to believe the nominalistically stated versions of our *current* scientific theories, then, it is likely that we will find ourselves committed to stronger assumptions about the nature of space and time than are accepted by most working scientists.

All this serves merely to highlight the fact that Quine's notion of our 'best' theory, all of whose components are equally confirmed by our theoretical successes, is (as Quine surely realizes) an ideal. In fact, it is conceivable that all the theories we actually make use of (even when regimented as carefully as possible) will contain components (such as the assumption of the continuity of space-time or the assumption that properties such as temperature can be defined at points) whose contribution to our theoretical successes may not depend on their literal truth. In holding that mathematics is confirmed by its use in empirical science, Quine's view is that, in moving towards an ideal, fully regimented theory, ironing out all idealizations and falsehoods, we will still find ourselves making use of mathematics. Field's response is that, in such an ideal theory in which such idealizations have been ironed out, the mathematical hypotheses will ultimately be unnecessary. But both assume (despite recognizing the presence of literally false or empirically unsupported idealizations in the theories we actually use) that such an ideal—a theory that states, without recourse to any idealizations or falsifying assumptions, our literally believed theoretical worldview—is at least theoretically possible.

But what if it isn't? What if it turns out that anything general enough to be called a *theory* is bound to contain some assumptions that ought not to be taken to be literally true? Perhaps even at the ideal limit the presence of some hypotheses in our best scientific theory might be best explained without assuming their truth, even if we do not have a literally believed alternative theory which does not make use of these hypotheses. If that were so, then even if we could not dispense with mathematics in expressing our best scientific theories, the question of whether the mathematics used in those theories receives empirical confirmation would remain, recast as the question of whether the use of mathematical hypotheses is explicable without assuming the truth of those hypotheses. And while Field's dispensability project, if successful, would provide *one* way of explaining why the mathematical components of our scientific theories are useful without being true, it is far from clear that this is the *only* way in which the theoretical usefulness of mathematical hypotheses can be explained. The ultimate dispensability of mathematics might turn out to be beside the point.

Let us, then, assume for now for the sake of argument that P3 of the indispensability argument is correct. That is, we will assume that, despite Field's admirable efforts in questioning this premise, it is in fact correct that statements whose truth would require the existence of mathematical objects are indispensable in expressing our best scientific theories. If we accept P3, then the only way we can now avoid the conclusion of the indispensability argument is to reconsider P2, Confirmational Holism. As naturalists, if we are to reject this criterion it must also be on naturalistic grounds—that is, on the grounds that it is not justified according to our ordinary scientific standards.

In fact, recent discussions of the indispensability argument (in particular, Maddy 1992; Sober 1993), have thrown doubt on the scientific grounds for P2. I will discuss these, along with other concerns about the indispensability argument, in Chapter 5. For now I will simply note that rejecting P2 might well be consistent with the *spirit* of the Quinean idea (presented above in sect. 2.2.1, and followed to the letter by Field) that we are committed to believing the existentially quantified utterances used to express our best scientific theories *unless we can account for the presence of these utterances as merely practical.* Quine and Field both consider a proof of eliminability to be the only way of showing that our speaking 'as if' there are ϕs is merely practical. However, loosening this requirement a little, we might find that there is room for an approach that explains the *indispensable* presence of quantifier commitments to mathematical objects in our best scientific theories as of merely practical utility. On such an account, our ordinary scientific standards would justify an attitude to our best scientific theories that falls short of full belief in their literal truth, since even our best theories might include some utterances that are best thought of as merely useful fictions. But before considering the reasons we might have for such an approach to the mathematical utterances of our *empirical* scientific theories, we should consider the question of whether our *pure* mathematical and logical practices give us reason to believe in mathematical objects.

4

Naturalism and Mathematical Practice

Assuming that mathematical hypotheses are indispensable in formulating our best empirical scientific theories, proponents of naturalism have, in the indispensability argument, one route to mathematical realism. If they are right that naturalism requires us to believe our best scientific theories, then it follows that we ought to be mathematical realists, at least concerning those mathematical objects indispensably hypothesized by those theories. However, for those impressed by the autonomy of pure mathematical practice, this route to mathematical realism might seem rather too circuitous. Much of our mathematical theorizing takes place in the context of pure mathematics, without a view to empirical applications. Mathematicians, when working on these theories, apply their own standards of justification. If naturalism requires that we trust our best scientific theories to tell us what there is, then surely this naturalism should extend to our pure mathematical theories, and to the internal mathematical standards of justification accepted by practitioners in developing these theories? We should, then, on this view, look first and foremost to our pure mathematical theories, rather than to the theories utilized in empirical science, to discover which mathematical objects we ought to accept as existing. And since these theories tell us of the existence of a plethora of mathematical objects, it appears that naturalism already counsels mathematical realism, independently of the question of the indispensability of mathematics in natural science.

Indeed, one might think that this is a good thing for naturalists. For, if it follows from Quinean naturalism that the indispensability of mathematics in natural science provides the *only* reason for believing in mathematical objects, then it looks as if this naturalism is in conflict with pure mathematical practice. Many theories that are justified according to the internal justificatory standards of pure mathematics will not turn out to be indispensable in applications, and so, presumably, will not be justified according to the naturalist's standards. Further- more, the norms of parsimony at work in natural science would seem to speak in favour of adopting particular set-theoretic reductions of various systems of mathematical objects, which goes against the math- ematical practice of refusing to identify the objects of mathematical theories such as number theory with their set-theoretic counterparts. Noticing this and other apparent points of conflict between mathemati- cal and scientific justificatory practices, Penelope Maddy (1992: 279) has complained that 'the indispensability argument shortchanges unapplied mathematics' and 'misrepresents the methodological realities of the math- ematics that is applied'. Maddy's complaint, which is shared by many, is that the indispensability argument for mathematical realism leads to an implausible philosophy of mathematics, according to which, in contrast with their usual justificatory practices, mathematicians ought to look to natural science to discover which amongst alternative mathematical the- ories they ought to be working on, and should take empirical evidence, rather than mathematical proof, as the ultimate test of their mathematical theorems.

Are Quinean naturalists mistaken, then, in resting the question of whether we ought to believe in mathematical objects on the role of mathematical hypotheses in our empirical theories? Is there a tension in Quine's version of naturalism in focusing too narrowly on our 'empiri- cal' standards of justification while ignoring the standards of justification at work in pure mathematical practice? I will argue in this chapter that there is no such tension. For a plausible view of our mathemat- ical practices is available to the Quinean naturalist, which allows such a naturalist to respect pure mathematics as it is practised. On such a view, we can respect the internal mathematical standards that govern the appropriateness or inappropriateness of making various mathematical utterances in the context of our mathematical theorizing, without viewing those standards as justifying belief in the truth of the sentences thereby uttered. Before turning to this response, though, let us consider just why Quinean naturalism may be thought to be in conflict with unapplied mathematics.

4.1. Mathematical and Scientific Norms: A Conflict?

Quinean naturalists have assumed that naturalism requires one to believe in the objects posited by a particular mathematical theory only if the hypothesis that there are such objects is required in formulating our best empirical theories. Thus, for Quine, acceptance of mathematical objects is a grudging matter. We accept only the minimal amount of mathematics required for the smooth formulation of our scientific theories. And while this might well lead to the acceptance of a significant amount of ordinary mathematics, if there remain any unapplied theories that go beyond the needs of science, these should be set aside as receiving no empirical confirmation:

> Pure mathematics, in my view, is firmly imbedded as an integral part of our system of the world. Thus my view of pure mathematics is oriented strictly to application in empirical science. Parsons has remarked, against this attitude, that pure mathematics extravagantly exceeds the needs of application. It does indeed, but I see these excesses as a simplistic matter of rounding out. We have a modest example of the process already in the irrational numbers: no measurement could be too accurate to be accommodated by a rational number, but we admit the extras to simplify our computations and generalizations. Higher set theory is more of the same. I recognize indenumerable infinities only because they are forced on me by the simplest known systematizations of more welcome matters. Magnitude in excess of such demands, e.g., $\beth_\omega$ or inaccessible numbers, I look upon only as mathematical recreation and without ontological rights. Sets that are compatible with '$V = L$' in the sense of Gödel's monograph[1] afford a convenient cut-off.   (Quine 1986: 400)

In fact, Solomon Feferman (1992) has suggested that even this rather modest amount of set theory (ZF + $V = L$)[2] is perhaps unnecessary to provide

---

[1] '$V = L$', or the 'axiom of constructibility', is the claim that the set-theoretic universe V is identical with the universe L of constructible sets, which Gödel introduced in his proof that the continuum hypothesis (CH) is consistent with the ZFC axioms. L was there introduced as an alternative to the usual cumulative hierarchy V of sets. As L forms a model for ZFC + CH, it proves that CH is consistent with ZFC, on the assumption that ZFC is itself consistent. Assuming that the set theoretic universe V is *identical* with L is, however, usually considered to be unduly restrictive. The hierarchical construction of L *suggests* that it contains many fewer sets than does the full set-theoretic hierarchy, since at each stage in the constructible hierarchy it is stipulated that only those subsets of the previous stage are formed which can be defined by means of first-order formulae whose quantifiers range over sets present at the previous stage. In the 'full' hierarchy, by contrast, we suppose that *all* combinatorially determined subsets of the previous stage are formed.

[2] Since '$V = L$' implies the axiom of choice, 'ZFC + $V = L$' is equivalent to 'ZF + $V = L$'.

all the analysis we need for empirical applications. Feferman proposes a predicative system, W, a conservative extension of PA, which he claims can provide a foundation for analysis of the sort required for physics.[3] At any rate, it is likely that the Quinean account will provide confirmation for only some amongst the many mathematical theories that are accepted as respectable from a pure mathematical perspective.

Let us assume, for now, that Quine is right that empirical science requires us to accept the existence of Gödel's universe 'L' of constructible sets, but no more. Then the axiom '$V = L$', which says that the constructible sets are all the sets there are, receives empirical confirmation on the Quinean view. But, as Maddy has stressed (see her 1990: 134), although the assumption that $V = L$ provides answers for many open questions in set theory (most famously, the continuum hypothesis), set theorists working on extensions of ZFC tend to consider the constructible universe, L, as overly restrictive. Why, when forming sets in the iterative hierarchy, should we imagine that only those are formed that our rules are able to describe? Elsewhere in mathematics the trend has been away from rule-governed constructions and towards allowing arbitrary constructions. No less so in set theory. 'ZF + $V = L$' may be sufficient for the purposes of empirical science, but mathematicians certainly feel no need to stop their set theoretic explorations there.

The norm of ontological economy, which pushes Quine to accept $V = L$ in favour of more expansionary set-theoretic axioms, also implies some *reductionist* consequences that appear to be in conflict with the norms at work in our pure mathematical practices. One great advantage of set theory is that the universe of sets (even Quine's rather restricted universe L) appears rich enough to provide models for all of the mathematical theories that we care to work on. Whenever we have need of a particular mathematical theory in empirical science, then, we can always find a set-theoretic model of this theory whose objects can do duty for the objects posited by that theory. Once we accept the existence of sets, then, we have all the mathematical objects we need. Other mathematical objects (numbers, for example), can be supposed to to exist, from the Quinean

---

[3] Since W is proof-theoretically reducible to PA, Feferman suggests that the ontological commitments of W need not be understood platonistically, since we could understand PA as about our 'mental conception of the structure of natural numbers' (Feferman 1992: 451). Thus Feferman suggests that the indispensability argument loses its ontological bite. I will not, however, pursue this line of thought here, since my main purpose in presenting Feferman's example is to suggest that it is plausible that only very weak mathematical systems are required in order to ground all scientifically applicable mathematics.

reductionist perspective, only as sets of a particular sort, and not as objects in their own right.

On the Quinean picture, then, the claim that Peano arithmetic is confirmed by its use in empirical science amounts to the claim that we should accept the Dedekind–Peano axioms as truths about some particular set-theoretic model. Which particular model we pick does not matter, Quine thinks: all that is important from a scientific perspective is that we pick a model which is convenient for empirical purposes. Which objects we are talking about when we talk about *the* natural numbers in empirical science is a matter of stipulation, not of discovery: 'to say more particularly what numbers themselves are is in no evident way different from just dropping numbers and assigning to arithmetic one or another new model, say in set theory' (Quine 1969*b*: 43–4). From the perspective of pure mathematics, however, such an attitude to set-theoretic reductions appears unwarranted. We can find many different ω-sequences in set theory and, indeed, elsewhere, to do duty for the natural numbers—but why should we be *forced* to pick any one of these, and stipulate that any one of these *really is* the natural number sequence? Picking one such sequence, and saying that these are the objects we were talking about all along when doing arithmetic, would seem entirely arbitrary. The reductionist motivations that make such a stipulation appealing are a by-product of the worldview of empirical scientists. Pure mathematicians would take some convincing before accepting such a stipulation.

Aside from counselling an overly restricted ontology and a reductionism that seems at odds with pure mathematical practice, the Quinean naturalist view of mathematics also appears to get things importantly wrong about the confirmation of mathematical theories. The claim that mathematical theories receive their confirmation through their role in empirical science carries with it the suggestion that, when those theories are falsified, in at least some cases it might be the mathematical hypotheses they use that should take the blame. But, as A. J. Ayer (1936: 69) pointed out in response to J. S. Mill's empiricist approach to mathematics, mathematicians *never* seem to take the falsification of a scientific theory as providing any evidence against the truth of the mathematics used in that theory:

if what appears to be a Euclidean triangle is found by measurement not to have angles totalling 180 degrees, we do not say that we have met with an instance which invalidates the mathematical proposition that the sum of the three angles of a Euclidean triangle is 180 degrees. We say that we have measured wrongly, or, more probably, that the triangle we have been measuring is not Euclidean. And this is our procedure in every case in which a mathematical truth might appear to be confuted. We always preserve its validity by adopting some other explanation of the occurrence.

More recently, Charles Parsons (1983*b*: 383) has also pointed to the apparent insulation of mathematical theories from empirical falsification as evidence against the Quinean picture, on the grounds that 'the known or easily conceivable examples of empirical falsification of mathematical theories in *science* do not yield any instance or model of empirical falsification of pure mathematics'. To say that Euclidean geometry is in fact falsified by developments in theoretical physics simply flies in the face of mathematical practice. From a mathematical perspective, Euclidean and non-Euclidean geometries are pursued side by side. The fact that the parallel axiom does not form a part of our best empirical theory of physical space in no way sullies it from a mathematical perspective. Doesn't this suggest, then, that the pure mathematical theories receive their confirmation from another source, that mathematicians have reasons to believe the theories of pure mathematics *independently* of any use those theories might turn out to have in empirical science?

Indeed, if one looks at how mathematicians justify their mathematical utterances, they do seem to appeal to internal mathematical reasons that are entirely independent of issues of empirical applicability. Thus, Maddy (1997: 106) points out that,

If a mathematician is asked to defend a mathematical claim, she will most likely appeal first to a proof, then to intuitions, plausibility arguments, and intra-mathematical pragmatic considerations in support of the assumptions that underlie it. From the point of view of the indispensability theorist, what actually does the justifying is the role of the claim, or the assumptions that underlie its proof, in well-confirmed physical theory. In other words, the justifications given in mathematical practice differ from those offered in the course of the indispensability defence of realism.

Furthermore, as we have seen, these internal mathematical standards of justification actually appear to conflict with the standards of evidence at work in empirical science. If we adopted the internal standards of mathematics in guiding our beliefs, we would find ourselves believing *more* mathematics than is required for science. We would accept the existence of more *sets* than the minimal amount required for empirical science, and we would accept the existence of objects of other mathematical theories, such as number theory, without accepting any parsimonious reduction of those objects to sets. Is this not a clear case of conflict between Quine's naturalist philosophy and successful mathematical practices? And, if so, should we not as naturalists conclude, with Maddy (ibid.: 161), that 'if our philosophical account of mathematics comes into conflict with successful mathematical practice, it is the philosophy that must give'?

4.2. Reasons to Utter and Reasons to Believe

In identifying, in the previous section, a *conflict* between our successful mathematical practices and the Quinean view of mathematics as receiving confirmation only from its role in empirical science, we have implicitly been assuming that reasons to utter a sentence in the context of (pure) mathematical theorizing are best viewed as reasons to believe the sentence one thereby utters. If this assumption is correct, then mathematical norms governing appropriate theoretical utterances may well provide justification for our believing more mathematics than is used in empirical science. And if so, the existence of direct mathematical evidence for our mathematical theories would render the indispensability argument for the existence of mathematical objects obsolete. The best evidence for the truth of mathematical utterances would be given by the internal mathematical reasons cited by mathematicians in support of those utterances: that is, the proofs, intuitions, plausibility arguments, and intra-mathematical pragmatic considerations that Maddy mentions.

In resting the issue of whether we have reason to believe in mathematical objects on the question of whether *empirical science* provides us with such a reason, those who take the indispensability argument seriously must be rejecting the assumption that *mathematical* reasons to speak as if there are ϕs in the context of our mathematical theorizing count as reasons to *believe* that there are ϕs. And this goes not only for those grudging Quinean realists who accept the indispensability argument as the only reason to believe in mathematical objects, but also for unrepentant anti-realists such as Field, who reject the indispensability argument and conclude from this that we have no reason to believe in mathematical objects. Since this is one point where fictionalists and Quinean realists must be in agreement, it will be helpful to take a moment to outline an understanding of pure mathematical practice that is available to both sides of this dispute.

The understanding I have in mind views the practice of pure mathematics as involved primarily in (*a*) formulating mathematical concepts, and (*b*) inquiring into the consequences of the assumption that those mathematical concepts are instantiated.[4] On such a view, the question of whether this assumption is, as a matter of fact, true—that is, of whether there are ultimately any objects correctly described by our mathematical concepts—should be of no interest to pure mathematicians qua mathematicians (though it may of course be of interest to them in so far as they wish to apply mathematics, or in so far as they have philosophical leanings). And if the question of whether a given mathematical concept is in fact satisfied by any objects is not a matter for mathematical inquiry, then whatever answer that empirical science gives to this question need not conflict with anything in the practice of pure mathematics. According to this view of mathematical utterances, an existentially quantified sentence may be justified as mathematically *good* independently of the question of whether it is in fact true of any objects. It may be part of a good characterization of an interesting mathematical concept, or it may follow from other sentences that are taken as characterizing an interesting mathematical concept. The

---

[4] Related accounts of pure mathematics are presented by Hartry Field (1984) and Mark Balaguer (2001). On Field's (1984: 83) view, the knowledge sought by mathematicians in the context of pure mathematical theorizing is '(i) knowledge that certain mathematical claims follow from certain other mathematical claims or bodies of claims, [and] (ii) knowledge of the consistency of certain mathematical claims or bodies of claims and other knowledge of a basically similar sort', so that a mathematical utterance made in the context of developing a consistent theory is correct just in case it follows logically from the assumptions of that theory. For Balaguer (2001: 91), on the other hand, 'A mathematical sentence is objectively correct just in case it is "built into", or follows from, the notions, conceptions, intuitions, and so on that we have in connection with the given branch of mathematics.' The main difference in these two accounts concerns how much of our 'notions, conceptions, intuitions, and so on' can be packed into the 'bodies of claims' that count as expressing a mathematical theory. Field sometimes seems to suggest a purely axiomatic approach to theories (e.g. his 1998: 391, where he argues that a mathematical sentence is correct just in case it is 'a consequence of accepted axioms'), whereas Balaguer wishes to focus on wider conceptions of mathematical objects that may go beyond axioms. My talk of 'formulating mathematical concepts' is intended to allow the possibility that mathematical practice within a pure theory is constrained by more than just the bare axioms of that theory. However, given that, unlike Balaguer, I am happy with second-order formulations of our mathematical theories, in the case of categorical (second-order) axiomatizations such as the axioms for Peano Arithmetic, axioms might be sufficient to provide all the relevant constraints on our theorizing.

discovery that empirical science requires us to hold that some (and only some) such mathematical concepts are instantiated by mathematical objects need make no difference to the mathematical practice of inquiring into what would have to be true were anything to satisfy the assumptions of our pure mathematical theories. Indeed, even if it turned out that empirical science confirmed the existence of *no* mathematical objects, mathematicians could continue as before in their hypothetical inquiry into what would have to be true were there any things that satisfied the axioms of their mathematical theories.[5]

To defend this picture of mathematical activity, we will need to consider the kinds of reason mathematicians give in favour of their theoretical utterances. Must these reasons be seen as reasons to *believe* those utterances, or can they be viewed as reasons to accept those utterances as correctly characterizing interesting mathematical concepts (without regard to the question of whether those concepts are satisfied)?

4.2.1. Mathematical Proof

Consider the kinds of 'justifications' Maddy tells us are offered by mathematicians in support of their mathematical utterances. Maddy lists proofs, intuitions, plausibility arguments, and intra-mathematical pragmatic considerations in favour of underlying assumptions. Of these, mathematical proof surely provides the strongest prima facie justification for a mathematical utterance—with intuitions and plausibility arguments often utilized as evidence that a proof is obtainable (we will leave aside pragmatic considerations for now). The first question we must ask, then, is does a mathematical proof provide us with a reason to believe the conclusion proved?

The answer to this question might seem to be an obvious 'Yes'. After all, deductive mathematical proof is often cited as providing mathematical conclusions with an enviable degree of certainty that is difficult to come by elsewhere. But here we must be careful: most mathematical proofs establish

---

[5] Quine's aforementioned view of this kind of inquiry as 'mathematical recreation . . . without ontological rights' perhaps leaves the impression that there is something self-indulgent about this kind of ontologically carefree mathematical activity. But whether or not Quine himself thinks this, an appropriate degree of modesty in reflecting on mathematical practices would surely require us to respect the value of this 'mathematical recreation'. After all, allowing mathematicians free rein to develop mathematical theories without being impeded by ontological scruples has, as a matter of fact, enabled the development of a vast wealth of mathematical tools that have turned out to be empirically useful.

their conclusions on the basis of some assumptions (axioms, or alternatively just generally accepted mathematical claims). In such cases, the conclusion of a mathematical deduction can only be as certain as the assumptions from which that conclusion has been deduced. If we provide a mathematical proof based on assumptions, we can conclude (so long as we accept that our derivation system is sound) that the conclusion of the proof must be true *if* those assumptions are true. But the question remains of what reason we have to believe the assumptions from which the conclusion has been derived.

There are, of course, mathematical proofs whose conclusions are based on no undischarged assumptions. For example (with the help of suitable definitions), we can prove the conditional claim 'If the Dedekind–Peano axioms are true, then there is an even prime number.' But the conclusions of such proofs are logical truths that imply no existential commitments (empty domains are, at least arguably, logically possible, and if this is so then one cannot get existential commitments out from logic alone).[6] In so far as we have mathematical proofs of statements whose truth would require the existence of any objects, those proofs must depend on some assumptions. Such proofs can tell us what would have to be true of anything satisfying the concepts governed by the mathematical assumptions we begin with, but by themselves they do not tell us that anything exists that satisfies those assumptions. It is reasonable, then, to understand mathematical proofs as justifying claims about what does and does not follow from our mathematical assumptions, without regard to the question of whether those assumptions are themselves true.

4.2.2. Believing the Axioms

We must turn, then, to the question of what attitude we should take to the assumptions from which we prove mathematical results. In particular, the question that should interest us is that of what attitude we should take to the axioms of our mathematical theories. Must we view mathematical

---

[6] Even if one rejects empty domains, it is standardly assumed that domains containing only *one* object are logically possible, in which case the point remains that one cannot get *substantial* existential commitments from logic alone. See e.g. George Boolos's (1997: 246) argument against any reading of logicism according to which the truths of arithmetic are held to be *logical* truths: 'Arithmetic implies that there are two distinct numbers; were the relativization of this statement to the definition of the predicate "number" provable by logic alone, logic would imply the existence of two distinct objects, which it fails to do (on any understanding of logic now available to us).'

reasons for adopting a given collection of axioms as reasons for believing that those axioms are true of a domain of mathematical objects? Or can we interpret such reasons as speaking to something other than the *truth* of the axioms they are presented as favouring?

In choosing axioms for a mathematical theory, mathematical proof is perhaps somewhat less important than the other 'justificatory' considerations Maddy mentions: intuition, plausibility arguments, and intra-mathematical pragmatic considerations. This is not to say that proof is entirely irrelevant in justifying some choices of axioms: although it may seem odd to think that axioms are something that can be *proved* (surely axioms must be prior to proof?), axiomatizations do often emerge as the conclusions of proofs. For example, it may be proved that a particular collection of 'naturally occurring' mathematical structures are pinned down by a collection of assumptions (which then become their axioms). But when choosing axioms, such proofs are just one amongst several kinds of considerations that can be given in favour of adopting a given axiom system. The question we must ask is, need we interpret any of these considerations as considerations in favour of the *truth* of the axioms they recommend?

The picture of pure mathematical practice I am suggesting views mathematicians as engaged in (*a*) characterizing mathematical concepts, and (*b*) enquiring into the consequences of the assumption that these concepts are satisfied. The practice of choosing mathematical axioms falls under the first of these activities. What I would like to argue, then, is that reasons offered in favour of adopting a given collection of axioms can be viewed as justifying their value as characterizations of interesting mathematical concepts, implying nothing about whether these concepts are true of any objects.

Take, for example, axioms justified by proof, such as the (second-order) Dedekind–Peano axioms for arithmetic. Richard Dedekind (1888, trans. 1901*b*), first presents these axioms as a *definition* of a kind of system of objects (a 'simply infinite' system). He then proves that any two simply infinite systems are isomorphic, sharing the structure of our intuitive conception of natural numbers (as a sequence of objects with a unique first element and, for every element, a unique successor). This justification of the axioms establishes that they succeed in pinning down the essential structure of our pre-axiomatic *conception* of the natural number sequence. But does acceptance of this justification require us to accept that there *are* any such sequences? Dedekind himself brings further considerations to bear to argue in favour of the actual existence of a simply infinite system: he thinks that reflection on those things that could be objects of thought shows that there is at least one infinite set of things. However, this rather contentious argument can be viewed as extra-mathematical. In so far as Dedekind's mathematical *proof* is concerned, it shows only that the axioms suffice to characterize our standard conception of natural numbers, not that there are any objects satisfying that conception. The axioms are therefore justified as 'good' candidates for characterizing our concept of number, without being justified as being true *of numbers*.

Dedekind's proof is not, of course, presented as a proof *of the Dedekind–Peano axioms*: he is, after all, proffering these as genuine *axioms*, and he takes the proof as significant because it shows the axioms to characterize a unique structure. But perhaps there is room to ask for more than this—a genuine proof, or at least an argument, to establish that the axioms for arithmetic are *true*, and not just that they characterize the natural number structure up to isomorphism. An alternative account of axioms holds that genuine axioms should be immediately graspable *truths* about their objects. This was certainly Gottlob Frege's view: according to Frege, genuine axioms express 'fundamental facts of intuition' (Gabriel et al. 1980: 35). On this account, the Dedekind–Peano *postulates*, although true of natural numbers, should not be viewed as axioms since they are consequences of more fundamental facts of intuition that we can grasp as logical truths. And while Frege's own derivation of the Dedekind–Peano postulates from logical truths failed (since the 'logical truths' he started with included the contradictory Basic Law V (Frege 1967)), it has been shown (Parsons 1965; Wright 1983) that these postulates can be derived from Hume's principle ('The number of Fs = the number of Gs if and only if $F \approx G$'). If Hume's principle can be known to be true as a 'fundamental fact of intuition', then we have a justification for our mathematical axioms that goes beyond justification of them as characterizing interesting mathematical concepts: our justification by intuition will show them to be true of their objects, the natural numbers.

But do we know Hume's principle as a 'fundamental fact of intuition'? Crispin Wright (1997: 210–11) takes the principle to be explanatory of our concept of number. Once we have grasped this concept, on Wright's view we grasp that there are numbers, since we can know the right-hand side of the principle to be a truth of second-order logic for some Fs and

Gs. So, while Hume's principle, taken as an axiom, can be viewed, as we have suggested all axioms should be viewed, simply as characterizing a mathematical concept, this particular concept turns out to be one that we can know, as a matter of logic, to be instantiated. Our assumption thus far has been that there is a gap between having a concept and knowing that that concept is instantiated, and that the latter question needs to be answered by means of empirical inquiry. Wright's suggestion is that for at least some concepts (in particular, for the concept of number), one only needs to grasp the concept to know that, given our grasp of some second-order logical truths, the concept is true of some objects.

There is, however, an acceptable alternative reading of Hume's principle as true 'of our concept of number' that does not carry with it such ontological implications. We might think of Hume's principle as true of our concept of number in the sense that, *if there were numbers*, Hume's principle would have to be true of them. That is, presented with any purported number-forming operator #, taking concepts to associated numbers, we would only count this as a genuine *number-forming* operator if it satisfied the equivalence $\#F = \#G \equiv F \approx G$. But accepting Hume's principle as constitutive of our concept of number in this sense does not guarantee the existence of such a number-forming operator, any more than accepting the Dedekind–Peano Axioms as constitutive of our concept of number guarantees that there are any objects satisfying those axioms. Indeed, from a purely logical perspective, in a finite domain of size n, we know that no number-forming operator # (from concepts on the domain to objects in the domain) can exist that satisfies Hume's principle, since there are $n + 1$ equivalence classes of subsets of that domain, under the equivalence relation 'is equinumerous with', but only n objects in the domain that could count as possible numbers.

Similar considerations can be brought to bear on other purported *intuitive* or *plausible* grounds for accepting axioms. Where a realist may take our intuitions to be intuitions about mathematical objects, an alternative ontologically neutral account can view such intuitions as intuitions about our mathematical concepts. The prime case for this is set theory: Kurt Gödel (1947: 484) famously claimed that we have a perception-like intuition 'of the objects of set theory, as is seen from the fact that the axioms force themselves upon us as being true'. Accepting the phenomenon of mathematical intuition, an ontologically neutral reading could view such intuitions as intuitions that the axioms correctly characterize our iterative conception of set (a concept which, in Gödel's (ibid.: 474) words, is based on our grasp of the 'iterated application of the operation "set of "' to the integers or other well-defined objects). Indeed, despite his own platonism, even Gödel seems to concede that the question of the objective existence of sets about which we can have intuitions is ultimately irrelevant to the question of whether mathematical intuitions can be brought to bear in justifications of new set-theoretic axioms:

the question of the objective existence of the objects of mathematical intuition . . . is not decisive for the problem under discussion here. The mere psychological fact of the existence of an intuition which is sufficiently clear to produce the axioms of set theory and an open series of extensions of them suffices to give meaning to the question of the truth or falsity of propositions like Cantor's continuum hypothesis.   (ibid.: 484–5)

What matters, it seems, is that we can appeal to intuition to pin down more precisely our mathematical *concepts*, in such a way that we may be able to discover whether open questions such as the continuum hypothesis follow from our more precise efforts at characterizing those concepts. But our having an intuitive grasp of the content of our mathematical concepts in no way implies that we can grasp, by intuition, the existence of objects satisfying those concepts.

Turning finally to intra-mathematical *pragmatic* considerations, such as the mathematical fruitfulness or simplicity of a candidate axiom system, we have perhaps the easiest case for an ontologically neutral account. Here the onus is surely on the realist to explain the relation between mathematical fruitfulness and truth. After all, just because the axiom of choice has lots of fruitful consequences, why should *that* give us reason to believe it correctly describes the sets? For an ontologically neutral account, though, if we see mathematicians as involved in characterizing interesting mathematical concepts, fruitful consequences certainly count in favour of mathematical interest. Whether or not there is a universe of sets satisfying the axiom of choice, the assumption that there are such things allows for the development of a great deal of fruitful and interesting mathematics. In this development, why should mathematicians be held back by ontological concerns about what the mathematical realm is *really* like?

4.3. Against Recreational Mathematics

I have suggested that pure mathematical inquiry can be viewed as inquiry into the consequences of interesting mathematical concepts, without regard to the question of whether these concepts are true of any objects. To borrow Quine's phrase, we can view such inquiry as 'mathematical recreation . . . without ontological rights', preserving *ontological* questions as questions about which existentially quantified claims empirical science requires us to believe. On such a view, since the value of a pure mathematical theory as a piece of pure mathematics is independent of the question of whether that theory has been confirmed as true, we have an explanation of the autonomy of pure mathematical practice, and of the insulation of pure mathematical theories from empirical falsification. Falsified theories may still be considered mathematically good, since their goodness does not rest on their being true of any objects. Looking at the kinds of reason mathematicians give in support of their mathematical utterances, we have so far not found any grounds to take these as providing evidence for the *truth* of such claims. This speaks in favour of the recreational view of pure mathematics. But there are several objections to this picture of mathematical activity that must be considered before we can be happy to leave questions about the ontology of mathematics to empirical science to answer.

4.3.1. *The Obviousness of Elementary Mathematics*

On the Quinean naturalist picture that I am endorsing, the question of whether the utterances of standard mathematics assert truths is a highly theoretical matter: it will depend on their role in our best confirmed scientific theories. Before we know the answer to this question, we cannot know the truth of even the most elementary mathematical claims. That $2 + 2 = 4$, for example, will not be a matter of knowledge: at best, we can know that *it follows from the Dedekind–Peano axioms* that $2 + 2 = 4$,[7] leaving it to empirical science to establish whether the Dedekind–Peano axioms are in fact true of any objects.

This implication of the 'recreationalist' picture strikes many as implausible. Surely, the objection goes, we should take the truth of claims such as

---

[7] Or, that '*If there were numbers*, then $2 + 2$ would equal 4.'

$2 + 2 = 4$ as immediately given data, and look for a philosophical account of such truths as truths. Thus, according to Charles Parsons (1979–80: 152), it is 'a gross fact about arithmetic, that a considerable body of arithmetical truths is known to us in some more direct way than is the case for the knowledge we acquire by empirical reasoning'. Parsons (ibid.) suggests that the best explanation of this phenomenon is 'the hypothesis that we have direct knowledge of these truths because the objects they are about are given to us in some direct way'. The problem with the Quinean view, which rests the confirmation of even elementary arithmetic on its role in formulating the theoretical posits of empirical science, is that it simply does not fit this aspect of our experience. 'The empiricist view, even in the subtle and complex form it takes in the work of Professor Quine, seems subject to the objection that it leaves unaccounted for precisely the *obviousness* of elementary mathematics (and perhaps also of logic)' (ibid.: 151). Contrary to our suggestion, not all mathematics can be viewed as recreational (until proved otherwise): for at least some claims of elementary arithmetic, it is *obvious* to us that these claims are literally *true*.

The 'gross fact' to which Parsons appeals, however, is something that anyone attracted to the 'recreationalist' picture of mathematical practice will doubt. Parsons simply *assumes* that we do have a considerable amount of arithmetical knowledge. His claim is that some basic arithmetical propositions are *obviously* true. But if it is *obvious* that, for example, there is an even prime number, then it is likewise obvious that there are numbers, since this latter is a trivial logical consequence of the former claim. If this is right, then, as Mark Colyvan (2001: 117) has pointed out, it 'would mean that the debate over the reality of numbers that has been raging for over two thousand years has an obvious answer—Platonism is correct'. But surely the mere existence of a debate over this matter speaks against the claim that the truth of the arithmetic propositions in question is genuinely obvious? (At the very least, if their truth is obvious, it cannot be obviously so!) This would be too much even for many of those on the 'Yes' side of the debate over mathematical ontology to accept: 'Now I'm a Platonist, but I don't think that it is *obvious* that there are numbers' (ibid.).

If Colyvan is right, then it appears that the 'gross fact' in need of explanation is not so much the 'obviousness' of elementary mathematics, but rather, the *feeling* we have that much of elementary mathematics is obviously true. But here we have something that defenders of the 'recreationalist' view of pure mathematics can account for without accepting the truth of arithmetic.

Although no claim that implies the existence of mathematical objects can be obvious, Parsons is surely right to suggest that the propositions of elementary arithmetic have at least an air of obviousness about them. The equation '2 + 2 = 4' is something that is difficult to doubt, even for anti-platonists who would reject the closely related claim '$(\exists n)(n + 2 = 4)$' as carrying with it an unwarranted ontological commitment to numbers. But, despite its apparent indubitability, Colyvan suggests that our willingness to attribute 'obviousness' to such claims of elementary arithmetic might rest on a confusion. Perhaps what is obvious to us is just that certain propositions, including the proposition that $2 + 2 = 4$, follow logically from the assumption that there are numbers satisfying the Dedekind–Peano axioms.[8] But no immediate ontological worries arise from the thought that it may be obvious what *follows from* some hypotheses, so that it is obvious to anyone who knows some basic number theory that, 'If number theory is true, then $(\exists n)(n + 2 = 4)$.'

It might be objected that it is obvious to us that $2 + 2 = 4$ even before we know much number theory. Against this, Colyvan (ibid. 121–2) warns that we should be careful in attributing obviousness to sentences of basic arithmetic that we learn from an early age, since this early conditioning might create an illusion of obviousness: 'we learn the rudiments of number theory very young and without any concern for ontology. Consequently, when we come to consider examples from number theory in the context of deciding whether mathematics is a priori or a posteriori, our intuitions are corrupted by this deeply ingrained, undiscriminating, early training in arithmetic.' This is not to say that, were it not for our early training, we might have found *different* number-theoretic claims obvious. Perhaps, as George Orwell imagined in *Nineteen Eighty-Four*, a lot of painful deconditioning would shake our confidence in even this piece of basic arithmetic, but if this was what Colyvan had in

---

[8] How about mathematical truths that appear, on reflection, to be obvious or intuitive but which are not consequences of our axioms? The Dedekind–Peano axioms surely had that status *prior* to the axiomatization of number theory. In this case, the feeling of obviousness might be explained in relation to our pre-axiomatic conception of numbers. Thus, for example, Mark Balaguer (2001: 104) has argued that 'intuitiveness is a sign of [mathematical] correctness because correctness is determined by our intentions and our intentions are determined by the notions, conceptions, intuitions, and so on that we have in the given branch of mathematics'.

mind with this example, it would be hard to take it very seriously. If someone persistently asserted that $2 + 2 = 5$ and not 4, it is not clear whether we should credit them with a belief that $2 + 2 = 5$ rather than with a failure to understand what we mean by numerical singular terms. Colyvan's point, however, is somewhat different: our early training in basic arithmetic conditions us to accept claims about numbers as true without regard to the ontological commitments they bring with them, so that by the time we come to consider matters of *ontology*, we find it hard to take seriously the possibility that there may not be any numbers.

But might we not still find such claims as '$2 + 2 = 4$' obvious even if, by some strange quirk of fate, we had missed out on childhood conditioning and only come to consider them once we had the critical faculties required to recognize their ontological baggage? While Colyvan's warning not to place too much weight on intuitions about basic arithmetic is welcome, we might worry about resting our case against the obviousness of such claims solely on this hypothesis about the effects of our early training. It is fortunate, then, that there is another way of accounting for some of the apparent obviousness of the unconditional statement '$2 + 2 = 4$' that does not rely on a story about our susceptibility to childhood conditioning. It is common to justify our confidence in the truth of statements of (unquantified) elementary arithmetic, such as '$2 + 2 = 4$', by appeal to counting. The roots of basic arithmetic in counting suggests a further explanation of the obviousness of simple sums. When we say that it is obvious that $2 + 2 = 4$, it is plausible that we sometimes mean, not that it is obvious that *number theory implies that* $2 + 2 = 4$, but rather, that it's obvious that if I correctly count exactly two objects of one sort (for example, fingers I'm holding up on my left hand), and exactly two objects of another sort (for example, fingers I'm holding up on my right hand), then taking these together I will be able to count exactly four objects that are either of the first sort or the second sort. But this just makes adjectival use of the natural numbers, and such uses can be formalized without quantification over natural numbers.

$$((((\exists x)(\exists y)(x \neq y \ \& \ (\forall z)(Fz \equiv (z = x \lor z = y))) \ \&$$
$$(\exists x)(\exists y)(x \neq y \ \& \ (\forall z)(Gz \equiv (z = x \lor z = y)))) \ \&$$
$$\neg(\exists x)(Fx \ \& \ Gx)) \supset (\exists x)(\exists y)(\exists z)(\exists w)((((((x \neq y \ \& \ \cdot$$

$$x \neq z) \mathbin{\&} x \neq w) \mathbin{\&} y \neq z) \mathbin{\&} y \neq w) \mathbin{\&} z \neq w) \mathbin{\&}$$
$$((\forall t)(Ft \vee Gt) \equiv (((t = x \vee t = y) \vee t = z) \vee t = w))))$$

Although the logical formalization of such a claim is rather a mouthful, the claim that if there are exactly two Fs, exactly two Gs, and nothing that's both F and G, then there are exactly four Fs or Gs, is a straightforward logical truth. But this claim by itself does not imply the existence of mathematical objects. And if we view the sentence '$2 + 2 = 4$' as, on some occasions, *simply* being used to express claims of this sort (for example, as shorthand for a corresponding logical truth), the move to the quantified claim $(\exists n)(n + 2 = 4)$ will be unwarranted.[9] The superficial similarity of some quantifier-free claims of number theory to logically true generalizations about objects should not be taken to show that it is the truth of *number theory* that is justified by the obviousness of some of these logical truths.

When Parsons speaks of the obviousness of some claims of elementary arithmetic, then, it is plausible that what is obvious is not those arithmetic claims considered as part of full number theory, which, if true, carry with them ontological implications. We might find it obvious that certain conclusions follow from the axioms of number theory, or from our pre-axiomatic intuitive conception of number, or we might find adjectival analogues of sentences of basic arithmetic obvious. Alternatively, as Colyvan suggests, we might be under an illusion that the claims, considered as claims of full (platonistic) number theory, are obvious, just as a result of our familiarity from an early age with this theory. Our pretheoretic sense that some claims of arithmetic are obvious can thus be accounted for in several ways, without presupposing the existence of mathematical objects. But if this is the case, then it might still be (as Quine supposes) that the only reason we might have for believing (the highly non-obvious claim) that there *are* natural numbers stems from the central role such objects play in our physical theories.

---

[9] This is not to say that *all* uses of $2 + 2 = 4$ should be viewed as shorthand for logical truths of this sort, but only that, in some contexts, the bare arithmetic claim is put forward when a claim making adjectival use of numbers will suffice. Within number theory, however, $2 + 2 = 4$ should surely be viewed as a statement about *numbers* (from which it follows, for example, that 'There is a number which, added to itself, gives 4').

4.3.2. Naturalistic Scruples

A second objection to the 'recreationalist' interpretation of pure mathematical practice is that it requires us to view many mathematicians as either systematically mistaken in their mathematical utterances, or as misleadingly not really meaning what they say. For, in the context of doing mathematics, mathematicians regularly utter sentences whose truth would require the existence of mathematical objects, and do so without explicitly disavowing the truth of those utterances (for example by making clear that they are intended only as conditional on the supposition that there are numbers or sets). If mathematicians really believe the utterances they make in the context of mathematical theorizing, then the recreationalist view holds them to be mistaken. And if mathematicians do not believe those utterances, then shouldn't we expect them at least sometimes to be explicit about this?

This objection has been pressed by John P. Burgess against fictionalist views of pure mathematics. Fictionalists accept the 'recreationalist' view of mathematical practice laid out in this chapter. (I have labelled the view 'recreationalist' rather than fictionalist, simply because I take the view to be available as an account of pure mathematics even to realists, such as Quine, who ultimately disagree with fictionalists about the truth of our mathematical theories.) Burgess separates two kinds of fictionalist approach to pure mathematics, hermeneutic and revolutionary, and argues that both fail as accounts of mathematical practice.

Hermeneutic fictionalists hold that their interpretation of mathematicians as involved in working out the consequences of their mathematical assumptions correctly characterizes mathematicians' own views of what they mean when they utter mathematical sentences: 'The hermeneutic fictionalist maintains that *the mathematicians' own understanding* of their talk of mathematical entities is that it is a form of fiction, or akin to fiction' (Burgess 2004: 23). On this view, when mathematicians utter sentences such as 'There is an even prime number,' what they really *mean* are the hypothetical claims, 'If there are numbers, as characterized by the Dedekind–Peano axioms, then there is an even prime number,' or perhaps 'According to the story of number theory, there is an even prime number.' Burgess's objection to hermeneutic fictionalism is that there is no evidence that most mathematicians do mean their utterances in this less than committed way. And if they wish to claim that mathematicians should be so interpreted, hermeneutic fictionalists need some positive evidence that this is the case: 'the "literal" interpretation is not just one interpretation among others. It is the *default* interpretation. There is a *presumption* that people mean and believe what they say. It is, to be sure, a *defeasible* presumption, but some *evidence* is needed to defeat it' (ibid.: 26).

Revolutionary fictionalists, on the other hand, hold that while mathematicians may well intend their theoretical utterances to be taken literally as attempted assertions of truths, they are simply mistaken about this. The revolutionary fictionalist is thus involved in 'denying while doing philosophy what is asserted while doing mathematics, but not pretending that it never *was* asserted, or pretending that it was only asserted but wasn't really *meant* or *believed*' (ibid.: 28). Against this version of fictionalism, Burgess cites approvingly David Lewis's aforementioned objection to philosophical rejections of the claims of successful disciplines (see sect. 2.1.1). Following Lewis, Burgess (ibid.: 30) concludes that 'given the comparative historical records of success and failure of philosophy on the one hand, and of mathematics on the other, to propose philosophical 'corrections' to mathematics is *comically immodest*'.

I have discussed the issue of how much philosophical modesty is appropriate in Chapter 2, and in response to Burgess's concern, I need only reiterate what was said there. The 'recreationalist' account offers no revision to mathematical practices. Rather, it offers an interpretation of those practices that makes sense of mathematicians' judgements as to what counts as mathematically appropriate or inappropriate. Whether or not mathematicians *themselves* operate as 'recreationalists', conceptualizing their own practice as inquiry into what does and does not follow from assumptions that characterize interesting mathematical concepts, is simply irrelevant as regards this interpretation.[10] Indeed, it might well be the case that, when doing mathematics, adopting a straightforwardly realist attitude turns out to be pragmatically very helpful in stimulating inquiry into what follows from mathematical assumptions. If so, then even if Burgess is right that many mathematicians do see themselves as asserting truths about a realm of mathematical objects, so that the recreationalist account of mathematical practice is best viewed as revolutionary rather than hermeneutic, we

---

[10] In fact, given the variety of metaphysical views amongst mathematicians, it is likely whether the recreationalist interpretation turns out to be 'hermeneutic' or 'revolutionary' will vary depending on which mathematician one claims to be interpreting.

need not criticize such mathematicians qua mathematicians for working on the basis of this misconception. A philosophical interpretation of mathematical practice need not impinge even on mathematicians' own conception of their practice. Proposing a philosophical 'correction' to the interpretation of mathematical practice while advocating the preservation of that practice (and allowing mathematicians to adopt whatever attitude to that practice they find practically useful) does not amount to immodesty of comic proportions. Rather it can be viewed as an appropriate use of naturalistic philosophy as continuous with science in helping to provide an understanding of one aspect of human activity.

4.3.3. Consistency and Consequence

A final objection to the 'recreationalist' picture, and perhaps the most pressing, holds that, even if some mathematical practices can be interpreted from a perspective that remains ontologically neutral about the question of whether our mathematical theories correctly describe mathematical objects, not all such practices can be interpreted from that perspective. In particular, on the recreationalist view, part of what makes for a *good* axiomatic theory is that the axioms one starts with are *consistent*. And part of what makes for an appropriate utterance in the context of such an axiomatic theory is that one's utterance is a *logical consequence* of the theory's axioms. So the recreationalist account is committed to the *truth* of various claims about the logical status of our mathematical theories (claims concerning consistency and logical consequence). And commitment to the truth of these claims carries with it implicit commitment to the truth of some claims concerning mathematical objects (either in stating what one means by consistency and logical consequence in terms, for example, of the existence of mathematical models, or alternatively in justifying such claims by appeal to facts about mathematical models).

Recently, for example, essentially this objection has been presented against instrumentalist accounts of the use of mathematics in empirical science by Michael D. Resnik (1995: 173 n.6), who notes that 'even if we replace truth with truth in a story, we want some constraints on our stories. They should be consistent, and what is true in them should follow logically from their premises. Stating and proving that various stories have these properties will require a background mathematics.' And focusing just on pure mathematics, Michael Potter (2007: 19) has noted that whatever background theory we use to provide, for example, counterexamples to claims about what follows from the assumptions of a given mathematical theory, 'we cannot be implicationist about [that theory] as well, because that simply postpones the problem: at some point in the process there needs to be something we can assert as *true*, not just conditionally'.

This objection is essentially the objection to Field's use of mathematics to justify metalogical claims, as discussed in sect. 3.2.1. The concern there was that, either we view the claim that a theory is consistent as the claim that it has a mathematical model (in which case, a belief in the consistency of a theory is itself a belief in the existence of mathematical objects), or even if we do not accept this reduction of claims about consistency and logical consequence to claims about mathematical models, our justification of such claims will depend on our accepting the truth of some claims about mathematical models. So, the objection goes, either way, our acceptance of certain beliefs about the logical status of our mathematical theories will commit us to the existence of some mathematical objects, and hence to a non-recreational account of at least some mathematical theories.

My response to this objection is, then, simply to adopt Field's answer, as sketched in Chapter 3. This involves, first, rejecting the reductionist view of claims about consistency and logical consequence as claims about set-theoretic models. Rather, following Field, I take claims concerning consistency to be irreducibly modal, holding that we grasp the idiom 'it is consistent that' through its inferential role. Secondly, again borrowing from Field, I note that our reliance on background mathematical theories such as set theory in justifying claims about consistency and consequence (for example, by providing models of the axioms of a theory, or providing countermodels that show that a given sentence is not a consequence of our theoretical assumptions) is reasonable *so long as we have reason to believe such theories to be consistent*. If our chosen set theory implies the existence of a model of the axioms of some other mathematical theory, this allows us to conclude that that theory is consistent *so long as set theory is*. So on the assumption that it is reasonable to believe that our background set theory is consistent, our acceptance, as against the backdrop of an axiomatic theory, of set theoretic models as providing evidence for claims about consistency and logical consequence will also be reasonable, even if we do not believe in sets.

I conclude, then, that nothing in our pure mathematical practices requires that we view pure mathematicians as involved in anything more than searching for axioms that characterize interesting mathematical concepts, and inquiring into what does and does not follow from the assumption that there are objects satisfying those concepts. The question of whether the theories developed in the context of pure mathematics are actually *true* of any objects can be left, as Quine suggests, as a matter for empirical science to decide; whether or not our mathematical theories receive scientific confirmation as true need make no difference whatsoever to their status as interesting parts of pure mathematics. In so far as our concern is with ontology, then, and in particular with the question of whether we have reason to believe that there are any mathematical objects, the issue is properly approached by naturalists as a question concerning the appropriate attitude to our empirical, scientific theories. Must we follow Quine in taking all components of our best scientific theories, including their mathematical hypotheses, to be confirmed by our theoretical successes, or is their room, against Quine's holist assumptions, to pick and choose amongst those hypotheses, holding only some of them to be confirmed as true or approximately true? It is to this question that we will now turn.

5

Naturalism and Scientific Practice

The direct argument from the indispensability of mathematical posits in our pure mathematical theories to the existence of the objects posited was blocked in the previous chapter by showing that our standards for assertibility for sentences of our pure mathematical theories fall short of providing us with reasons to believe that those sentences are true. From the perspective of pure mathematics, the question of whether there really exist objects about which our mathematical theories assert truths is of no consequence for the mathematical questions that interest us. We can, it was argued, understand *pure* mathematical theorizing as inquiry into what follows logically from the assumption that there are mathematical objects of a particular sort, without regard to the question of whether there are in fact any such objects. Hence it is no criticism of pure mathematical practice to define mathematics as 'the subject in which we never know what we are talking about, nor whether what we are saying is true' (Russell 1901: 84). But, since we can account for the practices of pure mathematics without supposing that sentences uttered in the context of our pure mathematical theorizing are true, it follows that the only naturalistic argument that can be given for the existence of mathematical objects is indirect, via their presence as indispensable posits in other theories outside the context of pure mathematics. And, given the apparent indispensability of mathematical posits in our empirical scientific theories, it is empirical science that provides the most promising prospects for an argument for the existence of mathematical objects.

In this case, Quine thinks that naturalism requires us to believe in all those objects posited by our empirical theories, since he thinks that our reasons to speak as if P is true in the context of our empirical scientific theorizing *just are* reasons to believe that P. For, what else could 'trusting science' amount to than accepting as true those sentences we use to state the assumptions of our best scientific theories? If this is right, then if S is a sentence whose literal truth would require that P, then if S is indispensable in formulating our best scientific theories, we ought to believe that P. To say that the truth of a sentence is confirmed by our ordinary scientific standards of evidence just is, on this view, to say that that sentence is indispensable to the best formulation of our best scientific theory. Quine's naturalism thus requires us to believe (at least until we have found a better alternative) all theoretical hypotheses used in formulating our current best confirmed scientific theories, together with all their consequences. A reason to speak as if P is true, in the context of our best scientific theorizing, cannot, on this view, be distinguished from a reason to believe that P.

This aspect of Quine's understanding of science has come under attack in recent years, on the grounds that it leads to an implausible picture of scientific practice. Objectors have argued that, in contrast with Quine's own picture, one can clearly discern a distinction in our scientific theories between those assumptions whose truth we ought to believe and those whose presence in our successful theories can be accounted for by appeal to reasons other than their literal truth. It appears that is sometimes convenient, for scientific purposes, to speak as if P is true, even if one has independent reason to disbelieve P, or if one has doubts as to the literal truth of P. Hence, even in empirical science, a reason to speak as if P is true cannot *always* count as a reason to believe that P. If this is right, then it would simply be in *conflict* with the naturalistic aim to understand science on its own terms to impose a picture of scientific theories whereby the truth of all sentences used in formulating our most successful current theories is considered as equally well confirmed by their presence in those theories. Quine's confirmational holism is therefore, on this view, in conflict with his naturalism.

But if confirmational holism is mistaken, then the indispensability argument for the existence of mathematical objects needs to be revisited. The mere presence, in our best presentations of our scientific theories, of sentences whose literal truth would require the existence of mathematical objects, will not give us reason to believe that there are such objects, if those sentences are not amongst the parts of our theories whose literal truth should be considered as confirmed by our ordinary scientific standards. And in fact, if we look at the ways in which mathematically stated hypotheses are treated in the context of our scientific theorizing, there are some prima facie grounds for thinking that the truth of these hypotheses is *not* generally considered as confirmed by our theoretical successes. Thus, several recent criticisms of the indispensability argument have stressed the special place mathematical hypotheses appear to have in our scientific theories (see e.g. Maddy 1992, 1997; Sober 1993; Vineberg 1996). If these objectors are right about the confirmational isolation of mathematical posits in our theories, then we will have grounds for questioning the inference from the indispensable use, in formulating our scientific theories, of sentences whose literal truth would require the existence of mathematical objects, to the existence of the objects required for their truth.

If these naturalist critiques of Quine's confirmational holism are correct, then it appears that Quine is too quick to assume that naturalism requires us to be scientific realists. And, if a gap can be found between the naturalist's requirement to believe those theoretical hypotheses that are confirmed according to our ordinary standards of confirmation and the scientific realist's requirement to believe the face-value truth of all the sentences used in formulating best scientific theories, then naturalism need not imply mathematical realism, *even if mathematically stated hypotheses are indispensable to our best scientific theories*. In the remaining chapters of this book, I will exploit this gap, arguing that we can account for our reasons to include mathematical hypotheses in our scientific theories without assuming that we ought to believe that these hypotheses are true. Hence scientific naturalism does not give us reason to believe in the existence of mathematical objects. In this chapter, though, I wish just to consider more closely the objections to Quine's confirmational holism that seem to suggest that scientific confirmation is a more complicated matter than the holistic view suggests.

5.1. Scientific Confirmation and Mathematical Posits

Quine's confirmational holism requires him to interpret the naturalist's commitment to trusting science as a commitment to believing the truth of all sentences used in formulating our best scientific theories. But if confirmational holism is mistaken, then we will need to look again at the position of mathematical assumptions in our scientific theories, in order to consider whether their truth should be considered as confirmed by our scientific successes. And if we do look at the role played by mathematical assumptions in our scientific theories, there are some intriguing hints that suggest that the special role of mathematical hypotheses in our theories might set them apart, confirmationally, from other theoretical assumptions.

Elliott Sober (1993), for example, points out that the very same *pure* mathematical statements are often assumed as a backdrop to all competing scientific theories. And, taking confirmation of theoretical hypotheses to be essentially contrastive (where observation O confirms hypothesis H over H' iff $P(O/H) > P(O/H')$, Sober (1993: 45) suggests that if the same pure mathematical statements are required in order to formulate each of our competing hypotheses, then the mathematical statements we make use of can receive no confirmation from their presence in the hypothesis we end up choosing, in the light of such contrastive tests: 'If the mathematical statements M are part of *every* competing hypothesis, then, no matter which hypothesis comes out best in the light of the observations, M will be part of that best hypothesis. M is not tested by this exercise, but is simply a background assumption common to the hypotheses under test.' We might think of such pure mathematical statements, required in order to formulate *any* of our empirical hypotheses, as what C. S. Peirce would call 'regulative assumptions of inquiry': such assumptions are required in order to get our theorizing off the ground, but may nevertheless lack any empirical support of their own. In Peirce's work, for example, one such assumption is that there are determinate answers to the questions into which we inquire. As Cheryl Misak (1901: 141) explains, 'the justification for the regulative hypothesis is merely one of "desperation"—if we do not make it, we will "be quite unable to know anything of positive fact" (*CP* 5. 603, 1903). Such an assumption is one we must "embrace at the outset, however destitute of evidentiary support it may be" (*CP* 7. 219, 1901 [see Hartshorne and Weiss 1932])'. If the very same mathematical hypotheses are *required* in order to enable us to formulate *any* testable hypotheses, then on this view, those hypotheses lie beyond the reach of serious empirical testing. And if theoretical confirmation means survival in the light of rigorous empirical tests, we might well question whether the pure mathematical hypotheses of our theories should be thought of as confirmed alongside our other theoretical hypotheses.

Contrary to Quine's view, then, the mere presence of mathematical hypotheses in our theoretical assumptions is not, on Sober's account of confirmation, enough for us to be able to consider those hypotheses as *confirmed* by our tests of such theories, for most of those theoretical tests will not be designed to question the background mathematical hypotheses on which our competing hypotheses rely. On Sober's view, if we *are* to provide any genuine empirical support for mathematical hypotheses, then we must formulate tests that allow us to decide between competing background mathematical hypotheses. But in this case, we might still think that *some* such tests *are* possible for some of our mathematical hypotheses. Since a non-Euclidean, as opposed to Euclidean, geometry forms the backdrop to Einstein's gravitational theory, for example, we might think of the crucial experiments confirming Einstein's theory over Newton's as also confirming the truth of the non-Euclidean geometry used.

However, if our question is whether there is any contrastive, empirical experiment which confirms the existence of any abstract mathematical objects, the example of Euclidean versus non-Euclidean geometry will not provide us with an answer. For what is usually taken to be confirmed by the success of Einstein's theory over Newton's is that the geometry of physical space is non-Euclidean—that is, that the axioms of a non-Euclidean geometry are true when interpreted about physical points and straight lines. But the question of mathematical realism concerns the existence of abstract mathematical objects about which our mathematical theories assert truths: anti-platonists are happy to admit that the assumptions of our mathematical theories are sometimes true *of non-mathematical objects*. But this does not establish the existence of any distinctively mathematical entities. If Sober is right that confirmation has to be of one hypothesis in contrast with a competitor, then if we are to find empirical confirmation of the existence of mathematical objects, we need to find cases where what are put to the test are alternative, competing hypotheses concerning abstract mathematical objects.

An example considered by Sober looks more hopeful as a case where it is a genuinely mathematical hypothesis that receives empirical confirmation. Sober considers the possibility of confirming the mathematical hypothesis that '$2 + 2 = 4$' as opposed to all the alternative hypotheses, '$2 + 2 = n$', by counting four apples, first as two pairs, and then as four. '$2 + 2 = 4$' is indeed a hypothesis about mathematical objects,[1] the natural numbers, which, in the light of various assumptions about how to determine the cardinalities of sets of physical objects by counting will have implications

---

[1] Or, at least, can be taken to be. We will ignore for now the possibility considered in sect. 4.3.1 of viewing this claim as elliptical for a related logical truth.

for the result of the counting experiment. So it looks as though this case provides us with an example where a hypothesis concerning abstract mathematical objects—the natural numbers—can be subjected to the kind of contrastive testing that Sober's account of confirmation requires.

But, although this appears to meet Sober's criterion for a genuine contrastive experiment, Sober argues, perhaps somewhat surprisingly, that we do not really put the mathematical hypothesis to the test in such cases. The reason Sober gives for this is that, if somehow we counted the apples and ended up counting three rather than four, we would not consider the hypothesis $2 + 2 = 3$ as receiving confirmation (and thus consider the experiment as disconfirming the hypothesis that $2 + 2 = 4$), but would rather look to some mistake elsewhere in our assumptions about the nature of the experiment. But if we never consider the recalcitrant evidence as disconfirmation of the pure mathematical hypothesis, and only as disconfirmation of the bridging assumptions that allow us to apply that hypothesis, then we cannot, Sober thinks, see such experiments as confirming their mathematical hypotheses when they do succeed.

Despite Sober's initial focus on contrastive testing, his discussion of this case where we do seem to have constructed a genuinely contrastive test of competing mathematical hypotheses suggests that a further principle of confirmation is at work. According to Sober (1993: 53), a theoretical hypothesis cannot take the credit for a theoretical success if it would never be blamed for the theory's failures. 'The fact that we do not doubt the mathematical parts of empirically *un*successful theories is something we should not forget. Empirical testing does not allow one to ignore the bad news and listen only to the good.' We cannot view a hypothesis as confirmed by a theoretical test if we would always ignore any apparent disconfirmation.

This approach to confirmation has Popperian roots. Indeed, suggesting that we could never come up with any observational evidence that would speak against the pure mathematical hypotheses adopted in formulating our empirical theories, Alan Musgrave (1986: 90–1) has also argued, on Popperian grounds, that there must be something wrong with the claim that the truth of such mathematical hypotheses is confirmed by our empirical successes:

Imagine that all the evidence that induces scientists to believe (tentatively) in electrons had turned out differently. Imagine that electron-theory turned out to be wrong and electrons went the way of phlogiston or the heavenly spheres. Popperians think this *might* happen to any of the theoretical posits of science. But can we imagine natural numbers going the way of phlogiston, can we imagine evidence piling up to the effect that there are no natural numbers? This must be possible, if the indispensability argument is right and natural numbers are a theoretical posit in the same epistemological boat as electrons.

But surely, if natural numbers do exist, they exist of necessity, in all possible worlds. If so, no empirical evidence concerning the nature of the actual world can tell against them. If so, no empirical evidence can tell in favour of them either.

On Musgrave's view, then, it is no wonder that mathematical hypotheses are never blamed for theoretical failures. The insulation of mathematical hypotheses from theoretical disconfirmation is inevitable, since no empirical observation of contingent facts about the physical realm could ever tell us anything about what is necessarily true of the mathematical realm.

One might worry about Musgrave's slide from the claim that mathematical objects exist of necessity to the claim that we cannot have empirical knowledge of these objects. For it is at least arguable that we can have some empirical evidence for necessary truths, even though these truths do not vary with the empirical facts. Perhaps our evidence of how things *are* in our world can also give us reason to believe that this is how things *must be*, across all worlds.[2] And even if Musgrave is right that we cannot have empirical knowledge of necessarily existing objects, one might still worry about Musgrave's reliance on the premise that mathematical objects exist, if they exist at all, of necessity. Indeed, this premise is something that many indispensability theorists will reject. Thus, although they disagree about the question of whether mathematics is dispensable, both Hartry Field (who rejects the indispensability of mathematics) and Mark Colyvan (who claims that mathematics is indispensable) suggest that the question of the existence of mathematical objects is a contingent matter.[3]

---

[2] One plausible example of this is Kripke's claim that it is necessary, yet a posteriori, that Hesperus is Phosphorus.

[3] More precisely, in Field's case, Field (1989: 38–45) claims that the existence of mathematical objects such as numbers is not *logically* necessary (as, for example, it is logically consistent for there to be only finitely many things). Field questions whether we have a further notion of *metaphysical* necessity according to which the existence of mathematical objects may be thought to be necessary or contingent. Colyvan (2001: 134–40) explicitly plumps for the claim that the existence of mathematical

Either way, the indispensability theorist will wish to deny Musgrave and Sober's claim that empirical evidence could never tell against, or provide us reason to believe in, the existence of mathematical objects of a particular sort. For, the indispensability theorist will respond, we *can* imagine cases where the evidence does build up against our accepting the existence of mathematical objects of a particular sort. If our evidence for the existence of particular mathematical objects just is that we need to posit the existence of such objects in formulating our best empirical theories, then, if it turns out that we only need some very minimal mathematical assumptions to do science, surely the empirical evidence *does* speak against our accepting the existence of the objects posited in our more extravagant mathematical theories? For, Ockham's razor tells us that we should not multiply entities beyond necessity. In the light of this, if we can do science assuming only a very sparsely populated mathematical universe, then we have no reason to believe that the mathematical universe contains any more objects than this. Thus, as we saw in Chapter 4, Quine thinks that the empirical evidence speaks against the existence of sets beyond the universe of constructible sets, *L*. And if Feferman is right that still more modest mathematical assumptions suffice for empirical theorizing, the empirical evidence may speak in favour of less mathematics still.

Indeed, not only does the indispensability theorist assume that empirical evidence can give us reasons to accept or reject hypotheses about the extent of the mathematical universe, such a theorist is also willing to contemplate that the evidence may in fact mount up against the hypothesis that there are any mathematical objects. For, if mathematics turns out to be dispensable to our best theories, then the balance of evidence will speak against the hypothesis that there are any mathematical objects. Thus, in discussing Musgrave's objection, Colyvan (2001: 123–4) responds by imagining an experimental situation that would put the hypothesis that there are natural numbers to the test:

Suppose that Hartry Field has completed the nominalisation of Newtonian mechanics but that he and his successors repeatedly fail to nominalise general relativity. Let's also suppose that this failure gives us good reason to believe that general relativity cannot be nominalised. From this we conclude that mathematical entities

objects is contingent, citing Field's considerations, but suggests that the indispensability theorist could go either way.

are indispensable to general relativity, but not to Newtonian mechanics. In this setting, then, can we imagine an experiment to test the hypothesis that there are natural numbers? The answer is yes. Not only can we imagine such an experiment, we can perform it. In fact many such experiments have been performed over the last 80 years or so, for any experiment that confirms general relativity over Newtonian mechanics is such an experiment. In particular, the 1919 Eddington eclipse experiment is such an experiment.

Since Colyvan, as an indispensability theorist, would in this context view experimental evidence that spoke in favour of Newtonian mechanics over general relativity as speaking against the hypothesis that there are numbers, he is entitled, both by Musgrave's Popperian lights and on Sober's contrastive view of confirmation, likewise to view the evidence which confirms general relativity over Newtonian mechanics as confirmation of the hypothesis that there are such mathematical objects.

Musgrave's (and Sober's) Popperian objection fails, then, because it does not take the indispensability theorist seriously. Indispensability theorists such as Colyvan *are* willing to contemplate cases where the empirical evidence might simply speak against their assumption that the mathematical realm is richly populated (and, indeed, against their assumption that there are any mathematical objects at all).

What is interesting, however, is that while indispensability theorists such as Colyvan are happy to leave the question of which mathematical objects we ought to believe exist to empirical science to answer, it is not at all clear that the same can be said for scientists themselves. For, if the indispensability theorist is right about the status of mathematical assumptions as theoretical hypotheses waiting to be confirmed or disconfirmed, it is rather remarkable that scientists themselves do not behave as if they are testing the existence of mathematical objects alongside their other theoretical posits. As Penelope Maddy (1997: 157) has observed, 'science seems not to be done as it would have to be done if it were in the Quinean business of assessing mathematical ontology. If it were in that business, it would treat mathematical entities on an epistemic par with the rest, but our observations clearly suggest that it does not.'

Take, for example, the question of whether one ought to adopt a particular mathematical hypothesis in one's theory. Elsewhere in our scientific practice a norm of ontological economy prevails: one should think very carefully about positing theoretical objects of a particular sort, if it turns out that one could do the same theoretical work without assuming that there are such things. And Quine certainly thinks that the same should go for mathematical posits: we should adopt the minimal mathematical assumptions required for a smooth empirical theory. However, within empirical science (as compared with philosophical discussions of the indispensability argument), very little attention is paid to the question of minimizing the mathematical assumptions made by a theory. Indeed, scientists seem ready to adopt whichever pure mathematical hypotheses are convenient, without regard to the question of whether the same theoretical job could be done by a theory with less powerful assumptions.

Thus Maddy considers, in particular, the use of continuum mathematics in empirical science, where physicists seem ready to adopt the full resources of such mathematics in their descriptions of space and time, even in advance of establishing whether space really is continuous (and, as a result, even in advance of establishing whether such a mathematically rich theory is really necessary). 'As a rule,' Maddy (ibid.: 155) observes, 'physicists seem happy to use any mathematics that is convenient and effective, without concern for the mathematical existence assumptions involved . . . '. While Colyvan has suggested how scientists *could* put mathematical hypotheses to the test, the fact that they do not appear to do so provides a difficulty for naturalists who wish to take their cue from our best scientific practices when it comes to deciding which theoretical hypotheses are confirmed.

Maddy's examples are certainly suggestive: they do appear to indicate that the mathematical assumptions of our empirical theories have a special place. But perhaps the indispensability theorist can make room for this special place of mathematical assumptions in our theories, without conceding that those assumptions receive no confirmation from our theoretical successes. Of course, it might be countered, mathematical hypotheses are *bound* to be treated somewhat differently in our theories from assumptions concerning ordinary spatiotemporal objects: this simply reflects the different nature of the objects posited. And of course empirical scientists will not themselves worry too much about the strength of the mathematical theories they utilize: for it is surely the job of mathematicians working on foundational issues to fill in the details regarding exactly how powerful the mathematics required for applications needs to be. On such a view, it is merely due to a very reasonable division of labour that empirical scientists feel free to adopt whichever mathematical assumptions will help them in their theorizing, leaving mathematicians to answer the question of whether the same work could be done with fewer such assumptions.

On this view, then, the special status afforded to our mathematical assumptions does not mean that our mathematical assumptions do *not* receive confirmation when our theories are successful. Never mind the subtleties that go into testing individual theoretical hypotheses, it will be argued, what we are ultimately interested in is the big picture, the package of theories that we have reached as a result of applying such tests. And if we have reason to believe such theories, then, the Quinean will claim, we have reason to believe their mathematical components, regardless of how those components were originally introduced into our theories. Noticing that the mathematical assumptions of our theories appear to have a *special* place is not, then, enough by itself to force us to abandon Quine's confirmational picture, for their special treatment might tell us nothing about their ultimate confirmational status. We need some independent reason for thinking that this picture is mistaken.

5.2. Does the Indispensability Argument Conflict with Scientific Practice?

Attention to the special treatment afforded to mathematical assumptions in our theories is not enough, then, to overturn Quine's confirmational holism. What is needed is some independent reason for thinking that we ought not believe all the assumptions of our best scientific theories. If we can show, on naturalistic grounds, that by the lights of our own theoretical standards we have reason to doubt, or at least to withhold belief from, some of the sentences used in formulating our best scientific theories, then we can raise again the question of whether the special position of mathematical posits in our theories gives us any reason to withhold belief from hypotheses whose truth would require the existence of mathematical objects.

If scientists make use of a sentence S in formulating their preferred scientific theory, ought we, then, always assume that they have reason (by their own lights) to believe that S is true? There are, in fact, many cases where circumstances seem to indicate that we should not always assume that scientists have reason to believe all their theoretical hypotheses.

Sometimes context tells us that they *cannot* really believe that their theoretical hypotheses are literally true, for example if the truth of their hypotheses would conflict with the truth of theoretical assumptions they have made elsewhere. This happens most clearly when scientists make use of explicit idealizations in their theories, which may be explicitly contradicted by other theoretical assumptions made elsewhere. In other cases, scientists may adopt a hypothesis as part of a successful theory, but then go on to question whether their hypothesis is really true, looking for further evidence that what they have supposed to be the case really is the case. This hesitance in accepting the truth of a theoretical component even in the absence of any conflict with other theoretical assumptions also speaks against the holist picture of confirmation, according to which the truth of all theoretical hypotheses is considered to be equally well confirmed by their presence in our best scientific theories. Penelope Maddy has argued that both these cases are standard in our scientific theorizing. If she is right, then either scientists are wildly mistaken about what is confirmed by their own scientific standards, or, perhaps more plausibly, the Quinean holistic picture needs revising.

5.2.1. *Indispensable Idealizations and Ontology*

Many of our actual scientific theories do not consist of bodies of straightforward truths about ordinary objects, but rather include hypotheses that, if interpreted as assumptions about such objects, are explicitly known to be false. Thus, for example, in our theoretical account of the trajectories of projectiles, for ease of calculation we may assume, as is known to be false, that air resistance is not a factor. In accounting for economic trends in societies we may assume, as is surely false, that individual agents are fully rational utility maximizers. And in order to have a tractable theory of the dynamic behaviour of fluids, we may assume, as is known to be false, that fluids are continuous substances. Thus, after pointing out that fluids are made up of discrete molecules, textbooks on fluid dynamics will typically go straight on to assert the '*continuum hypothesis*'(!):

that the macroscopic behaviour of fluids is the same as if they were perfectly continuous in structure; and physical quantities such as the mass and momentum associated with the matter contained within a given small volume will be regarded as being spread uniformly over that volume instead of, as in strict reality, being concentrated in a small fraction of it.   (Batchelor 1967: 4–5)

It is only once we have adopted the idealizing assumption that fluids are continuous substances that we are able to make sense of the idea of properties such as density, velocity, and temperature being defined *at a point* in the fluid. And having made sense of this idea, we can look for equations that describe the values of these properties as continuous functions of position in the fluid and time (see ibid.: 6), thus providing the means to express our hypotheses about the behaviour of fluids mathematically.

If we apply our idealizing assumptions to *actual* projectiles, economies, fluids, etc., we are able to get on reasonably well, making good predictions about aspects of the behaviour of each. And given that a degree of falsification can still lead to successful theoretical predictions (and might even be necessary in order to make any predictions), it may indeed be *rational* for us to adopt such literally false hypotheses in the context of our theorizing, even though we do not believe those hypotheses. But surely the 'confirmation' that our theories receive from our theoretical successes does not extend to the literal truth of these idealizing assumptions. Rather, in such cases, what is confirmed is just that our theoretical hypotheses, such as the continuum hypothesis in fluid dynamics, were good enough—that they got *something* right about the behaviour of actual fluids, projectiles, and economic agents, even if they were not completely correct. Thus, although the 'continuum hypothesis' requires us to assume, for the sake of formulating a tractable mathematical theory, that fluids are continuous, from the successful application of this hypothesis all that is concluded is that the hypothesis of continuity is good enough, not that it is true. As Batchelor puts it, 'there is ample observational evidence that the common real fluids, both gases and liquids, move *as if* they were continuous' (ibid., my italics).

Given that the *truth* of such idealized theoretical hypotheses is not confirmed by our theoretical successes in these cases, then, as Maddy has pointed out, if the *mathematical* assumptions of our theories are made in the context of such literally false idealizations, we should be wary of supposing that the truth of *those* assumptions is confirmed by our theoretical successes. If all that is confirmed is that fluid dynamics has got *something* right about the nature of real fluids, why should we assume that the assumptions it makes about the nature of mathematical objects are amongst the assumptions that are actually confirmed as true by our theoretical successes?

Perhaps, though, the fact that we do not see the assumption that ordinary fluids are continuous as confirmed by our theoretical success in this case just shows that we have not really got to the root of what is really going on when we apply such idealized assumptions as the 'continuum hypothesis' concerning fluids. Perhaps, in adopting this hypothesis, we do not assume *falsely* that actual, physical, fluids are continuous, but rather, assume, quite correctly, that the behaviour of such fluids is, at the macro-level, similar to the behaviour of ideal continuous fluids, about which the 'continuum hypothesis' asserts a truth. On such a view, we might see an idealized theory such as fluid dynamics not as making lots of literally *false* claims about the actual properties of physically existing fluids, but rather, as a collection of true universal generalizations concerning the behaviour of *ideal* continuous fluids, genuinely existing abstract objects that are appropriately related to physical fluids. Our mathematical hypotheses may then be taken to assert literal truths about these abstract, ideal objects.

In fact, such a view of idealizations is commonplace amongst many of those philosophers who take seriously the prevalence of idealizations in our theorizing. Thus, for example, noting that most of our usual scientific laws are simply false if taken as universal generalizations about physical objects and processes, Ronald N. Giere (2004: 745) has suggested that if we want to take our scientific laws as asserting truths, we ought to see them as truths about ideal objects, understood as abstract entities: 'If we insist on regarding principles as genuine statements, we have to find something that they describe, something to which they refer. The best candidate I know for this role would be a highly abstract object, an object that, by definition, exhibits all and only the characteristics specified in the principles.' Similarly, Nancy Cartwright (1983: 17) also suggests that idealized theories assert truths about ideal objects, which resemble, in some (and only some) respects, the physical objects to which they are applied: 'The fundamental laws of the theory are true of the objects in the model, and they are used to derive a specific account of how these objects behave. But the objects of the model have only "the form or appearance of things" and, in a very strong sense, not their "substance or proper qualities".'

If this is how we understand idealized theories, then it looks as though we can apply such theories to predict and explain the behaviour of physical objects and processes without hypothesizing any known falsehoods. For all that we need to hypothesize, in order to apply the theory of ideal fluids to 'common real fluids' is that the behaviour of such fluids is similar (in some relevant respects) to the behaviour of the ideal fluids in our theoretical model. And, in the light of the success of *this* theoretical assumption, perhaps we *should* consider the hypothesis that the ideal fluids of our idealized theoretical models exist as being confirmed by the success of our theory. For, in this case, in contrast with the previous case where we *knew* that our theoretical assumptions could not be true of physical fluids, we have no prima facie reason for thinking that our theory has got anything wrong about the true nature of the *ideal* fluids whose existence it posits. And if we do count our theory's success as confirming its truth as an account of the nature of ideal fluids (and of their relation to the 'common real fluids' whose behaviour they model), then the confirmation our theory receives as a true account of the behaviour of ideal fluids will extend to confirmation of the truth of its claims about the relations between these fluids and abstract mathematical objects. And so, for example, the existence of real numbers and real-valued functions *will* be confirmed, alongside the existence of abstract ideal fluids, by their presence as posits in our literally believed theory of the nature of those fluids.

Or will it be? A look at Quine's own discussions of idealization shows that things are not quite so simple on his view. For, although Quine recognizes the presence in our theories of assumptions whose literal truth would require the existence of ideal objects[4] (including, to borrow some examples from Quine (1960), mass points, frictionless surfaces, and isolated systems), he does not think that the truth of such assumptions *even as assumptions about abstract, ideal objects* is confirmed by our theoretical successes. For, as we noted already in sect. 2.2.1, even on Quine's view it is not always a straightforward matter to uncover the ontological commitments of our theories just by looking at the existentially quantified sentences we use to express our theoretical assumptions. For convenience, we might introduce quantified phrases into our theories simply as abbreviations for unquantified phrases, in which case our apparent quantifier commitments will be eliminable by replacing abbreviated expressions with their

---

[4] Or, at least, would require their existence if those assumptions are to be more than vacuously true. As Quine (1960: 248) points out, if we formulate our theory of mechanics in conditional form: $(x)(\text{if } x$ is a mass point then . . .)$, the non-existence of ideal objects 'does not falsify mechanics; [but] leaves such sentences vacuously true for lack of counterinstances'. But if our ideal theory is only vacuously true, the question will arise how it is that 'some of these conditionals, rather than others, still evidently impart useful scientific theory'

long-hand versions. Alternatively, we might make use of entire theories, the literal truth of whose existentially quantified hypotheses would require the existence of objects of a particular sort, knowing that we can in fact eliminate use of such quantifications by replacing our theories as a whole with alternatives that they are taken to approximate.

Such is the case, Quine thinks, with our use of theories that posit ideal objects such as frictionless planes, mass points, and so on. In speaking as if there are such objects, we do not thereby commit ourselves to *believing* that there really are such things. For in these cases, the objects to which we appear to be referring in our theories are merely convenient myths. Pretending that there are such ideal objects can provide us with useful ways of representing how things are taken to be with really existing objects. But the fact that we are only speaking figuratively when we speak as if there are frictionless planes is made clear when we see that we have an alternative theory available that does not assume that there are such things. In such a case, it is surely not the literal truth of our theory about the relation between ideal frictionless planes and actual physical surfaces that accounts for the theory's usefulness, but rather, just that that theory provides us with an oblique way of saying something true about the behaviour of objects moving on real surfaces, which can also be said directly without recourse to the hypothesis that there really are any (ideal) frictionless planes. What is *really* asserted, when one speaks as if to compare real planes with the ideal frictionless ones of a model, is just some claim about how real planes behave as friction approaches zero. And similarly with other apparent talk of ideal objects:

When one asserts that mass points behave thus and so, he can be understood as saying roughly thus: that particles of given mass behave the more nearly thus and so the smaller their volumes. When one speaks of an isolated system of particles as behaving thus and so, he can be understood as saying that a system of particles behaves the more nearly thus and so the smaller the proportion of energy transferred from or to the outside world.   (Quine 1960: 249)

Even outside explicit falsehoods, then, the literal truth of some claims made in the context of our empirical theorizing should not be considered as confirmed by our theoretical successes. We might be speaking *as if* there are objects of a particular sort, as a merely convenient way of representing how things are taken to be with real things. And the fact that we make use of sentences that apparently refer to mass points should in no way commit us to believing in mass points, if we are *only* using those sentences in a figurative manner, as a convenient way of expressing how things are taken to be with extended particles. In the case of merely *figurative* uses of theoretical hypotheses that appear to concern the behaviour of ideal objects, then, so long as we can find an alternative way of expressing the literally believed content that these convenient fictions allow us, when speaking figuratively rather than literally, to express, then we need not accept the existence of idealized objects as being confirmed by our theoretical successes. As Quine (ibid.: 250) puts it, 'Since the latter, if either, is the one to count as true, the former gets the inferior rating of convenient myth, purely symbolic of that ulterior truth.' In explaining away our use of the 'myths', showing them to be convenient ways of expressing more complex literal alternatives, we thus discharge any commitment to believing in the ideal entities posited in our idealized theories.

On Quine's view, then, the existence of ideal objects such as point masses, frictionless planes, etc., is not confirmed by our successful use of theories whose assumptions, read literally, suppose that there are such things. But this is not a counterexample to his confirmational holism. For Quine's holism is not the claim that we ought to believe the literal truth of all the theoretical hypotheses we in fact make use of, but only that we ought to believe the truth of the assumptions of our *best*, most carefully formulated theories. And, loose talk of frictionless planes and point masses aside, Quine thinks that when we express our best theoretical accounts, such convenient fictions will be *eliminated* in favour of the literally believed alternatives that express the true content gestured at by these myths. Hence Quine's emphasis on the *indispensability* of mathematical posits in formulating our scientific theories: we need not believe *all* the empirical hypotheses we make use of, but we must, on Quine's view, believe any theoretical assumptions that we cannot dispense with, in our best attempts at regimenting our theories, in favour of literally believed alternatives.

Is Quine right, though, to focus on the ultimate dispensability of figurative ways of speaking as the *only* reason for not taking the literal truth of theories that include such talk as confirmed? On Quine's view, if talk of ideal objects in abstract models is eliminable from our best statements of our ultimate theoretical assumptions, then we are not committed to believing in such things. But if, on the other hand, we *cannot* eliminate such talk, then surely, on the Quinean picture, we *are* committed to belief in abstract ideal objects of this kind. For, Quine thinks, the *only* way we can show theoretical hypotheses to be merely convenient fictions is to show exactly where their convenience lies—that is, by stating explicitly the literal content that these convenient fictions allow us to represent. If we cannot do this, that is, if such assumptions remain in our best theoretical accounts, then we must take those assumptions at face value, as part of the literally believed content of our theories.

If Quine is right that we can *only* discharge our apparent commitment to the literal truth of our theoretical hypotheses by showing how those hypotheses can be dispensed with in favour of alternatives that express in literal terms their intended true content, then despite Quine's own dislike of ideal objects such as point masses, it turns out that there is a good chance that he will have to accept some such things into his ontology. For Quine's own wager, that all talk of such ideal objects is ultimately eliminable from our best theoretical accounts, seems vastly overoptimistic. Can we be so sure that, given any theory that appears to account for the behaviour of real objects by comparing their behaviour to that of the ideal objects of some imagined or abstract model, we will eventually always be able to find a literally believed alternative, that captures the true content of the idealized theory and that explains our successful use of the idealization, without hypothesizing that there are any such ideal objects?

Quine's examples of limit myths suggest that there might be a general strategy for eliminating talk of ideal objects: idealizations that involve setting a small finite quantity (such as friction) to zero can be replaced by claims about what will be true of systems as that quantity approaches zero. Ernan McMullin (1985) labels such idealizations 'Galilean', noting that they follow Galileo's method of modelling the behaviour of systems considered in isolation from disturbing causes. Quine's Weierstrassian strategy of considering such theories as shorthand for true theories about what happens as the interfering factors approach a minimum may work very well for such Galilean idealizations, where we can make sense of the idea that the behaviour of real systems might approach some limit as the effects of disturbing causes are minimized. However, the success of this strategy in some cases only provides a general argument for the eliminability of ideal objects from our theories if *all* idealizations are Galilean.

Unfortunately, however, not all idealizations *do* seem to take this form. Thus, Maddy has pointed to fluid dynamics as an example of an idealized theory that cannot obviously be dealt with using the Weierstrassian limit technique. The idealized fluids treated by fluid dynamics are continuous substances. But real fluids are made up of discrete molecules. Applying the Weierstrassian 'limit myth' strategy to get rid of talk of ideal continuous fluids from our picture would appear to require us to state something true about the behaviour of real fluids as they get closer and closer to being continuous. But, as Maddy notes, it is entirely unclear how we would make sense of the idea of real fluids approaching this ideal, continuous, limit. If, for example, we were to understand this as a claim about what happens as the molecules of the fluids become more tightly packed together, the limit that we would be approaching would be a solid, and not a fluid at all!

Perhaps more plausibly, we could try and replace our theoretical talk of density, velocity, and so on as continuously changing properties defined *at points* in a fluid, with talk of limits of the average density (etc.) of regions in the fluid as the region gets smaller and smaller. Indeed, this is how physicists do treat these properties in actual fluids, where they only make sense when measured as averages over a region. But even this talk of limits breaks down when the regions get small enough. For, far from continuously approaching a limit, as we take smaller and smaller regions the number of molecules in a region begins to matter, so that measurements taken with more sensitive instruments will show wide fluctuations of average density (for example), as the volume over which the measurement is taken approaches a minimum. It is simply not true that the *actual* properties of average velocity, density, and so on approach a continuously changing limit as these properties are measured over smaller and smaller volumes. So even if we wish to apply a 'limiting' story to avoid talking about the velocity *at a point* in the fluid, we will still have to make the literally false idealizing assumption that the average density we measure over some macroscopic region is going to remain roughly constant as the region gets smaller, in order to treat velocity as a continuously changing property whose value 'at a point' is defined as the limit of the average value over arbitrarily small regions centred on that point.

At any rate, even if we did have a plausible account of what it would mean for one fluid to be 'more' continuous than another, such an account would surely be beside the point in trying to provide a literally true replacement for our theoretical talk of ideal, continuous fluids, since the applicability of the idealized theory surely does not depend on facts (if there are any) about how close the actual fluids under consideration are to being continuous. As Maddy (1997: 145) sums up, 'The real point is that fluid dynamics isn't more applicable to one fluid than another, depending on how closely that fluid approximates a continuum; rather, it provides a workable account of any fluid.'

Here, then, we have at least one case where our talk of 'ideal' objects in an abstract theoretical model cannot be obviously dispensed with in favour of a literally believed 'limit' story.[5] Furthermore, it is not even clear that such a literally true story, if found, would be preferable to our idealized alternative. We want theories that we can put to use. But if we tried to build the actual properties of actual fluids into our theoretical account, we would likely soon find ourselves encumbered with an unnecessarily complex and potentially intractable theory. Furthermore, we want theories to be explanatory. But if we did manage to formulate a tractable theory that took into account the actual molecular structures of particular fluids, it is plausible that this might ultimately lead to a loss in explanatory power, since such detail would be different given different fluids. We want, in fluid dynamics, a theory that accounts for the behaviour of *all* fluids, to the extent that these fluids behave similarly in similar situations. But insisting on adding detail about the molecular structure of individual fluids would lead to a loss in generality, and to a proliferation of theories that depend on the molecular properties particular fluids in question. What makes the idealized theory of fluid dynamics work is that, at the level of detail in which we are interested, fluids *do* behave as if they were continuous, and so a model which takes them to be continuous works well. Even, then, if we

---

[5] And other examples are not hard to come by. Take, for example, the idealized assumption mentioned earlier that human agents are all fully rational utility maximizers, as assumed in accounts of economic trends. We might think that such a theory would apply better the closer individual agents get to economists' ideal of being fully rational, so that the idealization of fully rational agents could be replaced by a story about how economies behave the closer their agents are to behaving fully rationally. But in fact the idealization works very well even if the behaviour of individuals is far from the ideal. Furthermore, economists have an understanding of why this should be, as in this textbook account: 'We shall never explain actions based on whim or because you got out of bed on the wrong side. However, random differences in behaviour tend to cancel out on average. We can describe average behaviour with a lot more certainty' (Begg 2003: 23–4). It does not matter to the success of our idealized model if *lots* of people behave extremely irrationally, so long as the various deviations from fully rational behaviour are themselves distributed randomly, in such a way as to cancel each other out.

did have a literally believed account of the behaviour of specific individual fluids, our best explanation of why *all* fluids behave similarly, despite their differing molecular structures, will still, most likely, return to the idealized model: these fluids behave similarly because they all behave *as if* they are continuous.

If this example has been correctly described, we have a case of an essential idealization. We currently have no literally believed account of the true nature of ordinary fluids that does the job of our current theory of fluid dynamics, and does so without hypothesizing ideal continuous fluids to which the behaviour of ordinary fluids can be compared. Furthermore, given that our current best explanation of the dynamic behaviour of fluids is that they act *as if* they were continuous, it is arguable that any alternative literally believed theory of fluids, which dropped the comparison with continuous ideal fluids, would suffer a loss in explanatory power.

This is not to say that it is impossible to remove any talk of ideal fluids from our theorizing: we could perhaps avoid any talk of the behaviour of *ideal* fluids in ideal models of our theory, if instead we supposed that our theory of fluid dynamics applied directly to *ordinary* fluids. But in this case, since our theory assumes that fluids are continuous substances, and since we know independently that ordinary fluids are not continuous, then we would not have dispensed with our talk of ideal fluids in favour of a true theory of ordinary fluids, but rather in favour of a theory that is false and known to be false. And if we think that our best theory should not be one whose assumptions are already known to be literally false, we should prefer a theory that compares ordinary fluids to ideal continuous fluids to one that falsely claims physical fluids themselves to be continuous. If this is right, then it looks as if the hypothesis that there are ideal, presumably abstract, fluids about which our theory of fluid dynamics asserts truths is *indispensable* to our best theoretical account of the behaviour of physical fluids. So if Quine is right that the confirmation our best theories receive is confirmation of the literal truth of all their assumptions, then if assumptions about the behaviour of ideal fluids are indispensable to our best theory of 'common real fluids', we ought to accept that such ideal objects exist.

But hold on a minute! Aren't our theoretical assumptions about ideal fluids still rather like our theoretical assumptions about ideal point masses or ideal frictionless planes? Shouldn't we expect our understanding of the success of our theory of ideal fluids to be analogous to our understanding of the success of these other theories? Yet Quine thinks that, since we can dispense with talk of point masses and frictionless planes in favour of a literally believed theory, we ought not take the existence of these latter kinds of objects to be confirmed by the success of theories that speak as if there are such things. For, the successful use of *such* theories does not require the existence of the ideal objects they posit, but only requires that, by adopting the fiction of point masses, we are able to provide a good representation of how things are taken to be with really existing, massive particles. According to Quine, speaking figuratively *as if* there are point masses can serve the theoretical purpose of representing the behaviour of extended massive objects as being thus and so, *regardless of whether there really are any point masses*. This is shown by the fact that such a theory can be successfully applied *even though* our literally believed account of the behaviour of massive objects does not support the existence of ideal point masses. And if point masses do not figure in our *literally believed* theory, then the success of an alternative theory that posits such ideal objects cannot be due to there really being such things. The theoretical clout of the supposition that there are point masses must be something that can be achieved regardless of whether such objects really exist.

What does this tell us about our assumptions concerning ideal continuous fluids, which cannot be dispensed with so easily? We do not have a literally believed alternative theory, that does not posit continuous fluids as ideal objects in an abstract model of actual fluids. But should we really take this absence as providing confirmation that the ideal fluids posited in our theoretical models do exist? Given that we know of cases where the success of a theory is not due to the actual existence of the ideal objects it hypothesizes, but rather due to the way in which these convenient 'myths' allow us to represent some facts about real objects, is this not enough to throw into question the claim that the existence of ideal continuous fluids should be considered as confirmed by the success of fluid dynamics? For, we might reason, we know of cases where adopting merely convenient myths in formulating our theoretical hypotheses can lead to successful theories that are (according to our more basic theoretical accounts) literally false, but that nevertheless can provide us with an indirect way of expressing some truths about objects that are taken to exist. So we know that the contribution of a theoretical posit to the success of a theory need not always depend on the existence of objects of the kind posited. And with this in mind, given their similarities, we might wonder whether the utility of postulating continuous ideal fluids is more like the utility of postulating point masses than the utility of postulating (say) electrons. Here too, we might think, we should see ourselves as speaking merely figuratively, and not literally, when we adopt the hypothesis that there are such things, in order to take advantage of the representational value of that hypothesis in allowing us to paint a picture of how things are with real fluids. The fact that we do not have an alternative literally believed account actually available to us, that does not assume the existence of ideal fluids, is not enough to show that it is not some *figurative* content of our theory of fluid dynamics that is responsible for its success, rather than its literal content (as a theory about the nature of the relation between abstract ideal and concrete real fluids).

Recognition of the theoretical utility of adopting hypotheses that are known to be false may, then, be enough to throw doubt on the claim that the truth of even our *best* theories is confirmed, if these theories themselves contain hypotheses whose utility may be down to something less than their literal truth. If the utility of a theoretical hypothesis is not always down to its truth, then we should be wary of considering the truth of all of the hypotheses used in formulating our best theories as confirmed by our theoretical successes. We will return to this issue in the next chapter, but for now it will suffice to point out that the successful use of known fictions should at least throw doubt on Quine's holistic assumption that the literal truth of our best theories is confirmed by their successes.

5.2.2. Agnosticism and Direct Evidence

A second example from scientific practice that appears to speak against confirmational holism concerns the attitude of agnosticism that scientists sometimes have regarding some of their theoretical posits, even outside the context of explicit idealizations. There are cases where our theories indispensably posit objects of a particular sort, but where scientists hold back from accepting the existence of such objects until they have some more direct evidence of their existence. Maddy's example is of atomic theory, *circa* 1900: although this successful theory indispensably posited the existence of atoms, it was only when Jean Perrin's Brownian motion experiments provided some more direct evidence of the existence of such objects that many scientists became convinced of their reality. Similar behaviour can be found amongst modern scientists: cloud chambers and particle accelerators are constructed in order to detect, and thereby confirm, the existence of the subatomic particles posited by our theories, even though the assumption that there are such particles already appears indispensable to those theories. It seems, then, that indispensable occurrence in a successful theory isn't always enough to convince scientists that they have reason to believe in the objects posited by our theories. In at least some cases, a more direct kind of evidence is required.

Three points are worth noting concerning this aspect of experimental practice. Firstly, it should be noted that, in calling the type of evidence sought in these cases 'direct' evidence, I do not intend to imply that the evidence is somehow unmediated by theory. In setting up cloud chamber experiments to detect quarks, we need to rely on a great deal of theory regarding unobservables in order to link an observed vapour trail to the presence of a quark. The sense in which such experiments can be thought of as providing 'direct' evidence is that they present specific phenomena that can be explained on the assumption that particular objects posited by our theory were present and behaved as the theory said they should behave. Furthermore, if we drop the hypothesis that such objects were involved in producing the phenomena in the way the theory predicted that they would be, then it becomes very difficult to account for the phenomena under consideration. Part of the difference between these cases of 'direct' confirmation of theoretical posits and the general theoretical confirmation our theories receive is that, not only are we saying that the theory in general fits our overall experiences, but that there are specific phenomena that would be entirely mysterious if the particular objects our theory posits in our account of these phenomena did not exist.

We have, then, something that looks like a local inference to the best explanation. If we accept the existence of quarks, then we have a good explanation of the vapour trail in the cloud chamber. Alternatively, if we continue to remain agnostic about their existence, the presence of the vapour trail appears miraculous. In the light of these alternatives (that is, a good explanation or an explanatory miracle), it appears that we are licensed to infer the existence of quarks. The second point to note, though, is that to account for this inference as inference to the truth of our *theory* concerning quarks would be rather too quick. In detection experiments, we infer the existence of an object or complex of objects posited by our theoretical account of the observed phenomenon, since the hypothesis that there are no such objects makes the observation appear mysterious. But does the fact that our observation would be mysterious were there no quark-like objects give us reason to believe the truth of our theory of quarks in its entirety? That is, would the observation be mysterious if our theory wasn't completely true?

Nancy Cartwright (1983: essay 5) has argued forcefully that even if we accept that such detection experiments give us reason to believe in some of the objects posited by our theory, we need not also take them as giving reason to believe our theory as a whole. Plausibly, all that the mystery introduced by the no-quark hypothesis does is to convince us that the correct explanation of the phenomenon will be one that posits (something like) quarks. That is, it pushes us to favour a quark-like hypothesis over a no-quark hypothesis. But we may be more convinced that quark-like objects are responsible for the occurrence of the vapour trails than we are that our particular theory of quarks is itself true in all of its details. To this extent, then, we might see detection experiments as providing us with more reason to believe in the existence of the objects detected than in the truth of our theory of those objects. Thus in this example, Cartwright thinks, we may infer quark-like objects as the likeliest *cause* of the observation, even if we think we lack a literally true theoretical account of the nature of quarks.

This leads us to a third point to note concerning detection and 'direct' evidence. Talk of detection appears to presuppose a causal account. It is natural to suppose, then, that the only direct evidence we can have for the existence of theoretical posits must involve a causal chain. Certainly, the reason that agnosticism about quarks seems untenable in the cloud chamber example is that if we don't assume their existence, we are left with an event for which we can find no cause. But although the fact that our theory posits quarks as a *cause* of the vapour trails does help to explain why it is that we think that the existence of those vapour trails would appear miraculous if we did not assume the existence of quarks, this does not automatically show that the *only* direct evidence we can have for the existence of theoretical posits is causal evidence.

We have suggested that a quark-like hypothesis is preferred to a no-quark hypothesis because it appears that the assumption that quarks (or something like them) exist and are related to the observed phenomena in roughly the way our theory claims them to be will be essential to any *explanation* of the cloud chamber trails. And certainly, if all explanation is ultimately causal, this will imply that detection experiments only allow us to detect causes of phenomena. But, given that our interest is ultimately in the question of whether we ought to believe in acausal mathematical objects, it would be question-begging to assume that *all* explanation is causal. The reason that causal considerations are important in the case of the explanation of the vapour trail as being caused by quarks is that such a causal story clearly loses all explanatory power if we suppose that the objects posited as causes do not really exist. If there are explanations of specific phenomena that require us to suppose that there are mathematical objects, then it is plausible that in such cases we also lose explanatory power if we go on to suggest that the mathematical objects posited by those explanations do not really exist. In fact, although I think that there *are* some genuinely mathematical explanations of empirical phenomena, I will argue later (in Ch. 9) that the question of the existence of the mathematical objects posited by these explanations makes no difference to their value *as explanations* of such phenomena. But for now, though, let us keep in mind that the causal element of the examples of 'direct' evidence we have considered should not *automatically* preclude some analogous form of 'direct' evidence for mathematical objects, in the form of phenomena whose occurrence is mysterious unless we suppose that such objects exist.

At any rate, whether or not 'direct' evidence must ultimately be 'causal' evidence, the practice of looking for direct evidence for the existence of some of the objects posited by our theories again presents a problem for Quine's holistic account of confirmation. On Quine's account, we are equally committed to belief in all the objects posited by our theory, be they quarks or elephants. But, as was the case with idealized theories, we have here yet another case where our observation of scientific practices suggests that the indispensable presence of a theoretical hypothesis in our overall best theory is not on its own considered as good enough reason to believe that hypothesis. If these examples of Maddy's are representative of good scientific practices, then it would appear that our ordinary scientific standards of evidence sometimes *require* us to hold back from belief in some of our indispensable theoretical assumptions, and even in some of the *objects* indispensably posited by a theory, even in the light of the success of that theory. Once more, then, it appears that Quine is mistaken about the requirements of naturalism. Trusting science to tell us what there is should not require us to believe in all of the objects posited by our successful scientific theories, if scientists themselves think that there are good reasons to remain agnostic about, or even to doubt, some of their theoretical assumptions.

5.2.3. Success and Truth: A Diagnosis

We thus have two distinctive situations where the successful use of a theory is not considered *by scientists* a sufficient reason to believe all of the assumptions of that theory. Our naturalistic commitment to understand science on its own terms should lead us to take notice of these examples, which appear to speak against Quine's confirmational holism. However, 'trusting science' is not always the same as 'trusting scientists': scientists may simply be misapplying their own standards in refusing to believe theories that are empirically successful. In order to show that Quine is mistaken about confirmation, then, we need to consider whether scientists are *right* in sometimes holding back from belief in objects posited by their theories. Is this attitude *reasonable*, on ordinary scientific grounds, or are scientists just being overly cautious when, for example, they hold back on belief in the existence of objects until such objects have been detected?

In the case of apparently indispensable idealizations, such as the treatment of fluids as continuous substances, it is pretty clear that scientists are right to hold back from believing these theories in their entirety. Given our wider theoretical beliefs concerning fluids, the *only* appropriate attitude to fluid dynamics considered as an account of actual fluids is to consider the theory as a theoretical model that is strictly speaking false, but is correct in how it represents some aspects of the behaviour of fluids. If such idealizations are genuinely indispensable, then confirmational holism must be weakened to some degree. We cannot be committed to believing in the truth of such obvious falsehoods.

Things became slightly more complex when we considered the possibility of viewing fluid dynamics as a true theory of ideal objects that are related to real fluids in appropriate ways. However, even in this case we suggested that the success of such a theory might be explicable even if we do not accept the existence of ideal fluids, just as the success of our theory of frictionless planes can be explained without assuming that there are such things. Speaking 'as if' there are ideal objects whose behaviour approximates the behaviour of physical things can, we suggested, be a useful way of representing how things are with non-ideal, physical objects.

Viewing indispensable idealizations as 'merely useful', though false, ways of representing how things are with really existing systems of objects is against the letter of Quine's confirmational holism, which requires us to believe in all the objects indispensably posited by our best scientific theories. But perhaps such an outlook can be made consistent with the spirit of the Quinean view of confirmation. Officially, Quine's doctrine holds that we should believe all the assumptions of our best theory, in the absence of anything better. But perhaps this tentative belief could be coupled with a further claim that some amongst those assumptions should not be expected to remain as we continue to refine our theory. Indispensable idealizations would provide an example of theoretical assumptions which, although adopted tentatively as part of our current scientific worldview, we can reasonably predict will not remain as we revise and adapt our theory in the future, taking into account its inconsistencies as best we can.

Unfortunately, though, if what I have said about the central importance of idealizations is right, then even this modified holism (whereby the promise of future dispensability speaks against the confirmation some hypotheses receive by their presence in our current theoretical package) will not save Quine's picture. For I have suggested that there is theoretical virtue in idealization, such that it is likely that some idealizations will remain indispensable even to our best theories, given our twin aims of predictive success and explanatory power. In discussing fluid dynamics, we mentioned the possibility that any explanation that was sufficient to account for the behaviour of *all* fluids (regardless of their microscopic structure) would have to do so by treating them *as if* they were continuous. Similarly, quite independently of the project of rejecting Quine's indispensability argument, elsewhere within the philosophy of science, Nancy Cartwright has argued that idealizations are sometimes essential for explanatory purposes.

In this context, Cartwright (1983: 139–41) draws an illuminating comparison between the construction of theoretical models and the theatrical staging of historical events. The constraints of theatre force certain distortions in staging historical events, if only in order to portray them in a short period of time in a limited space. Furthermore, careful compression of dialogue and events can 'get to the nub' of the historical events portrayed, even if they knowingly distort the historical record. Similarly, idealizations may be forced on us in science due to the constraints of theorizing, where we often do not have complete descriptions of the physical situation available to us, and would not be able to deal with such descriptions theoretically even if we did. Furthermore, it is at least plausible that a degree of idealization is essential in getting to the nub of physical processes. No two physical events are identical. Whereas blow-by-blow causal histories of events would be able to account for what happened in a particular case, in order to get general physical laws one must abstract from the details of specific cases in order to find common features about which laws can be formulated. In the case we considered of fluid dynamics, we said that what is common to fluids is that, at the macro-level, they behave as if they were continuous. Any account of the behaviour of fluids that misses this aspect is surely missing something. If Cartwright is right about the advantages of idealization, then it looks as though Quine's account of confirmation will need more drastic revisions if it is to deal with the possibility of the permanent presence of such indispensable instruments in our scientific theories: it is not enough for Quine to assume that, in the long run, such idealizations will be ironed out.

How about objects posited by theories in the context of theoretical assumptions that are not explicit idealizations? Are scientists ever right in remaining agnostic about the existence of some such objects posited by our successful theories until they have some form of 'direct' evidence (in the form of phenomena whose occurrence cannot be explained without assuming the existence of such an object) for their existence? Or are scientists simply misapplying their own evidential standards when they hold back from belief in objects posited by those amongst their successful theories that are not already known to be literally false?

Given the 'local' character of detection experiments, one might think that a scientific double standard *is* being applied. If it is acceptable to infer the existence of objects required by our theoretical explanations of *particular* phenomena, shouldn't the same be said also for the *global* case? If we are right that such detection experiments provide evidence via something like an inference to the best explanation,[6] then one might think that scientists are being overly cautious in drawing such an inference in specific cases but

---

[6] Strictly speaking, given that we have acknowledged the possibility of using such evidence to infer the existence of objects but not the truth of our theory concerning those objects, we should not talk about inference to the best explanation (implying the truth of our explanation in its entirety), but

not in the general case. For, after all, our current best scientific theory, as a whole, is the best explanation we have of the phenomena we have experienced, taken together. Why hold back from applying the inference in the case of our theory as a whole, and instead apply it only in these specific cases?

Having acknowledged the ubiquity of idealization in our theories, though, such a global inference (from the explanatory power of our overall theory to the truth of that theory in its entirety) would surely be unwarranted. If our theories do contain idealized assumptions, then the explanations that our theories provide of empirical phenomena had better not depend, for their success, on the *truth* of these idealizations. Rather, to the extent that our idealized theories provide a good explanation of observed phenomena it will be because the idealizations allow us to provide a good working model of some genuine processes, and not because the idealized assumptions are literally true. The case of indispensable idealizations gives us just one example where false theories may nevertheless be explanatorily valuable (and, indeed, predictively successful). But with this phenomenon in mind, we may well wonder whether there are other cases where the explanatory value and predictive success of our theory is due to some reason other than its truth. In particular, we may question whether the successes of some theory that assumes the existence of ϕs are really down to the fact that it gets things right about ϕs. Once we have recognized that a theory's predictive and explanatory successes are not always a result of its truth, the requirement of direct evidence seems quite reasonable.

A further reason for seeking local, 'direct' evidence for the objects posited by our theories is that we have examples that remind us that the indispensability of a posit in a successful theory is at best a defeasible criterion for the existence of the object posited. The case of phlogiston theory shows that we can have empirically successful theories that have got things very wrong when it comes to ontology. Furthermore, our current chemical theory accounts for why it was that the phlogiston theory was successful to the extent that it was, and provides a warning that, just because a theory appears to be successful in explaining the phenomena we have observed so far, this does not have to be because it has got things right in its basic ontology.

---

rather, inference to the existence of those objects required if we are to have an explanation of the phenomenon in question.

Anti-realist philosophers of science use such examples as part of a pessimistic meta-induction to argue that we should *never* feel confident about the chances that our current theories are even close to the truth. But we need not (and, as naturalists, should not) draw such a sceptical conclusion here. Just because successful theories *could* be wildly wrong, and just because some of our theories have been wildly wrong, in their ontological picture, this does not mean that it is never reasonable to believe a theory. Rather, the lesson we should learn from past theories that have been shown to be false is that there is always the possibility of uncovering new kinds of evidence that will undercut our belief that their successes have been a result of their truth. But by probing our theories more closely, and in particular by creating experimental phenomena that appear to cry out for explanation in terms of the objects and processes posited by our theories, we can increase our confidence that such counter-evidence will not be found. In the light of our experience of previous successful, but false, theories, then, holding out for more direct kinds of evidence, which would be harder to account for without the assumption that there are objects roughly of the sort posited by our current theories, seems a reasonable thing to do.

5.3. Cracks in the Argument: Ontological Commitment Revisited

Quine's confirmational holism means that he understands the naturalistic requirement to look to our best scientific theories to discover what we ought to believe as requiring us to believe all sentences used in expressing those theories. As a result, since Quine holds that a sincere belief that there are ϕs commits one to accepting the existence of ϕs, Quine's holism combines with his naturalism to imply that we ought to believe in all of the objects posited by our best scientific theories. In the mathematical case, because some of our successful theories indispensably posit mathematical objects, Quine concludes that we are committed to the existence of such objects.

But the examples of the previous section throw confirmational holism into doubt. If our theories contain indispensable idealizations, then we should not see these theoretical components as confirmed by our theoretical successes. And if there is a reasonable practice of looking for more direct forms of evidence for the existence of some of the objects posited by our theories, it looks as if theoretical hypotheses can be considered more or less confirmed depending on whether they themselves have been put directly to the test. It appears, then, that one might reasonably make successful use of a theory while holding back from belief in some of its component parts, either because they are known to be idealizations, and thus to be contributing to theoretical success for reasons other than their truth, or because it has not yet been established that their contribution to the success of our theory will be best accounted for by assuming the existence of their objects, so that it is reasonable to remain agnostic about the objects posited. The fact that we can recognize cases where the practical success of a theoretical hypothesis is not a result of its truth means that we should hold back from assuming, as Quine's confirmational holism does, that a practical decision to adopt a hypothesis as part of our theoretical worldview should always be understood as providing us with a reason to believe that hypothesis.

Having separated *our* ontological commitments in making use of a theory from the quantifier commitments of that theory, the indispensability argument for the existence of mathematical objects in its original form is undermined. We need to look more closely at the question of which parts of our scientific theories receive confirmation from our theoretical successes, in order to discover whether we ever have reason to believe theoretical claims whose truth would require the existence of mathematical objects. And, although we have not considered in any close detail the question of whether we have reason to believe the mathematically stated hypotheses of our empirical theories, preliminary indications suggest that we can be somewhat optimistic about the prospects for anti-platonism here. If sentences whose literal truth would require the existence of mathematical objects are present only in the parts of our theories that are best viewed as *idealizations*, then we might expect that the use of such sentences should not commit us to belief in the existence of mathematical objects. Alternatively, if it could be argued that it is only the existence of objects to which we have 'direct' access that is confirmed by our theoretical successes, then if it can be argued that we have no means of 'direct' access to mathematical objects (for example, if direct access has to be causal), this would also speak against the claim that the existence of mathematical objects receives empirical confirmation. Furthermore, the apparent special confirmational status of mathematical posits in our theories, as noted in section 5.1, might provide us with some independent reason for thinking that they are not confirmed by their presence as background theoretical assumptions. Prospects for an anti-platonist view of mathematics are thus wide open, if we reject the view that all our scientific hypotheses should be considered as equally confirmed.

In Chapters 7–9, I will argue that our ordinary standards of evidence give us no reason to believe in the mathematical objects posited by our mathematized scientific theories. To do this, I will argue that the existence of mathematical objects receives no confirmation from our theoretical successes, since those successes can be accounted for even by one who remains agnostic about the existence of the mathematical objects posited by those theories. My hope, therefore, is to show that, contrary to Quine's own view, naturalism does not require us to be realists about mathematical objects, on any reasonable understanding of our standards of theoretical confirmation. But before presenting this argument, we must face the possibility of a sceptical response to this revised understanding of the naturalist's demand to 'trust science' on matters of ontology, stemming from difficulties that arise once we allow for the possibility of an indispensable role for theoretical fictions. It is to this worry that I will turn in the next chapter.

6

Naturalized Ontology

In considering both pure mathematics in Chapter 4 and empirical science in Chapter 5, we have found reasons to hold back from believing some of the utterances made in the context of formulating our best mathematical and scientific theories. In both cases, though for different reasons, I have suggested that the value of speaking 'as if' a sentence is true in the context of developing a given theory might be due to something other than that sentence's literal truth. Thus, in the case of our pure mathematical theories, I argued that if we view mathematicians as primarily engaged in working out what follows from their mathematical hypotheses, from the mere fact that it can be convenient for mathematicians to work against the backdrop assumption that these hypotheses are true, we need not conclude that they have any reason to *believe* these hypotheses to be true. And as regards our *empirical* scientific theories, where theoretical 'goodness' does seem to have a somewhat closer relationship to 'truth', the varying attitudes scientists in fact have to their theoretical hypotheses suggests that even there it is not always clear that we ought to believe the truth-at-face-value of *all* utterances made in the context of expressing our best empirical theories. Scientists themselves recognize the advantages of a degree of deliberate falsification in allowing themselves to form tractable representations of phenomena. Furthermore, experience tells us that we should not be too quick to believe all the assumptions of our successful scientific theories, even if they are not deliberate idealizations or falsifications, since we know that in some such cases the successful use of our theory is not simply a result of the truth of its assumptions. In the absence of a closer understanding of the role our various theoretical assumptions play in allowing for successful predictions and explanations of phenomena, it may be reasonable to withhold belief from the truth of some of the existentially quantified utterances made in the context of our theorizing, at least until we have further evidence that the utility of these utterances is due to their literal truth.

Abandoning the default realist assumption that our scientific theories are best understood as bodies of truths makes the naturalistic ontological project somewhat complex. Rather than simply reading off our ontological commitments from the existentially quantified utterances used in formulating our best theories, we will have to find some way of separating out, amongst the objects posited by our theories, those whose existence we have reason to believe, and those that we can discard as mere artefacts of a convenient form of speaking. Indeed, returning to the debate between Carnap and Quine discussed in Chapter 2, our ontological project can be seen as an attempt to navigate a third way between the two. Carnap, recall, thought that a practical decision to use a particular linguistic framework for theoretical purposes should not commit us to believing in the objects posited by the sentences of that framework, since *merely* practical reasons to speak as if there are ϕs do not count as reasons to believe that there are ϕs. Quine, by contrast, argued that practical reasons are just some amongst the many reasons we may have for adopting a given theory, and count, along with the rest, as providing reasons for believing the assumptions of that theory. At least in the case of our best scientific theories, for Quine, practical reasons just *are* evidential. In pointing out that some of the assumptions of even our best theories do seem to be made on merely practical grounds, I have been suggesting, against both Carnap and Quine, that there is a distinction to be found in those theories between instrumental components, adopted *merely* for practical purposes, and those components whose presence in our best theory is evidence for their truth. In drawing this distinction, the hope, for an anti-platonist response to the indispensability argument, will be that the mathematical assumptions of our theories fall squarely on the merely instrumental side of this divide.

To get clearer on how to carry out the naturalist's ontological project in the light of the acknowledged presence of indispensable idealizations, I will in this chapter briefly outline a 'modelling' picture of scientific theorizing that gives a central role to idealizations. While one might (as discussed in sect. 5.2.1) take a realist attitude to theoretical models themselves, I will suggest an alternative, anti-realist approach to ideal objects. This approach, according to which we can reap representational advantages from ideal models by merely *pretending* that their objects exist and are related to real objects in appropriate ways, promises an account of how theories can be empirically successful without being literally true.

But with this promise comes a worry, which has been expressed most pointedly by Stephen Yablo (1998). If our theories are, as this approach suggests, full of merely instrumental hypotheses, whose value arises not from their literal truth but from their ability to represent, in an indirect way, how things are with really existing things, how can we ever hope to separate out those theoretical utterances we should take to be literally true from those that are merely useful fictions? Can we expect to be able to say whether, in uttering the law of universal gravitation, we mean to say that there *literally* is a function representing mass as a real number, or whether we mean this only *metaphorically*? And if, as Yablo thinks, there is no way of settling on an answer to this question, does it follow that the naturalist's project of ontology 'rests on a mistake'? In discussing Yablo's worry in this chapter, I will argue that his concern is ultimately unfounded, based as it is on an overly hermeneutic understanding of the naturalist's ontological project. But the response to this worry will be instructive in explaining just what *will* be needed to uncover the ontological commitments we incur in adopting our various theoretical hypotheses. In particular, I will conclude, carrying out the naturalist's project of ontology will require us to look for our best explanations of our theoretical successes, which can be found in a reflective, scientific understanding of science itself.

6.1. Models and Idealizations

My discussion of idealization in the previous chapter presented two ways in which idealizations can be used to represent physical things. First, an idealization can be an explicit falsification: we may falsely assume, of actual fluids, that they are continuous, in order to explain and predict their behaviour. Such a false assumption works because it is, in an inevitably loose sense, 'close enough' to the truth, and, coupled with a grasp of just where the falsifying assumption is likely to break down, skilled scientists can make use of this assumption in their explanations and predictions. This skill is somewhat like the skill exhibited by language users in applying metaphors: we have an idea, albeit a loose one, of how far we can 'play along' with the metaphor that Juliet is the sun, knowing, for example, that we should stop before concluding that she is 150 million kilometres from the earth.

The second use of idealization was in the provision of ideal models of empirical phenomena. Rather than assuming falsely of actual fluids that they are continuous, an ideal model is constructed whose objects include ideal, continuous fluids, whose behaviour is then compared with physical fluids to draw conclusions about their behaviour. The skill in applying these models is the skill exhibited in successful application of an analogy: physical fluids are held to be analogous, in important respects, to the ideal fluids of the model, and the scope of the analogy will determine how much we can conclude about the behaviour of physical fluids from consideration of our ideal model. While these two uses of idealization are on the face of it quite different, they are nevertheless closely related. Indeed, since we can always reinterpret false idealizations about actual objects as claims about the ideal objects of some theoretical model it would not, perhaps, be unreasonable to view all uses of idealizations in empirical science as ultimately explicable in terms of models and analogies.

The view that empirical science essentially involves the building of layers of theoretical models, which can be more or less realistic representations of empirical phenomena, is certainly not a new one, and has been presented in the philosophy of science literature by, for example, Mary Hesse (1963); Nancy Cartwright (1983); Ronald Giere (1988); and the various papers in Morgan and Morrison (1999). As we saw in the previous chapter, an assumption made by some of these writers is that the ideal objects of our models should be viewed as really existing abstracta. After all, if, in our arguments by analogy, we are comparing physical objects to the objects in some model, if those objects do not really exist, then there is nothing for us to draw a comparison with. Considering the use of *dispensable* idealizations, though, I have suggested that we might hope for an alternative account of ideal models that does not take their objects to exist. After all, we seemingly manage to achieve something by speaking as if there are ideal, frictionless planes even though, according to our *best* physical theory, we need not assume that there are such things, since we can dispense with such talk. Perhaps, then, there is an explanation of the success of model talk that does not require us to believe in ideal objects as abstracta.

In fact, focusing on the use of idealizations in representing physical phenomena through metaphor and analogy suggests a place to look for a candidate explanation of our model talk. Kendall L. Walton (1993) has presented an account of metaphor based on a more general account of fiction, and of how fictions can be used to represent. Walton's central notion, out of which accounts of metaphor and of fiction can be developed, is of games of make-believe or pretence. His central insight is that, by playing along with a pretence in appropriate ways, we can often succeed in representing how things are in the real world. Walton refers to such uses of pretence, to represent in a figurative way how things are taken to be with real things, as 'prop oriented make-believe'. I will present Walton's account in detail in Chapter 7, where it will be important to get clear on how uses of mathematics in empirical science can be accounted for from the perspective of pretence. For now, though, it will suffice to note that if we do take models to be convenient fictions, an account of models as fictions is available that does not commit us to belief in the objects posited by those models as abstract, fictional objects. If this account can be made to work, then speaking as if ordinary fluids are related in appropriate ways to the continuous fluids posited by some ideal model will not saddle us with accepting the existence of continuous fluids as abstracta. For, as Walton (1990: 396) puts it, 'Insofar as statements appearing to be about fictional entities are uttered in pretence, they introduce no metaphysical mysteries.'

Assuming, then, that our use of idealized models in empirical science does not commit us to belief in the existence of ideal objects as abstracta, the naturalistic approach to ontology will require us to accept the existence of only those objects posited outside the context of fictional models. But one might worry, as Yablo has, that this requirement to separate the literal from the merely fictional posits of our theories is something that we can never fulfil, since we lack any means of definitively drawing the literal/fictional divide. If we cannot navigate this divide, then it looks as though the naturalistic ontological project cannot be completed, since in problematic ontological cases we will have no means of deciding whether an existentially quantified utterance is meant literally or merely figuratively. It is to this worry that we will now turn.

6.2. Does (Naturalized) Ontology Rest on a Mistake?

In his (1998) paper 'Does ontology rest on a mistake?', Stephen Yablo comes to many of the same conclusions we have reached in the the course of our discussion so far. Returning to the Quine/Carnap debate on ontology, Yablo accepts, as I did, that Quine is right in responding to Carnap that practical decisions to speak as if there are ϕs can also be evidential, so that we can sometimes draw ontological conclusions from our reliance on existentially quantified claims in formulating our theories. However, bearing in mind the varieties of purposes served by theoretical utterances, Yablo points out that what Quine needs to show in order to establish his own position, whereby a decision to adopt a theoretical hypothesis in our best empirical theory always counts as a reason to believe that that hypothesis is literally true, is that practical reasons are *always* evidential. In particular, Quine must show that 'no other sort of practical reason is possible. There is no such thing, in other words, as just putting on a way of talking for the practical advantages it brings, without regard to whether the statements it recommends are in a larger sense true' (Yablo 1998: 241). But as we have seen, and as Yablo himself points out, there are many examples of cases where there *are* clear practical advantages to adopting a particular way of speaking for the purposes of theorizing, even when it is *known* that one's utterances, taken literally, cannot be true.

Indeed, Quine himself recognizes the practical value of speaking *as if* a given sentence is true even when such talk is not ultimately to be taken seriously. Quine (1978: 188−9) explicitly recognizes the wide use of figurative, non-literal language in much of our ordinary discourse: 'It is a mistake . . . to think of linguistic usage as literalistic in its main body and metaphorical in its trimming. Metaphor or something like it governs both the growth of language and our acquisition of it.' Falsehoods, whether they appear in the form of suggestive metaphors or theoretical fictions such as talk of mass points and frictionless planes, abound in our ordinary attempts to describe the world around us, and the practical reasons we may have for indulging in such falsehoods should not be taken as providing us with evidence for their ultimate truth.

As we have noted, in identifying practical reasons to speak as if there are ϕs with evidential reasons to believe that there are ϕs, in the context of our best scientific theories, Quine's assumption is that in such theories, metaphor and theoretical fictions will have been banished. While ordinary discourse may be full of merely figurative forms of speaking, whose ontological commitments are not to be taken seriously, in the context of formulating our best scientific theories, our task is to clear away such forms of expression, providing a straightforwardly literal description of the world as we take it to be. Thus, Quine (ibid.: 189) tells us, 'Cognitive discourse at its most drily literal is largely a refinement rather, characteristic of the neatly worked inner stretches of science. It is an open space in the tropical jungle, created by clearing tropes away.' But what if Quine is wrong about this? What if, as we have been suggesting, in formulating even our best theories, we find we have to include many sentences whose literal content may or may not be true, for the sole purpose of representing some metaphorical content as being the case? How, Yablo (1998: 245) asks, does Quine's naturalistic approach to ontology fare if we allow that, 'like the poor, metaphor will be with us always'?

6.2.1. Allowing for Representationally Essential Metaphors

Adopting Walton's account of metaphor and other theoretical fictions as 'prop oriented make-believe', Yablo argues that there are many cases where it is extremely useful, even indispensable, to adopt the pretence that real objects have properties that they do not have, or that they are related in various ways to other, merely fictional, objects, in order to represent, in an indirect or figurative way, how we take things to be with those real objects. For example, by pretending that Italy is a boot, we can describe the actual locations of real cities in Italy by describing their position on this imagined boot (ignoring artefacts of the metaphor, such as the size or the three-dimensional qualities of the imagined boot). Or by pretending that real fluids are continuous substances, we can describe their behaviour by means of equations governing changes in functions defined over these continuous substances (again ignoring artefacts of the metaphor, such as the microstructural properties of the imagined fluids). Alternatively, if we prefer to represent by analogy rather than metaphor, we can achieve similar ends by imagining a boot to which Italy can be compared, or imagining a continuous fluid, some of whose properties mirror those of the real fluid whose behaviour we wish to understand.

In all these cases, it is reasonable to think that the representational purposes of our various imaginings may be served regardless of whether the things we imagine to be the case are actually true: it is enough that our imaginings are appropriately constrained by the demands of the metaphor/analogy. What matters to the success of the pretences in these circumstances is not that their literal content is true (that Italy is a boot, that a given fluid is continuous, that there is a boot that resembles Italy in various respects, or that there is a continuous fluid whose behaviour is appropriately similar to some physical fluid), but rather that they are correct in their 'metaphorical content': playing along with the pretences to the appropriate degree allows us to draw some true conclusions about the geography of Italy or about the behaviour of physical fluids. Far from consisting of a single framework of equally confirmed theoretical hypotheses, then, on Yablo's (neo-Carnapian) view of science, our scientific theories consist of many bundles of theoretical frameworks, adopted for a variety of purposes. Viewing these frameworks as 'games of make-believe', the question of whether to believe a given theoretical hypothesis will come down to the question of its role in the theoretical framework to which it belongs. Is it merely part of the make-believe trappings of that framework, adopted because of some metaphorical, rather than literal, content they allow us to represent, or does it belong to some literally true core?

We are supposing, then, that there are two different purposes that may be served by our including a sentence S amongst the hypotheses of even our best scientific theory. One purpose may be to assert S's literal content, that is, to assert that S is true. But a second purpose may be indirectly to assert some figurative content S has, that is, to assert that the real world is such as to make our pretence appropriate (in the context of some make-believe). If this is right, then from the mere fact that scientists make use of an existentially quantified sentence of the form '$(\exists x)\phi(x)$' in order to express their theoretical picture of the world, we cannot straightforwardly conclude that, according to this picture, there really are ϕs. We need to know whether, when speaking *as if* there are ϕs, scientists are speaking literally or merely figuratively. If we wish to follow Quine's naturalistic approach according to which we should look to science to discover what there is, then, in the light of the possibility of representationally essential fictions, some modification is required. It looks as if we should count as existing all and only those objects whose existence is asserted in those parts of our theories that are to be taken literally, ignoring merely figurative uses of the existential quantifier.

So far so good. But now, Yablo asks, how are we to know which, amongst our theoretical hypotheses, should be taken as literally true and which should be viewed as adopted for merely figurative purposes? Unless we can answer this, then it looks as though we are at a loss when it comes to the question of which objects we ought to believe exist. It is this worry that leads Yablo to advocate a revised Carnapian scepticism about the prospects for answering ontological questions. According to Yablo, if we reject Quine's neat approach to uncovering ontology, whereby we simply read our ontological commitments off the existentially quantified sentences used in formulating our best theories (as, indeed, we should if we think that some of these sentences are not to be read as literally true), then it turns out that we will lack *any* means of identifying the genuine ontological commitments incurred in adopting our best theoretical accounts of empirical phenomena.

6.2.2. Separating the Literal from the Metaphorical

Yablo's sceptical argument is as follows. In order to uncover the genuine ontological commitments of our scientific theories, it appears that we need some way of separating off the metaphorical ('make-believe', 'idealized', or 'merely instrumental') components of our theories from those which are literally believed. Only then we can discover *our* ontological commitments, by looking to the existential commitments of the non-figurative parts of our theories. Now, perhaps in some cases we can discover which components are meant literally just by asking scientists for clarification: When you utter the sentence S in the context of your theorizing, do you mean that literally, or are you just speaking as if S is the case, in order to assert some metaphorical content S may express? But except in the most obvious of cases, Yablo thinks this is something that scientists will not in general be able to answer. For, Yablo (1998: 257–8) thinks, we often make utterances in a 'make-the-most-of-it spirit', whereby:

I want to be understood as meaning what I literally *say* if my statement is literally true—count me a player of the 'null game', if you like—and meaning whatever my statement projects onto via the right sort of 'non-null' game if my statement is literally false. It is thus indeterminate from my point of view whether I am advancing S's literal content or not.

Isn't this in fact our common condition? When speakers declare that there are three ways something can be done, that the number of *A*s = the number of *B*s, that they have tingles in their legs, that the Earth is widest at the equator, or that Nixon had a stunted superego, they are more sure that *S* is getting *something* right than that the thing it is getting at is the proposition that *S*, as some literalist might construe it. If numbers exist, then yes, we are content to regard ourselves as having spoken literally. If not, then the claim was that *A*s and *B*s are equinumerous.

It is therefore, Yablo thinks, sometimes *indeterminate* whether we really mean to assert *S*'s literal content, rather than some metaphorical content *S* might have. Worse still, if there is an answer to whether we mean to assert *S*'s literal content or some metaphorical content, it looks as though this answer itself depends on our already having an answer to the ontological question.

Thus, taking number talk as an example, Yablo's suggestion is that the question of whether we mean our number talk to be taken literally or metaphorically itself depends on the question of whether there are numbers. And it is precisely on this point that Yablo's argument gets its sceptical bite, against anyone looking (as we are) to adapt Quine's ontological naturalism to deal with theories that may contain non-literal components. Take, for example, the apparent assignment of numbers to massive objects. When we say that, for any massive object *a* there is a corresponding real number m_a, which represents the mass of *a* as a multiple of some specified unit mass, should 'there is' here be read literally or merely metaphorically? Presumably, it should be read literally if there are numbers, metaphorically if there are not. But in this case we find ourselves in a circle: in order to discover which objects we are committed to believing in we need to find a way of drawing the metaphorical/literal distinction, and in order to draw this distinction we need already to know which objects our successful use of our theory commits us to accepting. Thus Quine's advice as a naturalist, suitably adapted to account for the indispensable presence of non-literal theoretical components, 'is to countenance numbers iff the *literal* part of our theory quantifies over them; and to count the part of our theory that quantifies over numbers literal iff there turn out to really be numbers' (Yablo 1998: 258). If, as Yablo thinks, there is no way of escaping this circle, then the naturalistic approach to ontology is doomed.

Yablo (ibid.: 259–60) sums up his critique of the ontological project thus:

Quine's idea was that our ordinary methods could be 'jumped up' into a test of literal truth by applying them in a sufficiently principled and long-term way. I take it as a given that this is the one idea with any hope of attaching believable truth values to philosophical existence-claims. Sad to say, the more controversial of these claims are equipoised between literal and metaphorical in a way that Quine's method is powerless to address. It is not out of any dislike for the method—on the contrary, it is because I revere it as ontology's last, best hope—that I conclude that the existence-questions of most interest to philosophers are moot. If they had answers, Q [Quine's criterion of ontological commitment] would turn them up. It doesn't, so they don't.

The negative conclusion we are left with, then, is that in the absence of an independently drawn metaphorical/literal distinction, there is no hope for the naturalistic ontological project. And given that this is the only such project that has looked as though it stands any chance at success,[1] then there seems to be no hope whatsoever for the philosophical project of ontology.

6.2.3. Escaping Ontological Scepticism

Yablo's scepticism is too quick. According to Yablo, understanding the ontological commitments we incur in participating in a particular discourse depends on understanding the spirit in which we put forward our utterances in the context of that discourse. If we utter a sentence in the spirit of 'make-believe', then we should not be saddled with the ontological commitments of that sentence, literally construed. If, on the other hand, we utter a sentence sincerely, in order to assert its truth, then we *should* be understood as being committed to the objects its literal truth would require. Yablo's worry is that, even in the context of our scientific theorizing, we often leave open the question of whether we should be interpreted literally or metaphorically, holding that the proper interpretation of our utterances is to be determined by an independent resolution of the ontological question. And if the ontological question is itself tied in to the question of whether

---

[1] Yablo (1998: 229) opens his paper by pointing out that 'Ontology the progressive research program (not to be confused with ontology the swapping of hunches about what exists) is usually traced back to Quine's 1948 paper "On What There Is" '. If Yablo is correct about the failure of the Quinean research programme, then it seems we are left just with hunch-swapping.

we mean our utterances to be taken literally or metaphorically, then there seems no way out of this circle.

The first thing to notice is that Yablo's focus on what scientists take themselves as meaning to assert when they make use of a sentence in the context of their scientific theorizing is somewhat against the spirit of our naturalism, whereby our interest is not so much in what scientists say or believe, but rather, in what it is that their standards of evidence give them *reason* to believe. Yablo is, then, mistaken if he is assuming that carrying out the naturalist's ontological project requires us to uncover the spirit (metaphorical or literal) in which scientists *intend* their theoretical assertions to be taken. Naturalism requires us to adopt as our own those theoretical beliefs that are justified by our best scientific methods and standards. And the question of which theoretical hypotheses are so justified may be quite independent of the question of the spirit in which our theoretical hypotheses are originally intended. Thus, for example, the hypothesis that there are atoms may originally have been put forward by scientists as a merely useful instrument. But the fact that such a hypothesis was originally considered to be a merely practical instrument did not preclude our uncovering evidence that gave us grounds for taking the hypothesis to be confirmed as true. If this can be the case even with hypotheses that are initially *intended* as merely useful instruments, then we should not rule out that evidence may speak for, or against, our holding as literally true hypotheses about whose status (as metaphorical or literal) we are initially uncertain.

The question we need to answer, then, is not whether there is a fact of the matter about how we *intend* our theoretical utterances to be taken, but rather, whether there is a fact of the matter about how they *ought* to be taken.[2] That is, is it possible to discover which amongst our theoretical hypotheses we have reason to believe, and which it is reasonable to withhold belief from, or even disbelieve? In our attempt to chart a course between Carnap and Quine, we suggested that *some* 'ways of speaking' are

---

[2] It might be objected that our utterances *ought* to be taken however we *intend* them to be taken (I am grateful to Mark Balaguer for this point). In one sense of *ought*, concerning how we ought to interpret ordinary speech, this is surely right—charitable interpretation requires us to do our best to uncover what a speaker means to be saying by her utterances. But my point here is that the issue is not the hermeneutic one of correct interpretation at all—we are interested not in what theorists do mean, but at best in what they *ought* to mean by their utterances. What, that is, is the most reasonable attitude to take to the various sentences used in formulating our scientific theories?

adopted for merely practical reasons, whereas others cannot be considered as *mere* practical conveniences. What we need, then, in order to answer the ontological question, is some way of discovering whether the theoretical contribution made by a posit is merely due to the practical advantages the supposition that there is such an object brings (in, for example, allowing us tractable means of representing how things our with other objects whose existence we do have reason to believe in) or rather is due to there really being objects of the kind posited. And this is at least plausibly something that can be discovered by looking at the role played by posits in our theories, even if, in advance, there is no fact of the matter regarding whether practitioners intend to assert their existence literally or merely metaphorically.

The problem of distinguishing merely instrumental posits from really existing ones is certainly a difficult one. But, contrary to Yablo's suggestion, this is not, I think, because answering this question depends on a prior determination of what there is. For, in determining whether we should believe a sentence that, taken literally, would imply that there are ϕs, or only believe some metaphorical content which our utterance of that sentence may allow us to express, we can consider what it is about that sentence that contributes to its useful inclusion in our theory (and, in particular, whether it could still be useful if it was only some metaphorical content, and not its literal content, that was true). For any theory that, on a literal reading, posits the existence of ϕs, the question that needs answering is not whether there really are ϕs, but rather, whether we could make use of that theory in the way that we do, with reasonable expectation of theoretical success, if we supposed that there are in fact no ϕs. If not, then the successful use of the theory surely gives us reason for believing that the hypothesis that there are ϕs is more than a useful instrument: that is, that ϕs (or something like them) do exist. Alternatively, if we have a reasonable account of *how* the theory could be successful even if its supposition that there are ϕs is literally false, then this gives us reason for taking an instrumental attitude to the theory's assumption that there are ϕs. The difficulty of deciding this question depends on the difficulty of weighing up our alternative accounts of theoretical success, but Yablo has provided no principled reason why this *cannot* be done.

Indeed, as Lawrence Sklar has argued, the question of whether to view theoretical hypotheses as mere fictions or as literally true is not a matter of disconnected 'armchair' philosophizing, but is rather a central part of ordinary scientific practice. Thus, Sklar (2003: 431) asks,

How are we to determine if the characterization of a system within science is meant to describe the real system or if, instead, it is merely intended to provide a 'useful fiction' that is meant to have predictive value but not to characterize how things 'really are?'

And this question, Sklar claims, can only be answered

by consulting the science itself. Issues of the manner in which concepts and putative laws are intended to deal with the world cannot be decided upon a priori by the methodologist. Science is replete both with schemes intended to truly characterize 'how things are' and with other schemes intended only as knowingly false but useful models of the real situation. But only the science itself can do the job of explicating the intended purpose of its own descriptive and explanatory schemes.

Doing science, Sklar stresses, does not simply involve the blind use of theoretical hypotheses to draw out predictions, but also often involves developing an understanding of how it is that those hypotheses can be predictively successful. We might hope, then, to uncover more about which of our hypotheses should be taken literally, and which should be viewed merely figuratively, simply as part of our scientific understanding of science itself (of which naturalistic philosophy is a limiting case). In particular, when it comes to the mathematically stated assumptions of our theories, while it might not be obvious to us whether we ought to take these assumption as merely useful fictions, or as literal truths, an inquiry into the theoretical role of those assumptions might nevertheless allow us to answer the question of whether we have reason to believe them to be literally true.

How might such an inquiry proceed? How might 'consulting the science itself' allow us to decide which of our hypotheses we ought to take literally? On Sklar's view, we should look to our reflective understanding of why it is that our theoretical assumptions are predictively successful, in order to answer whether we ought to believe those assumptions to be true or merely useful fictions. And such a reflective understanding can be found in our ordinary scientific worldview, as when we attempt to explain, from the perspective of our more fundamental theoretical hypotheses, why it is safe in some contexts to assume, for example, that fluids are continuous or that space is Euclidean. Thus, Sklar (ibid.: 435) points out, 'there are major programs of science itself that are specifically designed to account for the fact that we are so successful in meeting our aims of prediction and explanation when we use theories that the fundamental science tells us cannot possibly be really correct in the contexts in which they are applied'. In such cases, we have at least a programme of scientific explanation of the successful use of theoretical hypotheses, which assumes that those hypotheses may not be literally true. And the fact that there is room in our scientific practice for such explanatory programmes, making use of our ordinary scientific standards of evidence and explanation to account for the success of theories that are not themselves believed to be literally true, makes it plausible that we can uncover naturalistic grounds for accepting or rejecting the literal truth of existentially quantified theoretical assumptions, in terms of our *explanations* of the successful use of those theoretical assumptions. For, the existence of such explanatory programmes suggests, first of all, that default literalism is not essential as an attitude to the assumptions of our scientific theories. Furthermore, they point to the possibility of applying ordinary empirical scientific standards to the question of whether to believe the existential assumptions of our theories.

Sklar's own examples of explanations of the predictive successes of theoretical assumptions involve accounting for the practical usefulness of merely figurative assumptions in terms of the claims of a *literally believed* underlying physical theory.[3] But if this is the only way in which we can expose merely useful fictions *as fictions*, then it looks as if a kind of ontological scepticism will reappear. For, if we take seriously our earlier suggestion that instrumental assumptions might be representationally essential even in our most fundamental theories, we will not be able to show *these* assumptions to be merely instrumental by providing a literally believed underlying account of why they should be successful if not true. Ontological questions will be unanswerable, in this case, not because there is no fact of the matter as to how we *intend* our assertions to be interpreted,

---

[3] This is primarily because the focus of Sklar's own discussion is reductionism. Against Nancy Cartwright's (1999) anti-reductionist account of a 'dappled' world, Sklar wants to show that we can have reason for giving a special status to our fundamental physical theories, viewing these theories as indicative of what's 'really' going on, even though these are not the theories we actually use in most of our scientific explanations. As a result, his focus is on showing that although such theories are not used to predict or explain many macroscopic phenomena, they do allow us to understand why the predictions and explanations we do give at these levels are good even if they are not, strictly speaking, true.

but rather, because we lack the means to provide an acceptable *explanation* of why the appropriate attitude to a given theoretical assumption is to see it as merely instrumental and not literally true. If our *only* means of showing that a theoretical assumption is not to be literally believed is by explicitly stating, in the context of a literally believed underlying theory, its metaphorical content, then Yablo's (and indeed my) suggestion that this cannot always be done will scupper the prospects of this project of uncovering our true ontological commitments via providing a scientific understanding of our theoretical successes.

But *must* an understanding of the contribution of a theoretical posit to a theory's successes always depend on our having a literally believed underlying theory to explain why a theory that posits such objects should be successful? Does answering the question of whether a theory's successes depend on the real existence of the objects it posits *require* us to have such an underlying, literally believed theory? My discussion of the kinds of 'direct evidence' we may have for theoretical posits should make us question whether the line between those posits whose existence we have reason to believe in and those we can coherently view as mere fictions must always be drawn with an underlying literally believed theory in mind. For, I suggested, sometimes evidence may require us to believe that there are objects of a particular sort even if we are not sure of the literal truth of our theory of such objects. With this in mind, within the philosophy of science, realists about entities (as opposed to realists about theories) have questioned the assumption that we can only answer ontological questions against the backdrop of a literally believed underlying theory. Such entity realists claim that there are cases where, even if we doubt the literal truth of a given theory, and lack any alternative literally believed account of the phenomena in question, we may nevertheless find that our understanding of that theory's successes requires us to assume that some of its objects exist. That is, even if we lack a literally believed underlying theory, we may still be able to discover, amongst the objects posited by our theories, a distinction between those posits whose existence we have reason to believe and those whose existence is not required for our theories to be successful.

Thus, although Nancy Cartwright is a thoroughgoing anti-realist about our ordinary scientific *theories*, arguing that those theories *must* to some degree falsify matters in order to explain phenomena, the lack of literally believed fundamental theories does not, according to Cartwright, preclude the possibility of uncovering some genuine ontological commitments when we try to understand why the theories we have succeed to the extent that they do. Cartwright wants to be a realist about (some of) the objects posited by our scientific theories, and thinks we can find evidence from the successes of our theories for believing in some of the objects they posit, even if we lack a literally believed underlying theory of those objects. If, for example, we posit objects in the context of successful causal explanations of phenomena, then Cartwright thinks that we *cannot* remain agnostic about the existence of the objects posited as causes, even if we have reservations about the literal truth of our theory concerning those objects. Such causal explanations would simply not succeed *as explanations* if we thought that the objects they posited as causes did not really exist. Similarly, Ian Hacking's (1983) defence of entity realism suggests that our *experimental practices* can give us reason to believe in ϕs even if we are sceptical about the literal truth of our best theory of such objects. Again, on Hacking's view, we cannot coherently view the hypothesis that there are electrons as merely fictional, in the light of our (largely successful) experimental attempts to manipulate electrons. Some existence claims may be present in our theories because of some figurative content they help us to express. But we cannot coherently continue to view such claims as merely figurative if we find ourselves manipulating the objects they claim to exist. You can't spray fictions! One way that we can discover that an existential claim is not to be taken as merely figurative, then, is by finding uses we put that hypothesis to that would not be served on the assumption that the existential claim is meant figuratively.

If Cartwright and Hacking are right that we can uncover reasons for accepting the existence of some of the entities posited by our theories even if we are unsure to what extent those theories may owe their success to reasons other than their literal truth, then this helps to sidestep a further sceptical worry we might have about the difficulty of discovering ontological commitments in theories that might not be literally true. Yablo (1998: 255) complains that any plausible approach to uncovering our ontological commitments will require us to embark on the potentially Sisyphean task of '*sequestering* the metaphors as a preparation for some sort of special treatment', so that we can set aside existentially quantified utterances made in non-literal contexts and instead focus our attention on uses of the existential quantifier that occur in our formulations of the literal parts of our theories. But if Cartwright and Hacking are right, then we do not have to make such a neat separation, for we can uncover some genuine ontological commitments even from within the midst of theories whose literal truth we may doubt.

Indeed, Yablo's own use of Walton's account of metaphor as prop oriented make-believe (which I will present in detail in Ch. 7) actually seems to *presuppose* that, in at least some cases, we can have explanations of theoretical successes that allow us to identify genuine ontological commitments *even in theories that are not intended literally*, and for which we have no non-literal alternative. After all, without providing a literally believed account of the theoretical contents that are accessible by means of our metaphors, Yablo himself offers an explanation of how it is that some non-literal ways of speaking can provide us with good, even indispensable, representations. Yablo's explanation of the importance of make-believe in our theorizing holds that non-literal theories are successful because of the restrictions that they place on the behaviour of real-worldly objects (props). But this explanation, if it is to make sense, surely requires us to believe in the existence of *some* of the objects posited in the context of make-believe hypotheses, even if many of the hypotheses our theories make concerning these objects are themselves literally false. We might not have a literally believed theory of ordinary fluids. But if we do not believe that *there are fluids* whose behaviour our theory of fluid dynamics represents, then we cannot make any sense of our scientific theorizing about such things.

It might be the case, we are supposing, that we cannot describe the kinds of objects whose existence we are committed to believing without appeal to some make-believe hypotheses, for example by saying that they are such as to make our theoretical hypotheses a good pretence. That is, we may suppose, Yablo could be right that we may not in general be able to give a description in purely literal terms of the objects to which we are committed. But so long as we can find some independent way of discovering which are the real-worldly 'props' in our theories (through the evidence we can have of direct interaction, for example, or less directly, through our attempts to account for a theory's successes), the lack of literal descriptions of these props does not prevent us from making substantial ontological claims. For, if Yablo is right about the representative power of metaphorical language, then we can say a lot about the nature of the objects to which we are committed by saying that they are such as to make our pretences appropriate.

6.3. Explanation and Ontological Commitment

Let us help ourselves, then, to Yablo's neo-Carnapian picture of natural science as consisting of a collection of linguistic frameworks, taking the form of 'make-believe games'. On this picture, we no longer take existential assertions as automatically ontologically committing. Putting forward an assertion in the context of a game of make-believe does not imply commitment to the literal truth of that assertion, but can be viewed rather, in Carnapian terms, as a practical decision to speak a certain way. Although we can agree with Quine that not all such decisions are purely practical (some also bring with them ontological baggage), we need not go so far as to say that *all* such practical decisions are ontologically weighty. As I have argued, the evidence of scientific practice speaks against this—there are many cases where indulging in a known fiction is extremely useful, perhaps even indispensable, to our scientific theorizing.

Following Sklar, I take the question of which theoretical utterances to take seriously to be answerable by looking to our scientific accounts of theoretical successes. In some cases these are already available. For example, we have some accounts of the successes of some literally false theories in terms of their relation to theories that are considered closer to the truth. We have indicators of how much we should believe of a given theory based on our theoretical accounts of the scale at which it should work and the points at which we might expect it to break down. We have indications that the posits of a theory are of more than just instrumental value when we have constructed experiments that provide more 'direct' evidence for the existence of those posits than is available from the general success of the theory. The practice of empirical science involves not just the use of theoretical assumptions to draw out predictions and give explanations, but also the provision of working accounts of what it is about those assumptions that makes them theoretically useful, and to what extent. This working understanding of scientific theories can be appealed to in part to make grounded judgements concerning the questions of to what extent we should take our theoretical utterances literally and to what extent we should accept their existentially quantified components as genuinely ontologically committing.

Elsewhere, and particularly in the case of mathematics, we may find that the question of what attitude to take to the theoretical assumptions made use of in formulating our theories is not explicitly considered by scientists. Nevertheless, embarking on the naturalist's project of providing a scientific understanding of science itself, we can still look to how such assumptions are used, and consider how we can explain the successful use of, for example, mathematical assumptions in our scientific theories. Having seen that mere presence in our best formulation of a successful scientific theory is not enough to guarantee the truth of an existentially quantified utterance, and that belief in the truth of such an utterance can be defeated in the light of a compelling explanation of its value as part of a merely instrumentally useful make-believe, we are compelled to consider how we can *explain* the uses of mathematics in empirical science before we pass judgement on the question of the existence of mathematical objects.

Indeed, despite his Quinean tendencies, Hilary Putnam has himself taken an *explanatory* route to realism. When Putnam (1975: 73) argues that realism 'is the only philosophy that doesn't make the success of science a miracle', he is departing from a pure Quinean position in order to defend the claim that science is true (for Quine, in contrast, the naturalist predicament is such that we have to assume that our theories provide our current best bet at the truth—that's just the boat we're in).[4] Putnam's argument is of the form advocated by our more thoroughgoing naturalist approach: he takes a look at scientific practice, notes that this practice is successful, and looks for an explanation of this success. For Putnam (ibid.: 73), the hypothesis of realism is 'part of the only scientific explanation of the success of science, and hence [is] part of any adequate scientific description of science and its relations to its objects'. The important step to note is Putnam's realization

---

[4] As we saw in Ch. 2, Quine frequently returns to the metaphor of Neurath's boat to make this point.

here that realism isn't a default position for anyone wanting to use the language of science,[5] but rather something that requires an argument, in the form of an explanation of the successful application of that language.

Where I propose to part company with Putnam, though, is in his suggestion that realism *is* the best explanation across the board. Once one notes the possibility of explaining the theoretical utility of make-believe games (in terms of their value in allowing us to represent their real-worldly props), as well as the actual existence of theoretical explanations of the success of theories that are known to be false, Putnam's blanket realism starts to look questionable.

Returning, then, to our fragmented picture of science as consisting of many 'make-believe frameworks' or ways of speaking, the question we need to ask is, does the successful use of a particular framework imply a literal construal of that framework? Our answer to this, I think, should not be Putnam's simple 'yes', but rather a case-by-case consideration of the role of posits in various theoretical components. If we start from a perspective according to which, for all we know, our scientific theories are just clusters of make-believe games, we will soon find, through our reflective understanding of our scientific practices, that this attitude cannot be sustained in the light of our theoretical successes. We will need some explanation of why these 'games' are as successful as they are. And, just as in Yablo's paradigm cases of make-believe, we saw that the theories were committed to the existence of the props that were invoked in our explanations of the success of these make-believes, in general we can take the commitments of a theory to be to just those objects whose existence we must assume in order to explain how these theories are successful.

In this way, we can hope that Yablo's controversial cases on the metaphorical/literal divide will yield to analysis. Although it may not be obvious the extent to which a picture we paint should be understood literally, we can ask how much of that picture would have to be correct in order to account for its success in our scientific theorizing. This does not mean that we will always be able to come up with a literal description to capture the literal content of the theory—the force of Yablo's point was that we cannot. But, from an ontological perspective, we can hope at least

---

[5] Compare this with the more belligerent Putnam of (1971), who stresses 'the intellectual dishonesty of denying the existence of what one daily presupposes' (ibid.: 347).

to separate the real-world props from the theoretical make-believe—to say that, in order to explain the success of this theory we need to accept the existence of an object x whose real-worldly properties are such as to make the pretence a good one. Discovering the worldly props our theories are meant to represent may be a difficult task, but surely not an impossible one. Applying the naturalist's approach to ontology is a tricky matter, but not, I think, one that rests on a mistake.[6]

---

[6] In a more recent discussion of the ontological status of mathematical posits, Yablo (2005: 98) himself appears to have moved away from his earlier ontological scepticism, positively asserting that 'numbers, as they appear in applied mathematics, are *creatures of existential metaphor*', and presenting an account of mathematics as metaphor which, while focusing primarily on the genesis of arithmetic, bears many similarities to the account I will provide in the next chapter. However, a footnote to this later work contains a nod to his earlier scepticism, where he states that he does not 'rule it out that '$2 + 3 = 5$ is a maybe-metaphor, to be interpreted literally if so-interpreted it is true, otherwise metaphorically. . . . I think that the existence issue can be finessed still further, but the margin is too small to contain my proof of this' (ibid.: 111).

7

Mathematics and Make–Believe

I have so far been concerned with outlining a naturalistic approach to ontology that takes seriously the possibility that even our best scientific theories will contain components whose theoretical utility is not attributable to their literal truth. The motivation for this approach has primarily been an appreciation of the immense utility of idealized models in empirical theorizing in allowing us to provide tractable representations of empirical phenomena. Such idealizations, by ignoring irrelevant features of those phenomena, can often allow us to 'get to the nub' of the general processes at work without leaving us bogged down in details of specific cases, and as such, may often be *better*, for both predictive and explanatory purposes, than more accurate literal descriptions. But if ideal models turn out, on occasions, to be theoretically preferable to more literal descriptions of empirical phenomena, then it is reasonable to think that such idealizations will remain even in our best theories, whether or not more literal accounts can be constructed.

The existence of apparently indispensable idealizations in our best theories provides some motivation for abandoning Quinean confirmational holism, but does not yet suffice to break the force of the indispensability argument for the existence of mathematical objects. In the first place, we have noted that a realist picture of scientific models, which views the objects posited by such models as really existing abstracta, is available according to which the indispensable use of ideal models in formulating our best scientific theories would count as evidence for the existence of ideal objects. If this is the best account of idealization available, then we need not abandon confirmational holism after all: our theoretical successes will confirm the existence as abstracta of the ideal objects posited by our theory. And secondly, even if (as I suggested in Ch. 6), an alternative anti–realist account of idealization as make–believe is preferable, so that the presence of indispensable idealizations in our theories would not count as confirmation of the existence of ideal objects such as continuous fluids, we would still need to do some work before we could conclude that the *mathematical* components of our theories are not confirmed by their success. In particular, we would need to show that the utility of the mathematical posits of our theories was more like the utility of the ideal objects posited by our ideal models than the utility of empirical posits such as electrons, before concluding that the existence of such objects does not receive theoretical confirmation.

Filling out the details of this response to the indispensability argument will be the work of the remainder of this book. In particular, in this chapter I would like to fill out the details of how Walton's account of fiction as make-believe can be used to provide an understanding of the utility of theoretical fictions (idealized models) which does not commit us to accepting the existence of fictional (ideal) objects, and to consider how this account can be extended to provide an understanding of the role of mathematical hypotheses in our scientific theories. Having presented an understanding of mathematical hypotheses as theoretical fictions, I will then go on (in Chs. 8 and 9) to defend this understanding of the special role of mathematics against more and less realist accounts of science.

7.1. An Anti-Realist Theory of Fiction

Recall the two uses of idealization considered in the previous two chapters. Idealizations can appear in our theories in the form of explicitly false assumptions about real things (we assume of real fluids that they are continuous), or alternatively as claims about the properties of ideal objects in ideal models. We can view this latter use of idealization as introducing ideal objects as theoretical fictions. In considering what the appropriate attitude is to the ideal objects posited by our ideal models, then, it is reasonable to consider the wider question of what attitude to take to the people, places, and things that populate our fictions in general. Setting aside for now the first kind of idealization (idealization as falsification), let us consider whether an account of ideal objects can be gleaned from an account of fictional characters.

There certainly does seem to be a close comparison between ideal objects and fictional characters. Characteristic of literary fiction is the ability of authors of fiction to generate their characters, and the fictional worlds they inhabit, simply by stipulating certain things to be true 'in the fiction' of them. Through his choice of various sentences in formulating the text of *Hamlet*, Shakespeare was able to make various things true, in the fiction, of Hamlet; there is no sense in asking whether Shakespeare had things right about Hamlet's behaviour, or the unfortunate events that befell him (although we may wonder whether it is plausible that any real person in similar circumstances would have behaved in the same kinds of way). Similarly with the ideal objects of ideal models: objects in these models are likewise given some of their properties *by definition*. It makes no sense to ask whether the fluids in a continuous fluid model really are continuous, nor whether the values of various properties built into the model are correct (although we may wonder whether these assumptions make the fluid in our model an appropriate representation of some real fluid). This is not, of course, to say that *everything* about Hamlet or about our continuous fluids must be explicitly stipulated. Our stipulations generate further fictional 'truths' through their logical consequences, and there may be further background assumptions implicit due to conventions of fiction-making/model-building that lead to more things being true in the fiction than are explicitly stated (Shakespeare did not need to stipulate that Hamlet was an ordinary, flesh and blood human being for it to be true in the fiction that he was).

Do such stipulations and background assumptions, made in the context of telling a story or describing a model, generate genuine (albeit stipulative) *truths* about the characters of the story or the objects of the model? Is 'truth-in-the-fiction', in other words, a species of *truth*? Certainly, there are realist accounts of fictional discourse that do take (some) such stipulations to be truths. For example, although Peter van Inwagen does not treat *all* utterances made in the context of fiction-making as true, he does think that, as a result of our stipulations, there are some genuine truths *about* fictional characters (such as, for example, that Hamlet's behaviour provides a good example of the Oedipal complex), that may be uttered in the context of wider discourse about fiction. And since he rejects, as I did in Chapter 1, the Meinongian alternative (defended by Terence Parsons), according to which the character Hamlet is a non-existent object, van Inwagen takes acceptance of such truths to commit us to belief in the genuine existence of fictional characters. If we transferred such a view to the ideal objects posited by our theoretical models, then clearly a 'modelling' view of the use of mathematics in science would yield no ontological gains: we would likewise be committed to accepting the existence of the abstract objects of our models. What we need, then, is an alternative view of the stipulations made in fiction-making, which does not see them as generative of any truths about fictional characters. Such a view is provided by Kendall L. Walton's account of fiction as make-believe.

7.1.1. Fictional Representations and Make-Believe

Central to Walton's account of fiction is the notion of pretence, or of games of make-believe. In writing literary fiction, for example, on Walton's view an author should be viewed not as *falsely asserting* the sentences that make up a given story to be true of some portion of the concrete, physical world that we inhabit, or, indeed, as *truly asserting* those sentences to hold of some abstract realm of fictional characters, but rather as merely *pretending* that the sentences they utter are true, and inviting the reader to indulge in this pretence. On such an understanding, it would be mistaken to take the text of Shakespeare's *Hamlet* as stipulating actual properties of an actual (though fictional) character: Shakespeare should be viewed as merely *inviting* us to imagine a character who behaves as the play describes, something that is, presumably, possible for us to do *even if there is no such character*. But the practice of pretence is more widespread than literature, and indeed Walton sees literature as just one amongst many examples of uses of pretence/make-believe for various purposes. The case that interests us, of course, is the use of theoretical models to represent how things are taken to be with real objects (such as the use of an ideal, continuous fluid model to represent the behaviour of real fluids). To understand how fictions, understood as games of make-believe, can be used to represent real objects, it will be helpful to consider Walton's wider account of representative uses of games of make-believe.

According to Walton, fictional representations represent their objects by prescribing imaginings concerning those objects. To use one of Walton's examples, a children's game of make-believe might prescribe its participants to imagine, *of tree stumps in a forest*, that they are bears. In this way, the game represents the tree stumps as bears. A novel such as *War and Peace* might prescribe readers to imagine *of Napoleon* that he 'was dreaming of the Moscow that so appealed to his imagination'. In this way, the novel represents Napoleon as dreaming of Moscow. And, returning to our examples of literally false idealizations introduced in Chapter 5, we might similarly see the 'continuum hypothesis' of fluid dynamics as a prescription to imagine *of real fluids* that they are continuous substances, thereby representing real fluids as continuous. In each of these cases, the reason that there is a prescription of a particular sort in play is different. The children may have explicitly decided, at the start of their game, to pretend that the tree stumps they encounter are bears. Tolstoy makes it the case that we ought to imagine of Napoleon that he was dreaming of Moscow by writing the sentence, 'Napoleon rode on, dreaming of the Moscow that so appealed to his imagination.' The prescription to imagine that ordinary fluids are continuous is established by including the 'continuum hypothesis' at the start of our textbook presentations of fluid dynamics. But in all of these cases the objects of our imaginings is fixed by quite ordinary means: the children can ensure that their prescribed imaginings represent *the tree stumps* as bears simply by pointing to the tree stumps. Tolstoy can ensure that his prescribed imaginings represent *Napoleon* by using the name Napoleon as we standardly use it, to refer to Napoleon. By providing examples of the kinds of fluids to which we take our theory of fluid dynamics to apply, we can pick out the appropriate natural kind whose properties our theory is meant to represent.

Such examples of fictional representation involve prescriptions to adopt make-believe hypotheses concerning the nature of *real* objects (the tree stumps; Napoleon; ordinary fluids). And strictly speaking, in these examples, all these representations also *mis*represent to some degree: they prescribe us to imagine of real objects that they are other than they really are. It is clear in these cases that we are sometimes being required to imagine something *false* concerning the nature of such objects: we know that the tree stumps aren't *really* bears; that the fluids aren't *really* continuous. But prescriptions to imagine need not, Walton thinks, always be prescriptions to imagine falsehoods: many of the claims about Napoleon that *War and Peace* prescribes us to imagine true of him may indeed be true. Furthermore, prescriptions to imagine need not, on Walton's view, always be prescriptions to imagine (perhaps falsely) *of real things* that they are in such-and-such a way. After all, in asking us to imagine things to be true *of Napoleon, War and Peace* is something of a special case amongst novels. It is certainly not only real (flesh and blood) people that are represented in novels. Far more common in literature are representations of purely fictional characters.

Thus, Cervantes' novel represents *Don Quixote* as tilting at windmills. But how (a realist about fictional characters might ask) can Cervantes succeed in this, unless there is some (fictional) character, Don Quixote, to whom the descriptions in Cervantes' text refers? Surely, if our novels contain representations of fictional characters, there must be some such things for our novels to represent? Similarly, on Giere's and Cartwright's understanding of idealizations in our scientific theories, such idealizations are best understood, they think, not as requiring us to assume, falsely, that ordinary, spatiotemporally located fluids are continuous, but rather, as requiring us to assume that the ideal fluids in some abstract model are continuous substances. But how, we might wonder, can we represent the ideal fluids in some ideal model as being continuous substances, if there are no such objects for us to represent? In such cases, we might think, there *must* be some fictional objects for our representations to be representations *of*. Furthermore, in these cases, we have no reason to think that our representations are also *mis*representations: if I represent real fluids as being continuous, additional knowledge about the true nature of such fluids shows my representation to be false in some respects; but if I represent the ideal fluids in some ideal model as being continuous, there is no further information that will show this representation to have got things wrong about the nature of its objects. (Indeed, at least on Giere's view, such ideal objects have the properties we ascribe to them simply *by definition*.)

Walton's notion of representations as prescriptions to imagine allows him to resist this line of thought, whereby representations must always be representations of objects that exist in some sense. If we think that representations must always be representations *of things*, then it is indeed tempting to think that Cervantes' novel refers to a (fictional) person, Don Quixote, and represents *him* as tilting at windmills. But if we understand representations merely as prescriptions to imagine, this surely removes the need for there always to be *objects* for our representations (considered as prescriptions to imagine) to represent. We do not need there to *be* a person, Don Quixote, in order for us to *imagine* that there is an errant knight of that name, about whose adventures we are learning when we read the novel. And once we make-believe that there is such a person, we can make-believe that many things are true of him. So there can be a prescription to imagine that Don Quixote tilted at windmills even if there is no one who can be said to be the object of our imaginings.

This, then, suggests a way of understanding our talk of ideal objects in models of our theories. According to the modelling view of idealizations, as presented by Cartwright and Giere, rather than supposing falsely *of real fluids* that they are continuous, we instead consider our theory of fluid dynamics as a theory about the properties of ideal fluids in ideal models (to which ordinary fluids can then be compared). This talk of ideal objects appeared to commit us to believing that there are such things as ideal, continuous fluids. But if we view the sentences we use in formulating the laws of fluid dynamics as analogous with the text of a novel, these sentences may generate a prescription to imagine (or make-believe) that there are fluids about which the sentences assert truths. And if we are only *making-believe* that there are such things, then our speaking as if there are ideal fluids should not be thought of as committing us to believing in such objects.

7.1.2. *Props and Principles of Generation*

In Walton's view, then, fictional representations are prescriptions to imagine that something is the case (Cervantes' novel represents Quixote as tilting at windmills if it generates a prescription to imagine that Quixote is tilting at windmills). But how is it, in general, that imaginings can come to be *prescribed* as a result of acts of fiction-making? We can take novel-writing as an example. It is, we suppose, a convention of novel appreciation (an understood rule of the games of make-believe we play with novels) that, in general, if the novel includes in its text a sentence S, then we should pretend that S, taken literally, expresses a truth. This can be defeated, of course, as when there are indications that the narrator is to be taken to be unreliable. But a general rule of thumb in 'playing along with' literary fictions is that we suppose that what is being revealed to us is the case, unless there are explicit indications otherwise. We can think of this rule of thumb as one of many implicit principles of generation for make-believe games surrounding novels. It tells us what we ought to imagine when faced with an author's text (presented as fiction). The actual texts of novels are needed to generate prescriptions to imagine, in the case of literary fictions. As such, they are what Walton calls 'props' in the games of make-believe that we, as appreciators, are invited to play when reading those novels: 'A prop is something which, by virtue of conditional *principles of generation*, mandates imaginings' (Walton 1990: 69).

Taking the texts of novels as props in our imaginative games, there are, of course, further principles of generation that mandate further imaginings. If we are to make-believe that S is true, and if T is a consequence of S, then in general we ought also to make-believe that T is true, for example. More importantly, for a given novel, there will be imaginings that will be prescribed not in virtue of principles of generation applied to the *text* as a prop, but in virtue of principles of generation as applied to *further* props aside from the text. For example, since *War and Peace* prescribes imaginings about *real* people and places, those very people and places can serve as props to generate further imaginings. *War and Peace* prescribes us to imagine some things of Napoleon that are not true of him. But to the extent that there is common knowledge about Napoleon that does not contradict these imaginings, we ought also to imagine many of those things to be true of Napoleon in the context of reading *War and Peace*, should the question arise. Tolstoy does not have to tell us such mundane things as that Napoleon was flesh and blood, that he ate and slept, that he travelled by the usual means available to nineteenth-century humans and not by teleporting . . . , in order for there to be a prescription for us to imagine such things, if we find ourselves entertaining such questions. Thus, aside from the texts themselves, real people and places can also serve as props by which the imaginings prescribed by literary fictions are generated.

Similarly with the objects (mis)represented in the other games of make-believe we considered. If we are to make-believe that tree-stumps are bears, then the tree stumps will serve as props in prescribing further imaginings. Thus, it is explicitly agreed in setting up our tree stump game that the tree stumps should be imagined to be bears, but it is a consequence of *how things are with the tree stumps* (as props in the game) that we should also imagine in this context that there is a bear over in that thicket. Similarly, it is explicitly agreed, in setting up the 'continuum hypothesis' of fluid dynamics, that fluids should be imagined to be continuous, uniform, substances, but it is a consequence of adopting this hypothesis that we should consider measurements of the average velocity (say) over a relatively large region as indicative of the value of the velocity at points within that region. And, as a result, correlations we may notice between average velocity and (for example) temperature as measured over macroscopic regions can generate prescriptions to imagine the truth of equations expressing these correlations in terms of the relations between continuous functions defined over points within the fluid.

The presence of real objects as props in our make-believe games means that the imaginings mandated by our make-believe games are not always transparent to us. I might not know that I ought to imagine a bear in the thicket, since I might not know that a tree stump is hidden there. I might be mistaken in imagining that there is a bear on the top of the hill, since what looks to me like a distant tree stump is actually a pile of stones. Now it might be the case that the sentences I utter in the context of playing such a make-believe game are all (taken literally) equally false (since, in this example, there are no bears in the vicinity). Nevertheless, to the extent that some are prescribed by the game (in virtue of its props and its principles of generation) and others are not, they can still be evaluated as acceptable or unacceptable. If there is a prescription to imagine that S is true, then we will say that S is *fictional* (in the context of a given game). We may be mistaken about what is fictional, and, through consideration of the props in our games, may come to new *hypotheses* about whether a sentence S is fictional in the light of the principles of generation of a given game.[1] Props and principles of generation combine, then, to ensure that even in games of make-believe we may be highly constrained as to which moves are appropriate.

7.1.3. Unofficial Games

In writing a novel, an author can generate prescriptions to imagine that such and such is the case with its characters, through, for example, including a given sentence in the text of the novel. But we also wish to say things apparently *about* the characters in such novels, that are not prescribed by the basic conventions of novel appreciation. This happens, for example, when we step outside the make-believe according to which we pretend that the events described in the novel really occurred. Outside this context we may make utterances that are not fictional within this make-believe,

---

[1] Note, then, that in this sense of the word 'fictional', being fictional, as Walton uses the term, does not necessarily imply being contrary to fact. Rather, the status of a hypothesis as fictional depends on there being a prescription to imagine that it is true, regardless of whether it really is true.

for example when we make utterances that appear to concern the relation of the characters of the fictions to other fictional characters or to real people. Walton (ibid.: 410) considers the following examples of such mixed utterances:

(11) Oscar Wilde killed off Dorian Gray by putting a knife through his heart.
(12) Most children like E.T. better than Mickey Mouse.
(13) Sherlock Holmes is more famous than any other detective.
(14) Vanquished by reality, by Spain, Don Quixote died in his native village in the year 1614. He was survived but a short time by Miguel de Cervantes.

These utterances are certainly not fictional in the make-believes generated by the creators of the various fictional characters they concern. After all, Wilde just isn't a character in *The Picture of Dorian Gray*; the fictional 'worlds' of E.T. and Mickey Mouse simply do not overlap (in the story of E.T., it is fictional that Mickey Mouse is a fictional character and E.T. is a real alien, but what is not fictional is that both are real). What are we to make of such utterances?

One *might* think that these utterances can be used to assert straightforward *truths* about fictional characters. Indeed, realists about fictional characters take such examples of apparent truths *about* fiction (as opposed to utterances made within the context of an explicit fiction), as presenting the best case for believing that there are fictional characters. Thus, while Peter van Inwagen is, as we noted earlier, a realist about fictional characters, he rejects the inference from the presence, in *Martin Chuzzlewit*, of the sentence (1) 'She was a fat old woman, this Mrs. Gamp, with a husky voice and a moist eye, which she had a remarkable power of turning up, and only showing the white of it,' to the existence of a fictional character, Mrs Gamp, about whom Dickens was asserting a truth. We might think that, in including this sentence in his fiction, Dickens is asserting of a person that she was fat. But van Inwagen (1977: 41–2) questions whether any assertion is genuinely being made in this case. After all, Dickens might only be *pretending* to assert that Mrs Gamp was fat. On the other hand, in talking *about* literature van Inwagen thinks that we do make some genuine assertions about fictional characters. Van Inwagen cites Dickens's preface to an 1867 edition of *Martin Chuzzlewit*, where Dickens claims that (2) 'Mrs. Sarah Gamp was, four-and-twenty years ago, a fair representation of the hired attendant on the poor in sickness.' This claim is outside the context of the fiction itself, and seems to assert (perhaps truly) *of the character* Mrs Gamp, that she was a good representation of a certain real type of person. Thus, according to van Inwagen, even if sentences uttered in the context of fiction-making are uttered in a spirit of pretence, so as not to bring with them genuine ontological commitments, our utterances, made in the context of literary theory, of sentences that, if taken at face value, talk *about* fictional characters are to be understood as sincere *assertions*. As such, they do carry with them commitments to an ontology that includes fictional characters (along with other theoretical entities, such as 'plots', 'sub-plots', and even 'novels'—as opposed to individual copies of novels).

These kinds of examples are particularly relevant to the use of ideal models to represent. While, in setting up an ideal model in fluid dynamics, we may start out by merely pretending that there are continuous fluids, when we go on to *compare* those fluids to the real fluids whose behaviour we wish to model, and use this comparison to draw conclusions about the real fluids, it appears that we are stepping outside the 'fiction' of the ideal fluid model in order to assert some truths. If we take it to be *true* that the fluid in our ideal model is a good representation of some real fluid, then surely such claims commit us to the existence of ideal fluids as theoretical objects, even if our initial stipulations in setting up the ideal model did not? Indeed, the whole point of developing ideal models in empirical science is to allow us to infer some truths about real objects: surely in these uses of models, mere pretence is not enough?

In the context of literary theory, Walton's response to this challenge again makes use of the notion of make-believe. Walton denies the truth of those claims of literary theory that appear to quantify over fictional characters, and denies that the purpose of engaging in such literary criticism is to assert truths about fictional characters. Instead, he thinks, the correctness of Dickens's use of the sentence (2) is also due to its *fictionality* in some make-believe game, rather than its truth. Of course, the game in this case cannot be the make-believe generated by Dickens's novel writing, according to which we pretend that the sentences of the novel are (by and large) true. In the context of this game, we are to pretend that Mrs Gamp is a real person, not that she is 'fair representation' of a kind of person that once existed. But aside from serving as props in these 'official' games generated by fictions—such as the game in which we are to imagine that Mrs Gamp was a fat old woman—works of fiction can, Walton argues, serve as props in further, 'unofficial' games. The implicit supposition, in literary criticism, that there are fictional worlds inhabited by characters created by their authors provides one such game. This supposition generates many prescriptions to imagine relations between these worlds, their characters, and reality. Such derivative games make sense of utterances such as (11)–(14) above: a derivative game in which the author of a fiction is a God-like creator/destroyer of some fictional world makes it fictional that Wilde killed off Dorian Gray; a derivative game in which the kind of psychological attitudes humans have in relation to other humans (fear; admiration; warmth) can also be had in relation to the characters that inhabit fictional worlds can make it fictional that most children prefer E.T. But we should not, Walton thinks, confuse the fictionality of these claims about the relations between real people and fictional characters with their literal truth. Like our utterances made in the context of official games, these utterances are also best thought of as moves in games of make-believe, albeit unofficial or derivative games.[2]

Such derivative games can make sense of the way in which the pretence that there are ideal continuous fluids about which the laws of our theories assert truths can be expanded to allow us to say things about real fluids. For in this case we need not restrict ourselves to the primary 'make-believe', according to which we just suppose that there are such ideal objects about which our theoretical laws assert truths. Seeing these objects as existing in their own 'ideal' realm may generate further imaginings concerning the relationship between those ideal objects and the real fluids of our world. Indeed, the possibility of 'unofficial' games helps to explain why it may be unclear, when we adopt the 'continuum hypothesis' in our theory of fluid dynamics, whether we are supposed to pretend, of real fluids, that they are continuous, or alternatively, to pretend that there are ideal continuous fluids, which resemble real fluids in some respects. Compare this case with the inclusion, in the text of *War and Peace*, of sentences apparently about Napoleon. On one reading, *War and Peace* requires us to pretend that lots of things that may or may not in fact be true *of Napoleon* are true of him. But if we indulge in the further unofficial

---

[2] Aside from Walton (1990), see Walton (1978) for a defence of the claim that we do not really (for example) *fear* fictions, but only participate in (sometimes very vivid) games of make-believe in which we, fictionally, are afraid.

'game' according to which literary fictions describe parallel universes, with their own unique casts of characters, the text of *War and Peace* is in this context pretended to be a literally true description of an alternative world, with its own inhabitant, Napoleon, distinct from the Napoleon who inhabits our own world. On this reading, then, the text of *War and Peace* is not to be imagined to assert truths about our Napoleon, but rather, to assert truths about some Napoleon character in a parallel universe. And indulging in this pretence allows us to consider how close a resemblance there is between this character and the real Napoleon. So *War and Peace* can be said to represent the real Napoleon in one of two ways, depending on our use of its text to generate a make-believe. In one way, it can represent Napoleon as being ϕ by prescribing us to imagine that Napoleon is ϕ. But in another way, it can represent Napoleon as being ϕ by representing its own Napoleon character as being ϕ, and implicitly suggesting that the real Napoleon resembles the Napoleon character in this respect. On Walton's view at least, the latter claim (that the real Napoleon resembles the Napoleon character in such-and-such a respect) is just as fictional as a straightforward prescription to imagine something that is known to be false of Napoleon, for it too occurs within the context of a make-believe game.

7.2. The Value of Make-Believe Representations

Why indulge in games of make-believe? In particular, what value is there in representing real objects as being thus-and-so, if we do not also believe that they are thus-and-so? The most important aspect of Walton's understanding of representations (and misrepresentations) as games of make-believe is his account of the value of participating in these games, and in particular, of the relation of these games to the props they utilize. Much of what Walton has to say here involves our use of props in make-believe games to aid us in appreciating the content of a representation: 'paint on canvas and print on paper lead us into exciting worlds of mystery, romance, and adventure and guide our travels through them' (Walton 1993: 39). This is surely the prime purpose of make-believe in the context of appreciating literature. Walton calls make-believe used in this way *content oriented*, since its main interest lies in contemplating the content of the make-believe.

7.2.1. Prop Oriented Make-Believe

What is of interest to us, however, is not so much content oriented make-believe, but what Walton calls *prop oriented* make-believe. This is when we use our make-believe games as a means for understanding the props that, together with principles of generation, generate those games. This *can* happen in literature: one can discover facts about London by reading the Sherlock Holmes stories (for example, that Bloomsbury is a fifteen-minute walk from Baker Street). But the Sherlock Holmes stories are primarily meant to be used in content oriented, rather than prop oriented, make-believe (we are interested in the content of the fiction for its own sake, independently of what it may or may not be able to tell us about crime investigation in London). A prime example of *prop oriented* make-believe is, on the other hand, the use of make-believe in metaphor, rather than in literature: it is by imagining Italy as a boot that we can locate Crotone by describing it as on the arch of the boot; or, in one of Walton's cruder examples, it is by imagining plumbing connections to be male and female sexual organs that we can say how it is that two pipes are to be fitted together (Walton 1993: 40). Our main interest in indulging in *these* make-believes resides in their usefulness in describing and understanding their props, rather than in the content of the make-believes themselves.

We noted above that what is fictional in the context of a make-believe will be in part constrained by facts about its props (the objects which, in conjunction with principles of generation, yield prescriptions to imagine). If we adopt the make-believe that Italy is a boot, then in the context of that make-believe, facts about the locations of cities make it the case that we ought to make-believe that Crotone is in the arch and not in the toe. And if, in the context of the make-believe, we pretend that Crotone is in the arch of the boot, there is a fact of the matter regarding whether we are *right* to so pretend, even though the sentence we use in the context of this pretence is, taken literally, false. But this means that our speaking as if Crotone is in the arch of the boot (as is literally false), can also be a way of indirectly representing some matter of fact: we represent the props in our make-believe (Italy and its towns and cities) as being the way *they* would have to be in order to make our pretence appropriate. For if we are right that it is *fictional* in our game that Crotone is in the arch of the boot, then in part this will be because of the actual location of Crotone. Uttering the sentence 'Crotone is in the arch of the boot' in the context of the game can then serve indirectly to assert that Crotone is in fact just where it would have to be in order for this utterance to be fictional.

On Walton's view, then, by participating in make-believe games, and entertaining hypotheses about what (given the rules of generation of our games) we ought to imagine concerning their worldly props, we can indirectly express hypotheses about the props themselves. Thus, in the game where tree stumps are imagined to be bears, our pretending to wonder whether there is a bear in the thicket in part involves us in genuinely wondering whether there is a tree stump there. Indeed, Walton identifies one *purpose* of uttering a sentence S in the context of a make-believe (in his terms, of *pretending to assert* that S is true), as being to indirectly express one's belief that such-and-such is the case with the props. For, as Walton (ibid.: 399) points out, 'Doing something is sometimes a way of claiming that it is proper or acceptable to do it.' Pretending to assert, in the context of a make-believe, that Crotone is in the arch of the boot is a way of claiming that it is acceptable to do so, given the rules of the make-believe. So part of what is achieved by our making this move in the make-believe is that it provides us with an indirect way of asserting that the props (Italy, Crotone) are such as to make this make-believe assertion appropriate.

This indirect use of make-believes to express truths about their props leads to a new sense in which fictional hypotheses can be said to represent real objects, aside from potentially misrepresenting them. So far, I have said that fictions can represent their worldly props as perhaps being *other* than they actually are, by prescribing imaginings about them that may in fact be false. But in some cases these misrepresentations can be used in an indirect way to make accurate representations of their props: when I misrepresent the thicket as containing a *bear*, I can thereby *truly* (though indirectly) represent it as containing a tree stump. And when I misrepresent a real fluid as behaving in a similar manner to some (non-existent) ideal fluid, I can thereby *truly* (though indirectly) represent it as having certain properties (those it would have to have to make my misrepresentation fictional in the context of the relevant game). In this sense, then, we can talk of make-believe games not just as *mis*representing their props (by prescribing us to make-believe that they are other than they are), but also as, via these misrepresentations, correctly representing them (as being the way *they* would have to be to make the pretence appropriate). It is this kind of use of make-believe games, in truly representing aspects of their props, that is of most interest in adapting Walton's theory to provide an account of how speaking as if a sentence S is true, in the context of our scientific theorizing, may be a way of representing some matter of fact.

Thus, returning for a moment to Stephen Yablo's discussion of the role of metaphor in scientific theories, Yablo uses Walton's understanding of how fictions can be used indirectly to represent how things are genuinely taken to be with their props to draw a distinction between the *literal* and *metaphorical* content of sentences. While the literal content of a sentence 'Crotone is in the arch of the boot' is simply false, its metaphorical content when uttered in the context of a make-believe, that is, what is indirectly said in this make-believe about the actual positioning of Crotone in Italy, is *true*. 'A metaphor on this view is an utterance that represents its objects as being *like so*: the way that they *need* to be to make the utterance pretence-worthy in a game that it itself suggests' (Yablo 1998: 247). Literally false, or fictional, theoretical assumptions can thus, on Yablo's view, be valuable in our theorizing due to their ability to represent, via their *metaphorical* content, genuine properties of real-worldly props. It will sometimes on this view be practical for us to speak as if a sentence S is true without believing that S (taken literally) *is* true, since doing so provides us a way of representing S's metaphorical content as being the case.

7.2.2. Modelling as Prop Oriented Make-Believe

My discussion of fictional representations was prompted by the thought that the ideal objects posited by ideal models, such as the ideal fluids of fluid dynamics, bear some important similarities to the characters who inhabit fictional worlds. Taking a realist view of fictional characters suggested a similar approach to ideal objects, according to which (as in Giere's and Cartwright's interpretation), such objects exist as abstracta. Walton's anti-realist view of fiction, on the other hand, suggests an alternative view of theoretical models. On such a view, in developing ideal models, our stipulations do not generate *truths* about ideal objects, but rather, prescribe us to imagine that certain things are the case. And by incorporating *real* objects as props in the games of make-believe we play with models, these props, in combination with the principles of generation of our games, may prescribe us to imagine certain things concerning the relation between those real objects and the objects supposedly inhabiting our models. On the account we have been considering, by uttering a sentence S that appears to concern the relation between real, concrete, objects and the objects of some ideal model, a theorist may succeed in representing some metaphorical content of S to be true. And if so, the value of uttering the sentence S might be indirectly to assert not that S is true, but rather, to assert S's metaphorical content, that is, that the real worldly 'props' in the game are such as to make the sentence S fictional. Utterances apparently about the relation between real-worldly objects and the ideal objects of ideal models are therefore seen to have their theoretical value not as a result of their literal truth, but rather, as a result of their ability to express some true metaphorical content. And by grasping this content, we are able to draw conclusions about the behaviour of real objects from our idealized theories, even if we do not accept the literal truth of all our theoretical utterances.

I will not be concerned here to say anything more in defence of Walton's account as a theory of fiction, or to justify the extension of this account to provide an understanding of the ideal models posited in empirical scientific theorizing. I hope that my discussion so far has made plausible the thought that (*a*) the ideal objects posited by ideal models in empirical science are in important respects analogous to fictional characters; and that (*b*) utterances within and about fiction, and even the use of such utterances indirectly to express contents that we take to be true, need not commit us to belief in the existence of fictional characters. For those who take idealizations to be significantly different from fictions, or who think that there is no hope for an anti-realist account of fictions and fictional characters, the remainder of this discussion will do little to move them to an anti-realist view of mathematics. My aim in what follows is, rather, to persuade those who do take it to be plausible that ordinary scientific modelling should be viewed as analogous to fiction-making, and that fiction-making does not introduce commitment to an ontology of fictional characters, that the use of mathematics in empirical science should be understood along the same lines.

7.3. Mathematics as Fiction

A fictionalist regarding the mathematically stated hypotheses of our scientific theories will wish to argue that the *value* of including such hypotheses in our theories is not down to their literal truth, but is rather down to their ability to represent how things are with the non-mathematical objects our theories posit. But is it really plausible that the value of adopting mathematical assumptions of our scientific theories may be due to something other than the literal *truth* of those assumptions? In particular, is it plausible that including mathematically stated hypotheses in our theories may be useful not because of their literal content (as claims about mathematical objects and their relation to the non-mathematical objects our theories posit), but rather because of their ability to represent the non-mathematical objects of our theories as being in such-and-such a way?

If we wish to answer this question in the affirmative, it is not enough to note, as we have done, that we know of *some* cases of literally false theoretical hypotheses that are representatively useful. For the examples considered so far, of our use of literally false theoretical models in allowing us to represent really existing objects, are perhaps sufficiently different from our uses of *mathematical* assumptions in formulating our scientific theories as to throw doubt on the claim that our representative use of mathematical assumptions in our theories is just more of the same. In particular, our discussions of false-but-useful theoretical models have primarily involved idealization: for the purposes of developing tractable theories, we suppose that there are ideal objects that, in Cartwright's (1983, 17) terms, 'have only "the form or appearance of things" and, in a very strong sense, not their "substance or proper qualities" '. I have suggested that, by merely *pretending* that there are such objects, we may be led (in the context of a prop oriented make-believe) to hypothesize that it is *fictional* (against the backdrop of this pretence) that some real-worldly objects resemble these ideal objects in some important respects. In such a way, the *pretence* that there are ideal objects allows us to make substantial claims about the real objects they are used to model: in hypothesizing (in the context of our fiction) that the ideal objects of our models resemble *real* objects in some relevant respects, we can indirectly express the claim that those real objects are such as to make this pretence appropriate. As such, by merely pretending that there are ideal objects of a particular sort, and pretending that they resemble real objects in certain respects, we may indirectly represent real objects as being in such-and-such a way.

If we wish to view our adoption of hypotheses whose literal truth would require the existence of mathematical objects as likewise part of a representatively useful make-believe, we cannot give the same account of the representative value of our make-believe in terms of a pretended relation of *resemblance*. For while, in developing our theoretical assumptions concerning ideal objects in ideal theoretical models, we explicitly construct our ideal objects as shadowy abstractions of real things, in the case of our mathematically stated empirical theories, it is not so clear that we can similarly view the mathematical objects posited by those theories as shadowy idealizations of really existing objects that they resemble. While this might be possible in some cases (for example, when we consider an 'ideal' triangle in some geometrical theory rather than a physical line drawing of a triangle), in many cases the objects supposed to exist by our mathematical theories resemble the non-mathematical objects whose properties we wish to use them to represent in no sense at all. Thus, for example, while we *might* try to think of small finite *sets* of physical objects as shadowy resemblances of the mereological sums of those objects themselves (abstracting away from incidental properties such as their spatiotemporal location, for example), it would be difficult to find non-mathematical objects to resemble all the transfinitely many sets that we suppose to exist in the context of doing set theory.

If, then, the purpose of positing the existence of mathematical objects, in the context of our scientific theorizing, is simply to provide merely fictional representations of non-mathematical phenomena, our understanding of how such fictions can represent cannot generally be in terms of the representative value of pretending that the objects they posit *resemble* really existing objects. Rather, we will need to provide some account of how the supposition that there are mathematical objects such as sets can be used to make substantial claims about the nature of non-mathematical objects, even if these claims are *not* expressed in terms of the resemblance between mathematical and non-mathematical objects. In order to make the case for viewing the *mathematical* assumptions of our theories as merely useful fictions, we will, then, need to make a case for seeing *these* assumptions as having some true representative content, even if they do not represent by means of resemblance. Following Walton's account of representation as prop oriented make-believe, we will need to find some way in which 'making-believe' that there are mathematical objects in the context of our scientific theorizing may allow us to place restrictions on the non-mathematical objects posited by our theories, when considered as props in our make-believe.

7.3.1. Make-Believe in Mathematical Theorizing

How might Walton's account of the representative value of uttering sentences in the context of a prop oriented make-believe be used to account for the value of uttering *mathematical* sentences in the context of our scientific theorizing? Consider Hilary Putnam's favourite example of a mathematically expressed empirical law, Newton's Law of Universal Gravitation. Recall (from Ch. 1) that Putnam expresses the law as follows:

There is a force f_{ab} exerted by any body a on any other body b. The direction of the force f_{ab} is towards a, and its magnitude F is given by:

$$F = \frac{gM_aM_b}{d^2}$$

where g is a universal constant, M_a is the mass of a, M_b is the mass of b, and d is the distance which separates a and b.   (Putnam 1971: 338)

On the view we are suggesting, the *value* of uttering (in the context of our scientific theorizing) these sentences might not be to express their literal content (which would require the existence of real numbers and functions), but rather, to indirectly represent some *metaphorical content*, some non-mathematical fact about the relation between the bodies a and b.

Of course, Putnam himself thinks that our utterance can represent no such content, if we do not take the law to be literally true. For, he asks, what is the statement *about bodies* that is made by the Law of Universal Gravitation? 'It is just that bodies behave in such a way that the quotient of two numbers *associated* with the bodies is equal to a third number *associated* with the bodies. But how can such a statement have any objective content at all if numbers and 'associations' (i.e. functions) are alike mere fictions?' (Putnam 1975: 74) As mentioned in Chapter 1, Putnam goes on to complain that rejecting the existence of the numbers and functions posited by the law

is like trying to maintain that God does not exist and angels do not exist while maintaining at the very same time that it is an objective fact that God has put an angel in charge of each star and the angels in charge of each of a pair of binary stars were always created at the same time!   (ibid.)

By viewing the representative uses of our theoretical utterances in terms of their status as moves in a prop oriented make-believe, I hope to show that, by merely *pretending* that God has put an angel in charge of each star (and, likewise, by merely *pretending* that there are numbers associated with bodies) we *can* sometimes indirectly represent some objective content to be the case.[3]

In order to make sense, in Walton's terms, of the representative uses of mathematically stated theoretical laws such as the Law of Universal Gravitation, then, we need to find some game in which such theoretical utterances may be thought of as fictional. One way we *might* think about doing this is to view the sentences used to state our theoretical laws as themselves generative of a make-believe game. That is, in attempting to extend Walton's account of the representative uses of prop oriented make-believe to cover our mathematically stated scientific theories, we might wish to start by considering the sentences used in formulating the laws of those theories as on a par with the sentences that make up the text of a novel. In this case, our mathematically stated theoretical laws would generate prescriptions to imagine that those laws are true, just as the sentences laid down by novelists in writing novels generate prescriptions to imagine the literal truth of what is written.

This, however, will not do. For part of the force of Walton's notion of prescriptions to imagine is that, if there is a prescription to imagine that *S* is true, we are to avoid investigation into whether *S* really is the case, and, indeed, set aside any information we have that shows *S* to be false (we suspend our disbelief). But if this were the appropriate attitude to the hypotheses of our scientific theories, we would never be able to revise

---

[3] This kind of response to Putnam's challenge is certainly not new. See e.g. Melia (2000: 470), who suggests that we can communicate a theoretical picture by asserting something to be the case (e.g., that God put an angel in charge of each star) and then *taking back* some of the consequences of our original assertion (e.g. that God exists and angels exist). In discussing the representative uses of make-believe in the remainder of this chapter, I will be drawing heavily on discussions of Melia and also of Mark Balaguer (1998), concerning the ways in which we may use mathematical utterances to express some non-mathematical content. By extending Walton's notion of prop oriented make-believe to the case of our mathematically stated theories, though, I hope to be able to say something a bit more systematic about how it is that our mathematically stated theoretical utterances may be used to paint a picture of how things are with the non-mathematical objects posited by our theories.

our theories in the light of recalcitrant data. And this just does not ring true: we simply do not (or at least, should not) take the same uncritical attitude to the sentences used to express our scientific theories that we take to sentences such as 'Holmes lived at 221b Baker Street,' that occur in the text of novels.

Does the *testability* of our scientific laws mean that we should not, then, view the sentences used to express these laws as *fictional*? It would be too quick to assume that since these laws appear to be testable they are not, nevertheless, best viewed as also fictional in the context of some make-believe. For we have noted that one purpose of making an utterance in the context of a make-believe can be indirectly to express the hypothesis that one's utterance is fictional. And if sentences S and T are used indirectly to express two alternative *hypotheses* about what's fictional in the context of a game, then these hypotheses *can* be put to the test, even though their literal content may be equally false in each case. Thus it can be *fictional* that there is a bear in the thicket and not fictional that there is one on the hill, even though *in fact* there are no bears in either place. So the fact that an utterance is considered to be open to refutation does not conflict with that utterance being expressed in the context of a fiction.

The testability of the sentences that make up our mathematically stated empirical scientific theories does not, then, show that these sentences should *not* be viewed as mere fictions. But it does show that mathematically stated empirical laws such as the law '$F = \frac{gM_aM_b}{d^2}$' cannot *themselves* be considered as generative of a make-believe game. Rather, if we wish to consider the representative value of such theoretical laws as allowing us indirectly to express hypotheses concerning what is fictional in some make-believe, we will need to find some *further* generative principles of a make-believe, according to which our mathematically stated theoretical laws may or may not turn out to be fictional. In particular, we will need to find *some* theoretical suppositions which, given facts about the non-mathematical 'props' our theories concern, will generate prescriptions to imagine that sentences such as our usual theoretical laws are true, but which will not themselves be likewise open to empirical testing.

What we need, then, is a make-believe game that would allow us to view the kinds of sentences used to formulate our scientific theories as indirectly expressing hypotheses concerning what is fictional in that game. We need, that is, to tell some story about how mathematical objects relate to non-mathematical objects, so as to allow us to view our mathematically stated scientific laws (which appear to concern the relations between numbers, functions, sets, and non-mathematical objects) as hypotheses concerning what is fictional in this story. But we have such a story, in set theory with non-mathematical objects as urelements. If we suppose, *of whatever non-mathematical objects there are*, that they are precisely the urelements of such a theory, that is, that they can be collected together into sets in the way our mathematical theory describes (in its axioms), then this supposition by itself generates many further prescriptions concerning what we ought also to suppose.[4]

How is it that facts about non-mathematical objects can generate the *fictionality* of utterances in the context of set theory with urelements? Well, if there are some non-mathematical objects satisfying a non-mathematically characterized predicate ψ, then from our supposition that the non-mathematical objects form a set, together with the subset axiom, it will follow that there is a set consisting of precisely those non-mathematical objects satisfying ψ. So our 'make-believe' according to which non-mathematical objects are precisely the members of the set of urelements U in our set theory will generate a prescription to imagine the existence of a set $\{x \in U : \psi(x)\}$. And further applications of our set-theoretic axioms to our hypotheses concerning what kinds of non-mathematical objects there are will generate further more complicated prescriptions to imagine that sets of a particular sort exist. Rather than take the mathematically stated hypotheses of our empirical scientific theories as *themselves* generating our fiction, then, we may take some axiomatic

---

[4] Indeed, although we use many branches of mathematics in expressing empirical hypotheses, the fact that these branches can all be developed in a set-theoretic setting means that we can hypothesize that set theory with urelements is *all* we need in order to view the assumptions of our ordinary scientific theories as hypotheses concerning what is fictional in this game. Thus, for example, when our mathematically expressed theories include the expression 'the number of *F*s', we can read this in our set-theoretic setting as 'the cardinality of the set of *F*s', where the cardinal numbers can be viewed as particular sets. When our mathematically expressed theories include functions from non-mathematical objects to real numbers, we can view these functions as sets of ordered pairs taken from the set $U \times \mathbb{R}$, the Cartesian product of the set of non-mathematical objects U with the set of real numbers. Although there are debates over whether the objects posited by mathematical theories outside set theory should really be viewed as sets, we can at least find set-theoretic *surrogates* for the objects of any mathematical theories we may wish to apply. The existence of such surrogates shows that if we stick with set theory with non-mathematical urelements as our basic background pure mathematical theory, against which our substantial empirical utterances may be viewed as hypotheses concerning what is fictional, we are unlikely to leave any application of mathematics out.

presentation of set theory with urelements, together with the assumption that the urelements are just whatever *non-mathematical* objects there are, as the principles of generation of a make-believe. Then *how things are with the non-mathematical props* will make fictional some utterances in the context of this make-believe. And similarly, by hypothesizing that a given utterance is fictional in this make-believe, we can indirectly represent a hypothesis concerning how things are with the non-mathematical props.

Thus, to take an elementary example, taking my fingers as objects, it is *fictional* (in the context of the supposition that the axioms of our set theory, with all non-mathematical objects as urelements, are true), that there is a 1−1, onto function f from the *set* of fingers of my left hand to the *set* of fingers on my right. *Discovering* that this is fictional (that is, that there is a prescription to imagine that this is the case) involves applying the rules of generation of the fiction to its worldly props. The rules alone tell me to suppose that the non-mathematical objects (whatever they may be) form a set U, and that, for any set and any predicate in my language, there is a subset of U that contains precisely those objects satisfying that predicate. So I know that there is a set R containing all and only the fingers of my right hand, and a set L containing all and only the fingers of my left. Relative to a chosen definition of ordered pair in our set theory, the rules also tell me that there is a set $R \times L$ of precisely those ordered pairs $\langle r, l \rangle$ such that $r \in R$ and $l \in L$, and that that all arbitrary subsets of this set also exist. But to answer the question of whether, amongst these subsets, there is one which is a 1−1 function from R onto L, I need to examine the objects I started with—my fingers—which function as props in generating the *fictionality* of my utterance concerning the existence of such a function.

This simple example is not particularly interesting in itself, but it does help to show how non-mathematical objects, as worldly props, together with the supposition that those objects, whatever they are, are the urelements in a standard set theory with urelements, serve to generate prescriptions to imagine that there are sets of a particular kind. More complicated imaginings will also be prescribed, depending on what non-mathematical objects there are. Furthermore, our own *beliefs* about what non-mathematical objects there are will require us to utter certain mathematical sentences S, against the backdrop assumption that non-mathematical objects can be formed into sets, as indirectly expressed *hypotheses* concerning what is fictional in our game. If there are space-time points, then given a choice of a pair of points at a time as a unit of distance, it might, for example, be fictional that there is a function that maps each pair of points at a given time to a real number representing the distance between them as a multiple of the chosen unit.[5] Similarly, we might wonder whether other qualitative properties can be represented quantitatively by means of such functions, whether, for example, there is a function that represents the mass of any given object as a multiple of the mass of some chosen unit. (Note that, under the supposition that all non-mathematical objects are urelements in our set theory with urelements, the question of the mere *existence* of functions relating these objects to real numbers will be in no doubt. What is of interest is which, among these many functions, can be said to represent theoretically relevant properties of non-mathematical objects.) Having adopted the hypothesis that there *are* functions representing distances, masses and so on, we can then wonder how the values of these functions should be thought of as being related, against the backdrop of this hypothesis. Thus we may wonder whether $F = \frac{gM_aM_b}{d^2}$ is fictional in the context of our make-believe. When we adopt this hypothesis as a theoretical assumption, and put it to the test, we are, according to this picture, not so much concerned with testing its truth, but rather with testing its fictionality: are the *non-mathematical* props of our theory such as to make this hypothesis fictional?

7.3.2. The Fictionalist's View of Scientific Theorizing

I have been suggesting, then, that the *value* of uttering, in the context of our scientific theorizing, a sentence whose literal truth would require the existence of mathematical objects, may just be that it provides us with a way of representing, indirectly, our utterance to be *fictional* in the game of set theory with non-mathematical objects as urelements. And given that the fictionality of such an utterance will, in general, depend not just on the supposition that the axioms of set theory with urelements are true (where the urelements are just all the non-mathematical objects there happen to

---

[5] Note that we may reserve judgement here on whether there are *in fact* any space-time points. What matters for this example is that the *hypothesis* that there are such things automatically generates further imaginings in the context of our supposition that whatever objects there are can be formed into sets. So to the extent that we are willing to suppose that there are such objects, we should likewise be willing to suppose that there are whatever *sets* of those objects that our set theory with urelements would require there to be.

be), but also on *how things really are* with these non-mathematical objects, by representing the assumptions of a mathematically stated scientific theory as *fictional* one may also (indirectly) express hypotheses concerning the nature of the non-mathematical objects one's theory concerns. In this way, then, we may consider that the value of adopting a mathematically stated scientific theory is in allowing us indirectly to express some non-mathematical, or nominalistic content as being the case. And rather than *believing* the literal truth of the utterances that make up one's mathematically stated scientific theory, we may wish to advocate mere *acceptance* of our theoretical utterances as useful ways of expressing some true nominalistic content. A fictionalist about mathematics will not believe the literal truth of the (mathematically stated) utterances that are used to express our ordinary empirical theories, but will, instead, believe that those utterances get things right in their picture of how things are with their *non-mathematical* objects. In short, we might say, fictionalist will assume that our scientific theories are *nominalistically adequate*, but not that they are true.

My argument in the remainder of this book will be that (regardless of whether scientists in general see themselves as merely 'pretending' that there are mathematical objects in order to represent some true non-mathematical content) nothing in our scientific practice speaks against adopting such an attitude to our theoretical utterances. That is, it will be argued that we can make sense of the kinds of empirical theories we have developed, and the uses to which we put those theories, even if we hold, as the mathematical fictionalist does, that such theories are *merely* nominalistically adequate, and not that they are true. Mark Balaguer (1998: 131) has called such a view of our scientific theories 'nominalistic scientific realism', where this is understood as 'the view that the nominalistic content of empirical science—that is, what empirical science entails about the physical world—is true (or *mostly* true—there may be some mistakes scattered through it), while its platonistic content—that is, what it entails "about" an abstract mathematical realm—is fictional.'

Holding that what makes our scientific theories good is not their *truth* but that they represent some true nominalistic content makes mathematical fictionalism importantly analogous to constructive empiricism, according to which it is the fact that our scientific theories are correct in their empirical/observable content, rather than their truth, that makes them good. Indeed, the terminology of 'acceptance' and of 'nominalistic adequacy' has been deliberately chosen to emphasize the parallel between mathematical fictionalism and constructive empiricism, as alternatives to standard scientific realism. But the similarity between mathematical fictionalism and constructive empiricism raises some concerns: we might wonder whether our reasons for viewing mathematical posits as theoretical fictions might extend to reasons for taking a fictionalist attitude to all unobservable theoretical posits, so that mathematical fictionalism collapses to constructive empiricism. And, given that there are well-developed objections to constructive empiricism, we might wonder whether those objections will apply equally to mathematical fictionalism. I will turn to these issues in the next chapter, where I will argue that the view of mathematical posits as theoretical fictions can be held independently of constructive empiricism, and is a more attractive view of empirical science.

8

Mathematical Fictionalism and Constructive Empiricism

According to the fictionalist view I have been developing, the appropriate attitude to our scientific theories is *acceptance* that they are correct in their representation of the non-mathematical objects they concern, but not *belief* in their literal truth as accounts of the relations between mathematical and non-mathematical objects.[1] Unless it is possible to dispense with mathematical posits in our scientific theories, then, mathematical fictionalism must part company with standard scientific realism, according to which we ought to believe that our best scientific theories are true or approximately true. Rather, in holding that our theories are at best 'nominalistically adequate', the fictionalist attitude is, as I have noted, importantly analogous to another instrumentalist approach to empirical science, constructive empiricism. In this chapter, then, I would like to discuss the extent of the analogy between these two instrumentalist views, considering in particular how much of Bas van Fraassen's characterization of the constructive empiricist's attitude to empirical science can be carried over to a characterization of the fictionalist attitude I recommend. I will also consider how some standard objections to the constructive empiricist's recommended attitude of immersed acceptance might be adapted to apply to my version of mathematical fictionalism, and how such a fictionalist can respond to such objections. Having compared these two instrumentalist approaches to science in this chapter, I will then, in Ch. 9, consider the question of how to choose

---

[1] Given our discussion of the ubiquity of models in scientific theorizing, this is, of course, something of a simplification. In fact, our theories will often include layers of idealized models, whose objects, though non-mathematical, are likewise to be viewed as theoretical fictions. For now, though, let us accept the simplification that the non-mathematical content indirectly represented by our mixed mathematical/empirical theories is literally true. We will return to this issue in Ch. 9.

between realism, fictionalism, and constructive empiricism, arguing that mathematical fictionalism provides the best explanation of the success of our scientific theories.

8.1. Characterizing Nominalistic Content

On the view developed in the previous chapter, our mathematically stated scientific theories can be used to express, indirectly, some nominalistic content. That is, utterances made in the context of expressing those theories can be viewed as indirectly asserting that the non-mathematical objects our theories posit are the way *they* would have to be in order to make our theoretical utterances fictional in our make-believe of set-theory with urelements. Outside of the context of Walton's particular theory of fiction, a similar notion of nominalistic content has been developed by Mark Balaguer, who argues that, if a mathematically stated empirical theory *were* true, then it would be true in part in virtue of how things are with the mathematical realm, and in part in virtue of how things are with the physical realm, these two realms being causally isolated from each other. On Balaguer's (1998: 135) view, the nominalistic content of a theory is just that the physical realm is configured in just the way *it* would have to be in order for our overall theory to be true (regardless of how things are with the mathematical realm): 'The nominalistic content of a theory T is just that the physical world holds up its end of the "T bargain", that is, does its part in making T true.' I take it that Balaguer's notion of nominalistic content is coextensive with my own—indeed, we can think of Balaguer's definition as providing another way of grasping what it would be for the theoretical utterances of empirical science to be *fictional* in the game of set theory with non-mathematical urelements. But can we do any better than these two rather loose characterizations of nominalistic content? Can we say more explicitly what the nominalistic content of a theory, or indeed of the utterances used to express that theory, amounts to?

In Chapter 7, I presented the claim that our theories are correct in their nominalistic content as the thesis that those theories are nominalistically adequate, and suggested that acceptance of our scientific theories, for a mathematical fictionalist, should amount to the belief that those theories are nominalistically adequate. The terminology of acceptance and of nominalistic adequacy was chosen with constructive empiricism in mind, and it is therefore natural to wonder whether fictionalists should (or can) adapt Bas van Fraassen's characterization of the analogous notion of empirical adequacy to flesh out the content of their claim that our mathematically-stated theories are nominalistically adequate, or that they are correct in their nominalistic content. Van Fraassen provides an explicit, technical definition of the empirical content of a theory, so we might hope that borrowing from this definition could allow us to be more explicit about the content of the fictionalist's belief that our scientific theories are nominalistically adequate.

8.1.1. The Constructive Empiricist's View of Science

Certainly, there is a very close analogy between the fictionalist's attitude to our mathematically stated theoretical utterances that I have been developing, and the constructive empiricist's attitude as outlined by van Fraassen. Like van Fraassen, as a fictionalist I doubt that we have reason to believe all the utterances made in the context of our empirical scientific theorizing. Nevertheless, I advocate, as van Fraassen does, total immersion in our standard theoretical world-picture, making use of our usual theoretical concepts even while rejecting the existence of some of the objects posited in characterizing these concepts. Thus, according to van Fraassen, we may find it necessary to characterize observable objects in terms of a *pretended* relationship between these objects and the unobservable objects posited by our theories. But this immersed acceptance of our theoretical characterizations of observable objects should not be thought of as committing theorists to belief in the unobservable objects posited in our theoretical descriptions:

In the constructive empiricist alternative I have been developing, nothing is more natural, or more to be recommended than this total immersion. . . . It may be the case that I have no adequate way to describe this box, and the role it plays in my world, except as a VHF receiver. From this it does not follow that I believe that the concept of very high frequency electromagnetic waves corresponds to an individually identifiable element of reality. Concepts involve theories and are inconceivable without them, to paraphrase Sellars. But immersion in the theoretical world-picture does not preclude 'bracketing' its ontological implications.   (van Fraassen 1980: 82)

Similarly, the version of fictionalism I advocate recommends the adoption of the terminology of our mathematically stated scientific theories (and in particular, of set theory with urelements) in our empirical descriptions of the world. And in doing so, we might find that we have no adequate way of describing a similarity between the Fs and the Gs except by saying that the *sets* containing each are *equinumerous*.[2] Nevertheless, immersion in a theoretical picture which sees the world 'as if' there are sets does not, I claim, preclude bracketing off its ontological implications, and taking a different attitude to those theoretical utterances whose literal truth would require the existence of sets than we do to those utterances that do not concern sets.

While the fictionalist view I have been developing advocates immersion in our theoretical worldview for the purpose of doing science, speaking *as if* there are sets in the formulation of our theories, as well as in using those theories to draw out empirical consequences, an adherent of such a fictionalism will not advocate belief in the set-theoretic utterances made in the context of our scientific theorizing, but will only consider these utterances as *fictional* against the context of the generative assumption that the axioms of our chosen set theory (with non-mathematical objects as urelements) are true. Like van Fraassen, then, the fictionalist sees acceptance of our theoretical worldview as involving something less than belief in all our theoretical utterances. But whereas van Fraassen's interest is in the (theory-drawn) line between the observable and unobservable posits of our theories, the mathematical fictionalist's interest is in the (similarly theory-drawn) line between our theory's mathematical and non-mathematical

---

[2] The question of whether we can describe this similarity without appeal to sets will depend on what resources we allow into our language otherwise. If we allow ourselves second-order quantification, then we can state what it is for the Fs and the Gs to be equinumerous without talking about sets—this presumes, of course, that Quine is wrong when he charges that second-order logic is really just set theory in sheep's clothing—although we do of course in this case find ourselves talking about properties and functions. Alternatively, if we allow plural definite descriptions and the plural relation 'are equinumerous with' into our language, the assertion that the Fs are equinumerous with the Gs would be expressible in our language without any apparent commitment to objects over and above the Fs and the Gs. The introduction of sets is perhaps more elegant than these alternatives, its ontological cost being offset by a vast simplification in 'ideology' (in the sense that we can say more without introducing complexities such as second-order quantification or plural idioms into our underlying logic). But whereas Quine considered this practical reason for choosing the language of sets to be a reason to believe that there are sets, we might instead see this trade-off between ontology and ideology as a reason to be wary of reading too much of our metaphysical commitments into the language we choose to use.

posits. That is, if we take our base mathematical theory to be set theory with urelements, the line that interests the fictionalist is that between the sets and the non–sets (urelements). So while, for constructive empiricists, acceptance of our scientific theories involves 'no more belief . . . than that what it says about observable phenomena is correct' (van Fraassen 1980: 57), for mathematical fictionalists, theoretical acceptance involves no more belief than that what it says about the non–mathematical objects it posits is correct.

It certainly looks, then, as if the fictionalist's claim that accepting our empirical theories requires only a belief in their nominalistic content should indeed be characterizable in precise analogy with van Fraassen's own account of acceptance, the only difference concerning precisely where the line is drawn between those objects posited by our theories that we have reason to believe exist, and those whose existence does not receive empirical confirmation. But despite these striking similarities, the analogy between constructive empiricism, as presented by van Fraassen, and my proposed version of fictionalism concerning the mathematical posits of our theories cannot be taken any further. For, in presenting constructive empiricism, van Fraassen makes heavy use of mathematical assumptions. So from the perspective of mathematical fictionalism, not only can we not believe empirical science; neither can we believe van Fraassen's metatheory in which he presents his account of empirical adequacy.

The problem comes with van Fraassen's *inflationary* view of truth and empirical adequacy as properties that *theories* can have or lack. On such a view, whether we believe *of a theory* that it is true, or only that it is empirically adequate, it looks like our belief will concern the nature of a kind of abstract object (a theory). And what does van Fraassen have to say about the nature of these scientific theories about which we may have beliefs? Here van Fraassen's account is heavily mathematical. Rejecting (as overly language dependent) a syntactic characterization of theories, van Fraassen is a proponent of the semantic view, according to which a scientific theory is standardly characterized by a class of abstract, set theoretic structures, its models.[3] So a belief concerning the properties of

---

[3] Van Fraassen himself is unclear about what to say about this standard presentation. Thus, noting that Patrick Suppes' original presentation of the semantic view is explicitly in terms of set theory, van Fraassen distances himself from the mathematical presentation of the view, without presenting any clear alternative account of the 'models' to which he refers: 'Although I do not wish to favour

a given theory (whether, for example, that theory is *true* or is merely *empirically adequate*) will turn out to be a belief concerning the nature of some mathematical objects (the theory's set theoretic models).

As well as specifying a theory's models, on van Fraassen's view in presenting a theory we also specify some components of those models (their empirical substructures) as candidates for direct representations of observable phenomena. Having specified these substructures, van Fraassen's notions of empirical adequacy and of truth can then be explicated in terms of the relation of these models and their empirical substructures to the world. Calling those structures that can be described in experimental and measurement reports *appearances*, van Fraassen (ibid.: 64) tells us that a

. . . theory is empirically adequate if it has some model such that all appearances are isomorphic to empirical substructures of that model.

Alternatively, a theory is considered to be true if it has

. . . a model which is a faithful replica, in all detail, of our world.   (ibid.: 68–9)

On van Fraassen's understanding of truth and empirical adequacy, then, even *false* theories are true *of some model* (or collection of models). Mathematical objects (be they models, objects in these models, or isomorphisms between parts of reality and substructures of these models) are thus essential to van Fraassen's account of how it is that false theories can represent the world. Against such a metatheoretical backdrop, the claim that our mathematically stated scientific theories, though literally false, are correct in the nominalistic content they represent would in no way remove any commitment to the existence of mathematical objects, since this claim would itself be claim about the relation between abstract mathematical models and the world.

For van Fraassen, then, to *accept* a theory will require one to hold some *beliefs* concerning abstract mathematical objects. This is because accepting a theory involves, in part, believing that it is empirically adequate, where empirical adequacy is understood as a substantial property of the theory's mathematical models.[4] Since this is the case, in characterizing the

any mathematical presentation as the canonical one, I am clearly following here [Suppes'] general conception of how, say, the theory of classical mechanics is to be identified.' (van Fraassen 1980: 66)

[4] Note that van Fraassen's own use of the semantic view of theories is not essential to this objection, which depends only on the characterization of empirical adequacy as a substantial property of *theories*

fictionalist's proposed attitude to our scientific theories we cannot make use of van Fraassen's own account of empirical adequacy in order to provide an analogous account of nominalistic adequacy. If believing that a mathematically stated empirical theory is nominalistically adequate involves believing something to be the case about its set-theoretic models, then in advocating that we *merely* accept our scientific theories (remaining agnostic about the mathematical objects posited by those theories), and thus that we believe those theories to be nominalistically adequate (and hence, believe a claim about the set-theoretic models of those theories), the fictionalist's proposed attitude will be self-defeating. If empirical science does not itself require us to believe in mathematical objects, our best metatheoretical account of the attitude we ought to take to our empirical theories does require us to believe in such things.

Indeed, as Gideon Rosen (1994) has pointed out, not only does this make van Fraassen's strategy unattractive to the fictionalist, this aspect of van Fraassen's account of empirical adequacy leads to a tension in constructive empiricism itself. For, Rosen argues, it appears that constructive empiricists who wish to remain agnostic about the existence of the unobservable entities posited by our theories are thereby required to remain agnostic about the existence of the abstract mathematical objects our theories posit. For, abstract objects, Rosen notes,

are unobservable if anything is. Experience cannot tell us whether they exist or what they are like. The theorist who believes what his theories say about the abstract must therefore treat something other than experience as a source of information about what there is. The empiricist makes it his business to resist this. So it would seem that just as he suspends judgment on what his theory says about unobservable physical objects, he should suspend judgment on what they say about the abstract domain.   (ibid.: 164)

In fact, van Fraassen (1974: 303) himself has suggested in the following fable that belief in the existence of abstract mathematical objects would be an idle wheel in our scientific theorizing:

as abstract objects of some sort. Even if we took a syntactic view of theories, perhaps holding that a scientific theory *T* is the set consisting of the deductive closure of its axioms, believing *of a theory* so understood that it has the property of being empirically adequate would likewise require us to hold some beliefs concerning mathematical objects. The semantic view of theories just makes the worry more evident. For while we might think that the essence of the syntactic view could be preserved in some way even if we abandon the set-theoretic setting, it is difficult to see how we might view the 'models' of the semantic view, if not as sets or, at the very least, as set-like structures.

Once upon a time there were two possible worlds, Oz and Id. These worlds were very much alike, and indeed very much like our world. Specifically, their inhabitants developed exactly the mathematics and mathematical logic we have today. The main differences were two: (a) in Oz, sets really existed, and in Id no abstract entities existed, but (b) in Id, mathematicians and philosophers were almost universally Platonist, while in Oz they refused, almost to a man, to believe that there existed any abstract entities.

They all lived happily ever after.

Surely van Fraassen's strict empiricism would require him to withhold belief in the existence of such idle wheels?

Agnosticism concerning the mathematical objects posited by our theories would seem to be, at the very least, a natural extension of the constructive empiricist's attitude, if not an essential part of that attitude. And it is certainly an attitude that van Fraassen appears to support. But if, as a constructive empiricist, one does suspend judgment concerning the truth of assertions concerning abstracta, one cannot even go so far as to *accept* our scientific theories, since, as we have seen, acceptance requires one to believe something positive about theories considered as abstract objects. 'The very act of acceptance involves the theorist in a commitment to at least one abstract object. Thus if empiricism implies nominalism we seem forced to the view that empiricism itself is incompatible with the practice of theory acceptance as van Fraassen understands it' (Rosen 1994: 165–6). By advocating acceptance of our scientific theories, understood as involving the belief that our theories *considered as abstract objects* have the property of being empirically adequate, it appears that van Fraassen undermines his own empiricist commitment to remain agnostic about unobservables.

The mathematical fictionalist cannot, then, take van Fraassen's account of the empirical adequacy of theories as true at face value (in order to adapt this account to provide a characterization of nominalistic adequacy). A belief in the empirical adequacy of theories, as defined by van Fraassen, is a belief about the nature of abstract, mathematical objects. To the extent that mathematical fictionalists think that the use of mathematical assumptions in our theoretical worldview is accountable for in terms of their being 'merely' a useful fiction, they must likewise think of the mathematical assumptions in van Fraassen's metatheory as also providing just a useful (rather than literally true) way of thinking about matters. Indeed, there are some intriguing remarks of van Fraassen's that suggest that he himself realizes the tension created in his view by his assumption that scientific theories *really are* just collections of abstract mathematical models. The semantic view of theories presents an alternative picture of science to that provided by the positivists, but still, van Fraassen (1980: 64) tells us, 'A picture is only a picture—something to guide the imagination as we go along.' This suggests that, in so far as we wish to use the metatheory in which constructive empiricism is presented, we should take a view of this metatheory that is analogous to that advocated for science itself: we accept the picture of theories as models as a way of generating concepts (such as empirical adequacy) by which we can describe and evaluate scientific theories, yet we hold back from belief in some of the ontological claims warranted according to that picture.

8.1.2. Deflating Talk of 'Theories'

At best, then, van Fraassen's own metatheory will provide us with a useful way of thinking about the notions of 'nominalistic adequacy' and 'nominalistic content'. But in so far as we wish to advocate acceptance of our mathematically expressed theories as requiring only the belief that our theories are nominalistically adequate, we cannot, as fictionalists, *define* nominalistic adequacy in analogy with van Fraassen's definition of empirical adequacy. Indeed, since it appears that believing in the nominalistic adequacy of theories will require us, at the very least, to believe in *theories*, it looks as if *whatever* account we wish to give of what it is to accept, as opposed to believe, our theoretical worldview will require us to endorse some claim about abstract objects (theories).

In fact, though, noticing that van Fraassen's approach involves an inflationary account of the *truth* of theories, as well as of their empirical adequacy, suggests a way forward for a nominalistically acceptable alternative account of these notions. For, just as nominalists will wish to deflate van Fraassen's account of what it is for a theory to be true, so as to avoid commitment to theories as objects, we may similarly look for a deflationary understanding of what it is for a theory to be nominalistically adequate, which likewise avoids commitment to theories as objects. So just as a deflationist about truth hopes to recast her belief, *of a theory*, that it is true, as consisting just in a collection of object-level beliefs (which can be expressed by asserting sentences that make up the theory), similarly, we might hope to recast the fictionalist's belief, *of a theory*, that it is nominalistically adequate as likewise consisting just in a collection of object-level beliefs (which can be expressed by asserting sentences that are part of the *nominalistic content* of the theory).

This deflationary move away from van Fraassen's account of truth and empirical adequacy as substantial properties of theories is something we have seen already, in the context of our discussion of Hartry Field's account of conservativeness, in Chapter 3. According to the deflationary account of the truth of theories presented there, a deflationist's claim *of a theory* that it is true should be understood as merely an indirect way of asserting the axioms of that theory (if necessary, by means of a device for infinite conjunction). On such an understanding of truth, when a realist philosopher of science holds that we ought to believe an empirical theory T to be true, we can read this claim as the claim that we ought to believe AX_T (where this is the conjunction of the theory's assumptions), and therefore to believe S whenever we have reason to believe $\Box(AX_T \supset S)$ (recall that '$\Box$' is to be understood to be a primitive modal operator on sentences). By contrast, anti-realist views of our scientific theories may be understood as denying that we ought to believe sentences such as AX_T, which are used to express our theoretical assumptions. A deflationist version of constructive empiricism may, then, view the constructive empiricist as wishing to remain agnostic about whether AX_T, on the grounds that we have no reason to believe the implications of that assumption concerning the existence of unobservable objects. And a deflationist version of mathematical fictionalism may likewise view the fictionalist as similarly wishing to remain agnostic about whether AX_T, on the grounds that we have no reason to believe the implications of that assumption concerning the existence of mathematical objects.

This deflationist account allows us to characterize the negative component of constructive empiricism and fictionalism. But in so far as constructive empiricism and fictionalism also involve a positive attitude of *belief*, what should our deflationary account say? Well, the constructive empiricist will want to believe our theory's *empirical content*, and a fictionalist will want to believe its *nominalistic content*. For the constructive empiricist, the empirical content of our theory will be the picture the theory paints of the observable objects it posits. And since our theory will itself allow us to draw a distinction between observable and unobservable posits, and also observable and unobservable properties, we can use this distinction to discover some theoretical utterances that can be thought of as part of the empirical content of our theory. That is, our theory will itself allow us to identify some sentences S as concerning only observable properties of observable objects (and, therefore, as part of the empirical content of our theory). So if S is such a sentence (call it an observation sentence), and $\Box(AX_T \supset S)$, then believing our theory's empirical content will require the constructive empiricist to *believe S*.

Is the constructive empiricist's proposed attitude of 'acceptance' of a theory T simply *equivalent* to believing any observation sentence S such that $\Box(AX_T \supset S)$? Unfortunately not, on van Fraassen's view, since in general our theory may place more restrictions on the observable objects it posits than can be expressed using only the 'observable' *vocabulary* of the theory. To use van Fraassen's example mentioned earlier, describing an instrument as a VHF receiver might *require* the vocabulary of very high frequency waves, such that there may be no purely *empirically* characterized concept that is true of an observable object if and only if it is (according to our theory) a VHF receiver. But this might mean that the *observable consequences* of a theory according to which there are observable objects satisfying the predicate 'is a VHF receiver' might themselves all be true in worlds where there *are* no instruments that our theory would describe as VHF receivers. Since our empirical language may not be very rich, then, our theory T may have a richer empirical *content* than can be expressed in terms of its empirical *consequences* (that is, the collection of observation sentences implied by the theory).

The constructive empiricist's 'acceptance' of a theory as empirically adequate, understood in our deflationary terms, will thus require *more* than just belief in the empirical consequences of that theory, since (simply in virtue of the paucity of our observational vocabulary) those empirical consequences can all be true even in cases where the observable phenomena are *not* as the theory represents them to be. Van Fraassen's own definition of empirical adequacy, in terms of an isomorphism between a theory's observable substructures and appearances, is meant to solve this problem, by removing the dependency of the notion of 'observable' on the predicates of our language. But our own deflationary analogue of constructive empiricism cannot make this move. Instead, the best we can do to characterize what more is required by acceptance of a theory is to view acceptance as not *just* belief in the empirical consequences of our theory, but also a belief that the observable phenomena are *the way they would have to be* for our theory to be a good representation. We might think of this further attitude as being what is required by (what van Fraassen calls) an attitude of *immersed* acceptance: we believe all the empirical consequences of the theory, but also commit to adopting the theory's *concepts* in our descriptions of empirical phenomena.

Is the same true for mathematical fictionalism? That is, must our 'immersed acceptance' of a mathematical theory involve us in more than just believing all its nominalistically statable consequences? Or can we hope to characterize the 'belief' component of mathematical fictionalism simply as belief in the truth of every nominalistically statable sentence S such that $\Box(AX_T \supset S)$? Consideration of the identifiable nominalistic content of *some* of our theoretical utterances might suggest that mathematical fictionalism does better than constructive empiricism here, since we can find clear candidates for their nominalistic content in terms of 'nominalistic counterparts', nominalistically stated sentences that are (against the backdrop of our mixed mathematical/empirical theory) provably equivalent to the mixed mathematical/empirical utterances they replace. However, as we will see, this optimism is short-lived. In fact, if we restrict our nominalistic language to a first-order theory, we can *prove* that there will be mathematically stated theories whose 'nominalistic content' (understood as the restrictions the theories place on the non-mathematical world) outstrips the collection of their nominalistically statable consequences.

When *can* we identify the nominalistic content of a theoretical utterance? The nominalistic content of a theoretical utterance is just what would have to be the case with the *non-mathematical* objects in order for our utterance to be fictional in our game of set theory with non-mathematical urelements. And there are cases where it is quite clear what restrictions a mathematically stated utterance, made against the backdrop of set theory with non-mathematical objects as urelements, places on the *non-mathematical* objects it concerns. For we can sometimes state the nominalistic content of a mathematically expressed sentence S in terms of a nominalistically acceptable sentence S' that will be *true* if and only if S is *fictional* against the background assumption of set theory with nonmathematical objects as urelements. This is the case when the axioms of our set theory allow us to prove the *equivalence* of S with S' in that theory.

Simple examples of this can be found in our assignment of numbers to collections of objects: when I utter 'The number of Fs is 5', for example, the literal truth of my utterance would require the existence of a natural number, 5, which is the cardinality of the set of *F*s. But, against the backdrop of set theory with urelements, the *F*s *can* be collected into a set, and sets *will* have cardinal numbers. And, against this backdrop, we can *prove* that 'The number of *F*s is 5' is true if and only if there are exactly five *F*s (where this latter claim can be expressed in first-order predicate logic without making any reference to numbers). For a fictionalist who questions whether there *are* any numbers, this equivalence *in the mathematics* of our mathematical utterance with a nominalistically acceptable claim may be used to indicate what it would be for 'the non-mathematical world' to hold up its end of the bargain (as it were). So if the purpose of my utterance of the sentence 'The number of *F*s is 5' is simply to provide a way of indirectly asserting that the non-mathematical objects are such as to make this utterance fictional, then we can view the nominalistic content of my utterance as the nominalistically acceptable claim that there are exactly five *F*s.

In cases, then, where a mixed mathematical/non-mathematical sentence *S* is *equivalent*, against the backdrop of our set theory with urelements, to some entirely nominalistically acceptable claim *S'*, we can view our utterance of *S* (made in the context of such a theory) as (perhaps correctly) *representing* its nominalistically acceptable counterpart *S'* to be the case, even if we do not believe that *S* itself is true. So, in cases where there are such equivalences to be found, if our interest is just in describing non-mathematical objects, we may view the *purpose* of our adopting a given mathematically stated utterance in our theory as allowing us to represent its nominalistically expressible equivalent as being the case.[5] A fictionalist who wishes to accept our mathematically stated scientific theories as having a true nominalistic content may in such cases identify the acceptance of *such* theoretical utterances as belief in their nominalistic counterparts.

One does not have to go too far, however, to find mathematical utterances where no obvious non-mathematical equivalent can be found. Joseph Melia (1995) takes the example of the sentence, 'The average star has 2.4 planets,' as one such case, since we cannot replace this sentence

---

[5] It is important to note that the various mathematical and non-mathematical claims are only equivalent in the context of our set theory with urelements: if we do *not* suppose that non-mathematical objects can be collected into sets, such that the number of *F*s equals the number of *G*s iff there is a 1–1 function from the set of *F*s onto the set of *G*s, then the truth of the nominalistically acceptable utterance 'there are exactly five *F*s' does not imply the truth of 'the number of *F*s equals 5'.

with an equivalent (in our mathematical theory) non-mathematical claim that expresses its non-mathematical content. To avoid commitment to *the average star* as an object, we may view our utterance of the sentence 'The average star has 2.4 planets' as a merely convenient shorthand for the claim 'The number of stars divided by the number of planets is 2.4'. And if we include *this* mathematical utterance in our theory, then a fictionalist about mathematics will wish to say that *its* presence is *also* accountable for as a merely convenient way of representing some further non-mathematical content as being the case. But what is this content? If our theory also included some assumption of a particular finite upper bound n on the number of stars, then against our backdrop of set theory with urelements, these mathematical assumptions would together be provably equivalent to a (very long) disjunction: 'The number of stars is 12 and the number of planets is 5; or the number of stars is 24 and the number of planets is 10; or the number of stars is 36 and the number of planets is 15; or . . . ; or the number of stars is n and the number of planets is m.' And this claim, of course, could (at least in theory) be expressed in first-order predicate logic, avoiding any apparent reference to numbers. We might, then, view our use of the mathematics as a convenient (indeed, practically indispensable) way of expressing this nominalistic content, as a non-mathematical counterpart of the mathematical utterance 'The number of stars is less than n, and the number of stars divided by the number of planets is 2.4.'

But our theory might *not* give us reason to put any upper bound on the number of stars. We might think we have very good evidence for the (fictionality of the) claim that the average star has 2.4 planets, but no evidence at all for the (fictionality of the) claim that the number of stars is less than n, for any finite n. In this case, our utterance of the sentence 'the average star has 2.4 planets' is not equivalent, in our theory, to any long finite disjunction of non-mathematical claims. At best, it is equivalent to an infinite disjunction. But if we do not have a device for infinite disjunction in our mathematically stated empirical theory, there will be no theorem in that theory which shows our utterance that the average star has 2.4 planets to be equivalent, in our theory, to some nominalistically statable counterpart.[6] So we cannot, in this case, find a non-mathematical

---

[6] Of course, increasing the linguistic resources of our theory to allow for infinite disjunction is possible—but our concern is with characterizing the nominalistic content of the theories we actually

claim that we can take to be the nominalistic content of our mathematical utterance.

Nevertheless, even in this case it appears that our mathematical utterance can be used to express some definite content concerning the non-mathematical objects (stars and planets) it posits, even if we cannot pin down this content in the form of a single non-mathematical sentence implied by the theory. For, against the backdrop of set theory with urelements, this mathematical utterance has a string of non-mathematical consequences that, though not themselves expressible as a single non-mathematical sentence (which by itself expresses the non-mathematical content of our mathematical utterance) nevertheless show that our mathematical utterance does place some restrictions on what non-mathematical facts concerning stars and planets can obtain. So even though we cannot find a nominalistically acceptable *alternative* to our mathematical utterance, in the form of a non-mathematical counterpart claim that is true if and only if our mathematical utterance is fictional, we may still see that utterance as expressing some definite non-mathematical *content*, in terms of its collection of nominalistically acceptable consequences.

So although we cannot always find, for any given mathematically stated sentence of our theory, an alternative entirely non-mathematical sentence that expresses *its* non-mathematical content (in terms of the restrictions the sentence places on how things are with the non-mathematical objects it concerns), the fact that such a sentence may, against the backdrop of our set theory with urelements, imply a definite collection of nominalistically statable *consequences* (whose truth would not require the existence of any mathematical objects), might tempt us to *identify* the nominalistic content of an utterance made in the context of set theory with urelements just as the collection of its nominalistically acceptable consequences. Certainly, if AX_{ZFU} is the conjunction of the axioms of our set theory with urelements, our acceptance of the 'nominalistic content' of a theoretical utterance S in the language of set theory with urelements will at the very least require us to believe every *nominalistically acceptable* sentence T such that $\Box(AX_{ZFU}$ & $S \supset T)$, since these sentences are surely amongst the restrictions S places on the non-mathematical realm, against the backdrop assumption of AX_{ZFU}.

---

use. For a standard scientific theory developed against the backdrop of set theory with urelements, this example shows that the nominalistic content of the claim in question cannot be characterized by a single nominalistic consequence of the theory.

Can we, then, simply *define* the nominalistic content of a mathematically stated scientific theory as consisting simply of the collection of all the nominalistically acceptable consequences of that theory (those nominalistically statable sentences whose truth would not require the existence of any mathematical objects)? Unfortunately not, for just as van Fraassen worried that the empirical content of a theory might not be exhausted by those of its consequences concerning observable posits that are expressible in its observational vocabulary, we have reason to worry that the nominalistic content of a theory might not be exhausted by its nominalistically acceptable consequences. As Joseph Melia (2000) has shown, at least if we restrict our nominalistically acceptable language to allow only first-order quantification, the collection of all the nominalistically statable consequences of a mathematically stated theory is not in general sufficient to pin down its nominalistic content (in terms of the restrictions it places on the non-mathematical world).

Melia considers two first-order theories of mereology, T and T^*. T is nominalistically stated, quantifying only over non-mathematical 'atoms' and regions of atoms considered as their mereological sums, whereas T^* also quantifies over functions and sets (i.e. T^* is expressed in the language of set theory with non-mathematical objects as urelements). It can be shown that T and T^* have exactly the same consequences in the nominalistic language. Yet T^* guarantees the existence of a *region* of a particular sort, whereas T does not. But it is plausible to view the issue of *what regions there are* as part of the *nominalistic* content of a theory. As a result, it appears that T and T^* differ in their nominalistic *content*, even though they have identical nominalistically statable *consequences*.

How does this happen? Melia's theory T is a nominalistic theory of mereology that says that there is no atomless gunk and implies that there are infinitely many atoms. More specifically, T contains the two-place predicate $x < y$, standing for the relation 'x is a part of y' (together with suitable axioms to ensure that $<$ is a partial order); the constant 1 (together with an axiom to ensure that 1 is the mereological sum of everything); and the predicate $\mathrm{Atom}(x)$ (together with an axiom saying that the atoms are precisely those objects containing only themselves as parts). T also contains an axiom ensuring that everything that there is is composed of atoms (i.e. there is no atomless gunk), and an infinite list of axioms ensuring that there are infinitely many atoms (this list reads: there is at least 1 atom; there are at least 2 atoms; there are at least 3 atoms; there are . . .). Finally, T contains a comprehension schema, which guarantees that, if there is an object satisfying the predicate F, then there is a region R containing all the Fs, such that everything that shares a part with R shares a part with one of the things that Fs.

T^* is a set-theoretic analogue of T. Thus, T^* includes the additional predicate Sx, which is used to pick out the sets, and adds the axioms of ZFC set theory to govern the use of the predicate Sx. T^* also contains all the axioms of T, but to avoid the interpretation on which T's infinitely many atoms are all just sets, T^* adds a list of axioms guaranteeing that there are infinitely many atoms that are non-sets (this list reads: there is at least 1 atom that is not a set; there are at least 2 atoms that are not sets; there are at least 3 atoms that are not sets; . . .). T^* adds to T's mereological comprehension schema all instances of that schema that include the vocabulary of set theory, and also an axiom asserting that the non-mathematical objects form a set. In short, T^* extends T by embedding it in ZFC set theory with atoms and regions of atoms as *urelements*.

A natural supposition is that, although T^* introduces sets into its picture, the added supposition that non-sets can be collected together to form sets should make no difference to any non-mathematical facts about how things are with the non-mathematical atoms and regions. And in one sense this is right: both T and T^* are identical in what they say in the limited vocabulary of theory T.[7] Nevertheless, there is an important sense in which T^* places more restrictions on how things can be with the non-mathematical atoms and regions than T does, since the added vocabulary of T^*, together with the extension of T's mereological comprehension schema to allow that, if there are non-mathematical objects satisfying a set-theoretic predicate ϕ, then there is a region containing all the (non-mathematical) ϕs, means that T^* implies the existence of kinds of regions whose existence is not implied by T.

More specifically, Melia calls a region R 'infinite and coinfinite' if both R and R's complement contain an infinite number of atoms. The truth of theory T does not guarantee the existence of infinite–coinfinite regions: the axioms can be true in a world containing countably many atoms, whose

---

[7] For details, see Melia (2000: app. 2), which shows that T is complete, and hence that T^* is (on the assumption, of course, that T^* is consistent) a conservative extension of T.

only regions are (*a*) for every finite set of atoms, a region containing the sum of those atoms; and (*b*) for every finite set of atoms, a region containing the sum of those atoms not in this set.[8] But theory T^* *requires* there to be infinite−coinfinite regions: since the non-mathematical atoms form a set, there is a 1−1 function f from this set into an initial segment of the ordinals. Consider the set $E = \{x : f(x) = 2n, n \in \omega\}$. This set is infinite, since we know that there is at least a countable infinity of atoms. By the comprehension schema of T^*, there is an infinite region R which is the mereological sum of these atoms. Furthermore, R's complement must also be infinite, since it contains (at least) for every $n \in \omega$, a unique atom x such that $f(x) = 2n + 1$.

The claim that there are infinite−coinfinite regions cannot be expressed in the limited vocabulary of T, and so T and T^* do not differ in their nominalistically stated consequences. Nevertheless, the difference between worlds in which there are infinite−coinfinite regions and worlds in which there are not certainly seems to be a difference in how things are with their non-mathematical parts: it is, after all, a difference concerning what kinds of *region* there are. The upshot of this is that 'there can be more to the nominalistic consequences of a theory than the set of sentences entailed by that theory in the nominalist vocabulary' (Melia 2000: 461).

Melia's example shows why the acceptance of our theoretical worldview as expressing a true nominalistic content may sometimes involve more than just than belief in the nominalistically stable consequences of our theories (infinite−coinfinite regions are analogous to van Fraassen's VHF receiver, in this respect). A fictionalist who makes use of set theory with urelements in her theorizing is committed to seeing the world 'as if' its non-mathematical objects can be collected into sets satisfying the axioms of our set theory. The fictionalist must, then, believe more than just the sum of the nominalistically stated consequences of this theory: she must also think that the non-mathematical objects are *the way they would have to be* in order for the theory as a whole to be true (for example, that there are non-mathematical *regions* that might only be describable in mathematical terms). The fictionalist must adopt the theory's methods of representing how things are with the non-mathematical objects, even while withholding belief in some of the objects posited in such representations.

---

[8] See Melia (2000: app. 1) for details.

Although a lot can be said, then, to pin down more precisely the nominalistic content of our scientific theories, ultimately our *full* grasp of the nominalistic content of our theory must be via our grasp of the claim that our theoretical assumptions are indeed *fictional* in our make-believe (that is, that the non-mathematical props are indeed the way *they* would have to be to make our theoretical utterances appropriate). And this should be no surprise: our mathematical language provides us not just with a useful way of representing how things are with non-mathematical objects, but also sometimes an *indispensable* way of doing so.[9]

8.2. Fictionalist vs. Constructive Empiricist Acceptance

For a fictionalist, then, accepting a scientific theory involves believing its nominalistic content, where this involves believing that the non-mathematical world is the way it would have to be in order to make our theoretical utterances fictional in the game of set theory with non-mathematical urelements. As we have seen, adopting such an attitude of acceptance involves the fictionalist in belief in all the nominalistic consequences of our scientific theories, but is not in general equivalent to belief in those consequences. While it is unfortunate that we cannot give a more precise characterization of the 'belief' component of the fictionalist's proposed attitude of immersed acceptance, one should not conclude that this weakens fictionalism as compared with constructive empiricism. For, as we have seen, it is arguable that van Fraassen's definition of acceptance in terms

---

[9] Indispensable, at least, if we restrict ourselves to first-order quantification. The mismatch between 'nominalistic content' and 'nominalistically statable consequences' that Melia points to is because our first-order mereological theory can only assert the existence of regions characterized by predicates in the language of that theory. Hence adding set theory, and allowing the existence of regions characterized by set-theoretic predicates, means that we can assert the existence of more regions. But perhaps our willingness to extend our mereological comprehension schema to include set-theoretic vocabulary just shows that we already view our first-order language as a limitation. That is, perhaps this shows that we really want to assert the existence of arbitrary mereological sums of atoms, regardless of whether we have a predicate in our language that applies to all and only those atoms. If we had a second-order mereological theory, then the added set-theoretic vocabulary might allow us to *derive* the existence of more regions than we previously could show to exist, but would not imply that *more* regions exist than are implied by our mereological theory. So if we thought that second-order quantification over arbitrary regions was nominalistically acceptable, then the 'nominalistic content' of our mathematical theory might not outstrip its nominalistically statable consequences.

of belief in the empirical adequacy of our theories is likewise unavailable to constructive empiricists, given its mathematical commitments. On the other hand, by providing an account of mathematically stated scientific theories as being developed against the backdrop of the props and principles of generation provided by the game of set theory with non-mathematical objects as urelements, the fictionalist view of mathematics has the advantage of tying 'nominalistic content' to more general notions of the 'metaphorical content' of fictional representations. Without any analogous account of the 'props' and 'principles of generation' of constructive empiricist science, constructive empiricism cannot likewise appeal to the wider notion of the metaphorical content of a fiction in order to clarify what is to count as the empirical content of a theory.

At any rate, let us suppose for now that fictionalists and constructive empiricists alike have done enough to make sense of their respective notions of nominalistic content and empirical content, so that we can grasp their respective notions of acceptance of a scientific theory. The natural question that now arises is whether any considerations render either one of these attitudes of acceptance any more plausible than the other. And here, the supposed acausality of the mathematical objects posited by our scientific theories does seem to introduce an asymmetry between fictionalism and constructive empiricism, which may be used to render the fictionalist's proposed attitude of acceptance more plausible than the constructive empiricist alternative. On the other hand, though, another disanalogy between mathematical objects and unobservable physical objects, the supposed necessity of mathematical objects, can be used to raise a concern for fictionalism that does not arise for constructive empiricism, throwing into doubt the coherence of the fictionalist's proposed attitude of mere acceptance. I will argue that this second supposed disanalogy does not render the fictionalist attitude incoherent, and that the first does lead to an advantage over constructive empiricism.

8.2.1. 'Makes no Difference' Arguments for Fictionalism

One reason often given for rating the prospects for anti-realism about mathematical objects higher than those for anti-realism about all unobservables is that there is a sense in which we should expect that the existence or non-existence of mathematical objects should make no difference to the success of our scientific theories. Mathematical objects are widely acknowledged to be acausal and non-spatiotemporal, if such objects exist at all. These supposed features put them in a somewhat different boat to electrons. Thus, a natural response to the constructive empiricist who is sceptical of electrons is to suggest that we should expect that the observed phenomena would be very different on the hypothesis that there are no such things: 'If there *were* no electrons, we wouldn't see that track in the cloud chamber.' But if such counterfactual considerations have force against those sceptical about the unobservable physical objects posited by our theories, no analogous counterfactual is available against those sceptical about the mathematical objects our theories posit. A mathematical realist who starts a challenge, 'If there *were* no numbers, then . . .' will find it difficult to finish this supposed counterfactual in a way that could trouble those sceptical of mathematical objects. Certainly, if there *were* no numbers, then many utterances made in the context of our ordinary scientific theorizing would not be true. But if we are looking for observable phenomena that we would expect to turn out differently depending on whether or not acausal, non-spatiotemporal numbers exist, then we will be hard pressed to find any.

As a result, 'makes no difference' (MND) arguments, based on the acausal character of mathematical posits, are very often presented as a rejoinder to the supposition that the existence of mathematical objects, like the existence of unobservable physical objects, is confirmed by the role of mathematical posits in our mathematical or scientific theories. Van Fraassen's (1974) fable of Oz and Id, mentioned earlier, is of this character, suggesting that the existence of mathematical objects would make no difference to our *mathematical practices* (a claim also made by Jody Azzouni (1994: 56), who pumps the intuition that mathematical objects have no epistemic role in our mathematical practices by asking readers to 'Imagine that mathematical objects ceased to exist sometime in 1968. Mathematical work went on as usual. Why wouldn't it?'). As they concern us here, though, the MND arguments that matter are those from the assumed acausality of mathematical objects to the conclusion that their existence or non-existence should make no difference to the behaviour of concrete, spatiotemporal physical objects. And here again there are many adherents to the claim that appearances would be the same whether or not mathematical objects existed (in a recent paper on MND arguments, Alan Baker (2003) quotes Terence Horgan (1987: 281–2); Brian Ellis (1990: 328); Stuart Cornwell (1992:

80); and Mark Balaguer (1998: 113)—all making claims of this sort). It is tempting, then, to conclude as Ellis (1990: 328) does that 'The basic reason for resisting abstract [objects] is that the world we can know about would be the same whether or not they existed.' This is a 'basic reason' that just isn't available to constructive empiricists in defending their own resistance to unobservable physical objects: we have every reason for thinking that, if there *were* no electrons, our observations might be very different.

8.2.2. Is the Fictionalist's Attitude Coherent?

I must confess that I am one of those who finds such reasoning appealing. But there are, as Baker rightly points out, some prima facie difficulties with using MND claims of this form to argue against mathematical realism. For proponents of the MND claim are asking realists to entertain a hypothesis that many such realists will claim to be nonsensical. The realist's mathematical objects are non-spatiotemporal. What, then, could it be to imagine them suddenly ceasing to exist in 1968? Of course, Azzouni has used some poetic licence in presenting the thought experiment in this temporally located manner. His colourful thought experiment is really trying to get at our intuition that, *even if there are* (and always have been and always will be) mathematical objects, *had there never been such things*, our mathematics (and, we may add, our science and indeed our experiences) would have unfolded in the same way as it in fact has done. But even *this* intuition will be challenged by many realists. For many (perhaps most) mathematical realists hold that the existence of mathematical objects is metaphysically *necessary*. But if this is so, then the MND argument requires us to defend the truth, not just of counterfactual, but of counterpossible assertions: 'If (as is metaphysically impossible) there were no mathematical objects, our experiences would have been just the same.' And the realist might well wonder on what grounds the truth of such a claim could be defended. Indeed, if David Lewis (1986: 111) is right, then 'nothing can depend counterfactually on non-contingent matters. . . . Nothing sensible can be said about how our opinions would be different if there were no number seventeen . . .'

Now it is not clear to me that, in discussions of the supposed necessity of mathematics, realists have made sufficient sense of the notion of necessity according to which mathematical objects are supposed to be necessarily existent. In debates between, on the one hand, Crispin Wright and Bob

Hale (who defend a necessity claim for mathematical objects) and, on the other, Hartry Field (who rejects the conception of mathematical objects as necessarily existent, holding that there is no well-worked-out notion of metaphysical necessity of the sort required by this conception), it seems to me that Hartry Field has the upper hand. I will not, however, need to enter the details of this debate here (except to note my conviction that if the existence of mathematical objects *is* in some sense metaphysically necessary, the realist has failed to establish this). For, as I have framed the debate between realists and fictionalists, the fictionalist is *not* required to argue for the truth of what, if the realist is right, will turn out to be counterpossible assertions concerning what the world would be like if there were no mathematical objects, despite the evocative presentation of MND arguments as involving such claims.

The question we are really trying to answer is, after all, *epistemological* not metaphysical: do the justificatory standards of our best scientific theories give us any reason to prefer the hypothesis of scientific (and therefore mathematical) realism to that of fictionalism? And this, I claim, is a question that can be answered in the negative even if we concede to the realist that mathematical objects might, for all we can tell, be *necessarily* existent. All we need to establish is that the existence of mathematical objects (necessary or not) is not something that our empirical experience and scientific standards of justification give us any reason to believe. That is, we are aiming to establish that the hypothesis of fictionalism is not unreasonable in the light of that experience and those standards. So, in so far as the fictionalist needs to defend a makes-no-difference claim, the claim that needs defending is just that adopting the hypothesis of mathematical fictionalism makes no difference to one's ability to adopt, reasonably, the methods and expectations of modern science.

This turns the focus, then, from the question of what the world would be like if there were no mathematical objects to the question of what it would be reasonable for one to *do*, as a scientist, if one adopted the hypothesis of mathematical fictionalism. In this way, we may hope to avoid begging questions about the ultimate metaphysical nature of mathematical objects. For all we know, mathematical objects *might* indeed be necessarily existent. The only claim the fictionalist needs to defend is that someone who didn't believe that our mathematically stated scientific theories asserted truths about such objects, and instead viewed their mathematical assumptions as representatively useful fictions, would not be unreasonable in relying on such theories in providing predictions and explanations of empirical phenomena.

But despite this epistemological turn, one might think that the challenge to make sense of counterpossibles remains for our assessment of the fictionalist's proposed attitude of mere acceptance. For, a fictionalist scientist is meant to believe only that our mathematically stated scientific theories are nominalistically adequate, where this at the very least requires us to believe that they are correct in their nominalistically acceptable consequences, but that, for all we know, those of their consequences whose truth would require the existence of mathematical objects might all be false. But if mathematical objects *are* metaphysically necessary, then the fictionalist scientist's supposition is just that some metaphysically necessary truths could, for all we know, turn out to be false. From the realist's perspective, then, it looks as though the fictionalist's hypothesis rests on a contradiction. If the realist is right about the special metaphysical status of mathematical objects (as compared with unobservable physical objects), then, whereas the constructive empiricist's proposed attitude of acceptance is coherent but unreasonable, the fictionalist's proposed attitude to our scientific theories is not even coherent.

This argument is, however, faulty, as can be seen if we try to unpack the 'contradiction' behind the fictionalist's hypothesis that the mathematical components of our theories might, for all we know, as a matter of fact be false. We are conceding, for the sake of argument, that the realist might be right that mathematical objects are (in some sense) necessarily part of the ultimate furniture of the universe. But what we need not concede is that we have any means of *knowing* of this necessity. I argued in Chapter 4 against the claim that mathematical objects are conceptually necessary: our having the concept of an ω-sequence in no way implies the existence of objects satisfying the Dedekind–Peano axioms, any more than our having the concept of a perfect God implies the existence of such a being. Nor has the realist provided any (non-question-begging) argument for the *reasonableness* of the hypothesis that mathematical objects are metaphysically necessary. But if mathematical objects are not *conceptually* necessary, then in entertaining the supposition that the mathematical assumptions of our scientific theories are merely fictional, the fictionalist is not guilty of entertaining any *contradiction* (there is nothing self-contradictory about supposing that the mathematical objects posited by our scientific theories do not exist, even if this supposition conflicts with metaphysical matters of fact). And in the absence of a realist argument for the *reasonableness* of the hypothesis of metaphysical necessity, in entertaining the supposition that the mathematical utterances of our scientific theories are merely fictional, the fictionalist is not violating any canons of rationality.

There is, then, nothing self-contradictory or prima facie unreasonable in the fictionalist's hypothesis that the mathematical utterances of our scientific theories might be *merely* fictional. And in fact, at least on Walton's view of fiction, one who defends this hypothesis does not even have to go so far as to *deny* that objects satisfying the descriptions of the mathematical posits of our theory exist. For, according to Walton, whether or not a hypothesis is *fictional* is a function of its role in our theorizing, and has very little to do with whether or not something exists that could be said to make that hypothesis true.

Thus, Walton asks us to suppose that, by some great coincidence, there was some actual boy Tom Sawyer who did and said all the things Mark Twain has his character Tom Sawyer doing. Walton argues that we should resist the temptation of regarding Twain as 'having, accidentally, written a novel about a real person'. The mere existence of such a person does not change the status, *as fiction*, of *The Adventures of Tom Sawyer*, on Walton's (1990: 109) view, since

> Mark Twain's novel does not prescribe any imaginings about the real-world counterpart of his character. Readers are in no way obliged or expected to imagine of the actual 'Tom Sawyer' that he got his friends to whitewash a fence, that he attended his own funeral, and so on. The fact that he happens actually to have done all these things has no bearing on what the novel asks us to imagine. This, at bottom, is why the real boy is not an object of the novel.

If Walton is right, then by analogy, in viewing our mathematically stated empirical theories as merely fictional, the mathematical fictionalist need take no stand on the question of the actual, metaphysical existence of a realm of objects satisfying the mathematical utterances of our empirical theories. Viewing the mathematical objects posited by our empirical theories as *mere* fictions requires us only to view our theories as prescribing us to *imagine* that there are such objects, and as prescribing imaginings concerning their nature (including their relations to real non-mathematical objects), rather than attempting to answer to the true nature of *actual* mathematical objects. So even if there happened to be a realm of mathematical objects that satisfied all the mathematical assumptions of our mathematically stated empirical theories, the existence of such objects (and even their *necessary* existence) would play no role in the fictionalist's account of our successful scientific theorizing. Whether or not there are such objects (and, indeed, whether or not they exist of necessity), the fictionalist's claim is that the hypothesis that there are such objects need play no role in our account of what we are doing when we make use of mathematical assumptions in our theoretical accounts of non-mathematical objects. For we can, the fictionalist thinks, account for the theoretical value of such utterances even if we view them as taking place against the backdrop of the *pretence* that set theory with non-mathematical urelements is true.[10]

8.3. Can We *Merely* Accept Our Theories?

I maintain, then, that there is nothing immediately contradictory or question-begging against the realist in our alternative fictionalist hypothesis concerning our scientific theories, and that something like the 'makes-no-difference' considerations can be used to favour that hypothesis as compared with the hypothesis of constructive empiricism. Yet, returning again to the analogy with constructive empiricism, we might still question whether it is really *possible* to be a fictionalist scientist. For, the fictionalist advocates that we hold an attitude that falls short of belief in the mathematical components

---

[10] Is the fictionalist conceding too much here? I hope to argue that fictionalism is a plausible alternative hypothesis to realism in making sense of our scientific activity. And I will wish to claim that showing this much will suffice to demonstrate that we have no reason to believe that there are any objects that would make true the existentially quantified mathematical utterances of our scientific theories. But as I have presented fictionalism, the hypothesis that the mathematical utterances of our theories are *merely* fictional does not rule out the existence, *or even the necessary existence*, of objects satisfying our mathematical assumptions. Still, if the fictionalist is correct that nothing in our scientific experience/activity speaks against the hypothesis of fictionalism, this will be enough to establish what I would like to show: that our successful scientific practices *provide us with no reason to believe* that there are mathematical objects. For, even if the fictionalist's hypothesis does not rule out the possibility of such objects, if that hypothesis is defensible, then mathematical objects (that is, objects matching the mathematical descriptions of our theories) will play no essential part in our scientific understanding of how our theories work to describe the world. So, as against the Quinean indispensability argument, the existence of such objects will receive no confirmation from the presence of mathematical hypotheses in our current theoretical worldview.

of our scientific theories. And there are those who will question whether it is genuinely possible to hold just the weaker attitude of immersed 'acceptance' that the fictionalist advocates. I will wish, in the next chapter, to argue that the fictionalist, who merely pretends, rather than believes, that the mathematically stated utterances of her scientific theories are true, can nevertheless reason in exactly the same kinds of way as does a realist scientist, developing her theories in the same manner, providing the same explanations of observable phenomena, and making the same predictions. That is, I will aim to show that adopting the fictionalist's proposed attitude to the mathematical posits of our theories should make no difference to our conception of reasonable scientific practice. Maybe this is so, but that it is so will suggest, to some at least, that the fictionalist's proposed attitude of *merely* supposing, or making-believe, that the mathematical assumptions of our theories are true cannot be distinguished from genuinely believing them to be so.

Paul Horwich has pressed this point as a general objection against 'epistemic' anti-realisms, views that advocate the continued use of our successful empirical theories, but hold that the proper, epistemically justified, attitude such theories might be something weaker than belief (that is, *mere* acceptance). In the light of their account of what it is to accept a theory, Horwich challenges such anti-realists to say what *more* would be involved in believing that theory to be true. And, in support of his pessimism regarding the prospects for answering this challenge, Horwich suggests that the instrumentalist's own understanding of what it is to *accept* a theory will tend to involve just the kind of psychological features that one would expect to be emphasized in any attempted definition of theoretical *belief*. Thus, Horwich (1991: 3) argues,

If we tried to formulate a psychological theory of the nature of belief, it would be plausible to treat beliefs as states with a particular kind of causal role. This would consist in such features as generating certain predictions, prompting certain utterances, being caused by certain observations, entering in characteristic ways into inferential relations, playing a certain part in deliberation, and so on.

'But that,' Horwich concludes, 'is to define belief in exactly the way instrumentalists characterize acceptance.'

If we wish to defend the claim that the fictionalist's attitude to our scientific theories provides a reasonable alternative to realism, then it looks as though we will need first to show that the attitude in question is a genuine *alternative*. For, if Horwich is right that using our theories in the way the fictionalist proposes (to make predictions, generate explanations, and generally to guide our inferences about the world), amounts to believing those theories, then the fictionalist is simply *mistaken* in thinking she does not believe in the mathematical objects posited by her theories, but only supposes, or makes-believe, that there are such things. Her actions belie her, for her immersed adoption of the 'make-believe' of set theory with urelements in describing the world around her show that she believes just as much as does the card-carrying realist.

In the context of our favoured version of fictionalism, then, Horwich's challenge is to show what it is about the fictionalist's proposed attitude to the mathematical assumptions of her theories that demonstrates it to fall short of an attitude of belief. And the fictionalist's explicit disavowals of utterances whose truth would require the existence of mathematical objects do not count here. Since the fictionalist can simply be mistaken about her own mental state, the fact that she *claims* to withhold belief from the mathematical assumptions of her theories in no way establishes that she does not in fact believe them. If we accept Horwich's challenge, then, we will need to find aspects of the fictionalist's *behaviour* that can be used to make sense of the hypothesis that she is merely making-believe, and not believing, that there are mathematical objects.[11]

And here it looks like we will face an insurmountable difficulty, given the general shape of the fictionalist's project. For in advocating an attitude of immersed acceptance what the fictionalist needs to show is that a fictionalist scientist can behave in *exactly the same way* as does the realist

---

[11] One might think that the fictionalist shouldn't even pause to consider Horwich's challenge. After all, it might be objected, it is pretty clear that fictionalist philosophers who explicitly deny the existence of mathematical objects do not believe that there are such things. If Horwich's account of the nature of belief renders mathematical fictionalists as self-deluded Platonists, then surely it is this account that should be found wanting. While I see the attractions of this quick line of response (suggested to me by Mark Balaguer), I think that the fictionalist can say something more explicit about the difficulty with Horwich's account. In particular, in the mathematical case, several similarities between the behaviour of ordinary scientists and the behaviour of those involved in straightforward games of make-believe suggest that, if Horwich's line of thought about the nature of belief is right, then it may turn out to be scientific realists who are deluded about their beliefs. So *either*, as Balaguer suggests, Horwich's challenge shows his account of the nature of belief to be inadequate, *or* it raises doubts as to the authenticity of the scientific realist's proposed attitude to the mathematically stated hypotheses of our scientific theories. Either way, the attitude to our scientific theories the fictionalist advocates turns out to be perfectly possible.

scientist, in developing, evaluating, and using her scientific theories. But then it appears that our desiderata pull in opposite directions. On the one hand, if we accept Horwich's challenge we will wish to show that there is some practically discernible distinction between the fictionalist's attitude (of immersed acceptance) to her theories and the realist's attitude (of genuine belief); but the discovery of any such distinction will speak against our claim that adopting the attitude of fictionalism makes no difference to one's ability to immerse oneself in the practices of modern science.

Rather, then, than accept Horwich's challenge to find something distinctive in the fictionalist's attitude to theories that shows it to be genuinely different from the attitude taken by self-avowed realists, the strategy I would like to take is to question Horwich's assumption that the attitude of self-avowed *realists* to their scientific theories should automatically be described as *belief* in the mathematical utterances of those theories. Horwich notes some behavioural features that might usually be taken to indicate that a person holds a particular belief, and notes that it is precisely *these* features that characterize the anti-realist's notion of immersed acceptance. In the light of this, it looks as though we will need to provide some positive argument for the claim that our *fictionalist* scientist does not, in fact, believe the mathematical utterances of her theories. But it is easy to turn this argument on its head. The fictionalist scientist advocates that we merely *pretend* that the mathematical assumptions of our theories are true, treating our mathematically stated theoretical utterances as moves in a game of make-believe, which can be used to express, indirectly, hypotheses concerning what is fictional in the game of set theory with non-mathematical urelements. Why not, then, consider the behavioural features characteristic of uncontroversial cases of make-believe? If these features are also characteristic of the behaviour of immersed participants in scientific activity with regards to the mathematical assumptions of their theories, then the realist who holds that we ought to *believe* those assumptions might equally well be challenged to find some behavioural indicator that the attitude she does hold genuinely amounts to *believing* the mathematical hypotheses of her theories.

How can we tell someone who is making believe that S is true, in the context of some game, from someone who genuinely believes the literal truth of S? If Horwich is right that people can be mistaken about what they believe, then we cannot simply ask them to clarify their attitude. Instead we must look at the way they treat the hypothesis: is there anything in their behaviour that suggests that they are treating this as anything other than a hypothesis about what is true? Consider, for example, the children who do not believe, but are merely making-believe, that the tree stumps are bears. One way of exposing this as make-believe, rather than belief, is to propose a refutation of the hypothesis 'The tree stumps are bears.' Thus, I might counter, 'That isn't a bear: it doesn't even have fur!' The fact that, in the context of the children's practice, this 'refutation' is not taken seriously is one indication that the appropriate description of the children's attitude is that they merely making-believe, but do not believe, that the tree stumps are bears. (This contrasts with a genuine refutation, in the context of the game, of utterances held to be fictional: the sentence, 'That isn't a bear, it's a pile of stones,' will be treated differently from, 'That isn't a bear, it's a tree stump,' in the context of the game in which tree stumps are bears.) Certainly, if *S* is one of the sentences used to *generate* the make-believe, then it will not be held open to refutation in the way that other utterances made within the context of the make-believe are.

A second distinctive aspect of make-believe is the way in which make-believes can define their objects. If I am pretending that there is a monster in the closet, then the features I pretend it to have are, in the context of this pretence, features that fictionally it does have. In this context, some questions about the monster will be 'trivially' answered: if I am making believe that it is green and hairy with big teeth, the question, 'Is it *really* green and hairy with big teeth?', will be considered a silly one—in the fiction, the monster is whatever I imagine it to be. This appears to contrast with objects about which I have genuine beliefs: hard-line Russellians aside, most of us are happy to concede that it might turn out that even our firmest beliefs about the descriptions satisfied by a particular object are false.[12]

A third difference between believing and merely making-believe that such-and-such is the case involves the amount of indeterminacy one is willing to allow. If I am making-believe that I am rich and famous, then I

---

[12] This is even true of objects introduced through a stipulative definition: if I decide to call 'Fred' the object, whatever it was, that caused a particular experience, even then I might be mistaken, in that there might be no such object picked out (but only, for example, a collection of objects). In contrast, if I resolve to make-believe that there is an object, Fred, satisfying a particular description, then (except, perhaps, through self-contradictoriness) there appears to be no way in which my make-believe definition of Fred can misfire.

might not have bothered telling myself a story about how that came to be. My make-believe may provide no determinate answer to the question of how it was I came to my current (make-believe) status, and as a result, one would be severely mistaken in thinking that one could discover how this status came about by further investigation. Indeed, in such cases where no determinate answer has been provided, I am free to stipulate a back story to fill in this gap. In contrast, such indeterminacy is not usually tolerated in the case of genuine beliefs: one might not *know* how a particular state of affairs came about, but if one really believes that the state of affairs obtains, then one cannot be satisfied with a merely stipulative story about why this is so.

A special case of such tolerance of indeterminacy in make-believes (and of the acceptance of stipulation as a solution to indeterminacy) comes with identity questions, as is illustrated with characters in novels. In *Jane Eyre*, the character of Bertha Mason, the first Mrs Rochester, is drawn rather sketchily: she is little more than the madwoman in the attic. In *Wide Sargasso Sea*, Jean Rhys tells the history of the first Mrs Rochester, filling out her background as a white creole heiress growing up in Jamaica in the 1830s. But is it really *the same* Mrs Rochester that Rhys is talking about? How did she know that this very character grew up in this way? These are silly questions: in Rhys's story, she is simply free to stipulate that it is *the* Mrs Rochester whose back story she is telling, so long as the story is consistent with Brontë's own sketchy presentation of the character as she appears in *Jane Eyre* (as Rhys herself says of Brontë's madwoman, 'She seemed such a poor ghost. I thought I'd write her a life').

But if such tolerance of *indeterminacy* and *stipulative freedom* are characteristic features of make-believe as opposed to belief, then we have the beginnings of a case for the hypothesis that the correct description of the attitude we actually take to the mathematical hypotheses of our scientific theories is that we do not believe them to be the case, but rather, merely suppose, or make-believe, that they are true. Regarding indeterminacy, if we *really* believed in numbers, sets, and so on, wouldn't we concern ourselves with the question of their precise identity conditions, not being content with holding that there is no determinate answer to the question of whether the number 2 equals Julius Caesar? On this criterion, Frege really was a true believer in numbers, displaying his genuine belief in numbers as objects by taking seriously, and seeking to answer, all conceivable questions concerning the identity of such objects. But such questions are of little concern to the scientists who make use of mathematics, or even to the pure mathematicians who develop the mathematics that gets used in applications. As Paul Benacerraf (1965) famously pointed out, there appears to be nothing in our mathematical practices that requires us to identify numbers with any one ω-sequence rather than any other.

If, on the other hand, we do wish to pin down more precisely the identity conditions for the objects posited by our theories, we are fairly free in stipulating such identity conditions, so long as the objects we pick to stand for (for example) the natural numbers satisfy the assumptions we have already made about those objects. Thus we can, for convenience, choose to stipulate that 2 in our mouths is the same as $\{\emptyset,\{\emptyset\}\}$, if we wish to find some *particular* referent for the numerical singular terms utilized in the context of our scientific theorizing. And wondering whether we are *right* in supposing that the number 2 whose existence we posited *before* making this precise identification *really was* $\{\emptyset,\{\emptyset\}\}$ all along, would, many would accept, be to ask a silly question: if we wish to identify 2 with a particular set, then our doing so is a matter of (constrained) stipulation, rather than discovery. And allowing for such stipulative freedom is, as we have noted, more characteristic to cases of make-believe than of belief.[13]

Similarly, we appear to indulge in just the kind of *definitional freedom* that is common to make-believe in our theoretical utterances that posit the existence of mathematical objects, allowing only considerations of consistency to get in the way of our hypothesizing that there is an object of a particular sort. As mentioned in Chapter 4, the set-theoretical backdrop to our mathematical theorizing might explain this freedom somewhat: in a set-theoretic setting, we can view the axioms of other theories as implicit definitions of properties of sets (such as, for example, the property of being a natural number system), and in that way can be happy that there are objects satisfying our definitions provided we assume that there are enough sets. But what about sets themselves? While we are keen to conform our axioms for set theory to our intuitive conception of set, and in particular

---

[13] Jody Azzouni provides an rich and compelling account of the role of stipulation in filling in mathematical indeterminacies in his (1994). Azzouni (2004: 59–61) also takes this aspect of mathematical posits to show that they are more akin to fictional, than real, objects, although his own account of fiction departs from ours in holding that, in making existential claims concerning fictional characters, we are not indulging in the make-believe that there are such objects, but rather, are asserting true claims that use the existential quantifier in a non-committing manner.

to choose axioms that conform to our idea that, at each stage in the set hierarchy, sets consisting of *all* possible combinations of sets in the previous stage occur, we saw in Chapter 4 no essential role for the notion of sets as independently existing objects in restricting our choice of axioms. That is, the question of whether there really are any objects satisfying the iterative conception is set aside. We might come to think that some of our axioms do not do justice to the iterative conception, but, unless it can be shown to be *contradictory*, the hypothesis that there are objects satisfying this conception is not something that we see as up for grabs in set-theoretic practice. Unless the hypothesis turns out to be self-contradictory, we are free to stipulate that sets exist and answer to that conception.

Finally, and perhaps most tellingly in the context of our scientific theories, our mathematical hypotheses exhibit just the kind of *immunity* to certain kinds of revision that we find in cases of make-believe. We noted already (in Chs. 4 and 5) the way in which mathematical hypotheses appear to receive special treatment when it comes to theoretical testing. The special place afforded to mathematical posits vis-à-vis confirmation/disconfirmation has been noticed again and again, and indeed has formed the backbone of many recent attacks on the indispensability argument for the existence of mathematical objects (see e.g. Maddy 1992; Sober 1993; Vineberg 1996; Peressini 1999). Such authors have stressed a peculiar insulation given to the mathematical hypotheses of our theories. The supposition that there are mathematical objects of whatever type we need in formulating our theories is automatically adopted by scientists, and is never given up in the light of theoretical disconfirmation. While we might learn of logical or calculational errors in the light of recalcitrant empirical experience, we never seem to take the failure of our theorizing to show that genuine mathematical consequences of consistent pure mathematical theories are false. Rather, empirical disconfirmation is taken, at best, to falsify the assumption that the mathematical objects in question are related to the non-mathematical objects of our theories in the way that our theory suggested. But this behaviour is just what we would expect of someone who was merely adopting the supposition that there are mathematical objects as a useful way of representing non-mathematical objects, without regard to whether this supposition is true. Such a person would not put the hypothesis that there are sets satisfying the axioms of set theory with urelements to the test, but would only test the hypothesis that such-and-such an utterance is appropriate against the backdrop of this hypothesis (that is, that such-and-such an utterance is indeed *fictional* in the context of the make-believe of set theory with non-mathematical urelements).

There is, then, at least a prima facie case for seeing the standard attitude adopted by scientists to the *mathematical* hypotheses of our scientific theories to be more akin to make-believe, or mere supposition, than it is to belief. And note that this is in contrast with our theoretical hypotheses whose truth would require the existence of unobservable physical objects. Horwich might well be right that there is nothing distinctive about our behaviour with regards to *these* theoretical assumptions (that, for example, we put our theoretical assumptions about electrons to the test in much the same way as we test our assumptions concerning observable physical objects). But as regards the mathematical assumptions of our theories, if Horwich's line of argument is right and attitudes such as belief are to be defined in purely behavioural terms, then there is a case to be made for questioning whether even the most dyed-in-the-wool self-proclaimed scientific realist/mathematical platonist *really* believes the mathematical components of her theories. The special treatment that mathematical assumptions receive in the context of our scientific theorizing do not show our attitude to them to be significantly different to the attitude we might take to the generative assumptions of a more explicit make-believe.

I do not wish to make this case here, however, but prefer to take this discussion to suggest that, at least against the mathematical fictionalist, Horwich's complaint that the attitude the fictionalist claims to take to our scientific theories is really just one of belief is far from having been established. If Horwich is right that it is our behaviour that indicates whether we genuinely believe a hypothesis, then it is not clear that the standard behaviour of empirical scientists should be viewed as indicative of belief in the mathematical components of their theories: perhaps the fictionalist's proposed attitude to our scientific theories is, after all, the default. On the other hand, if we take it to be implausible that, on Horwich's account, a dyed-in-the-wool self-proclaimed scientific realist could turn out, despite her avowals to the contrary, not to believe the mathematical hypotheses of her scientific theories, the same will go for the self-proclaimed fictionalist who, Horwich thinks, might turn out to be a realist. If this is the conclusion we draw, then it is Horwich's account of belief that is found wanting. Either way, Horwich has failed to establish that the fictionalist's proposed attitude is impossible.

In the absence of a conclusive argument to the contrary, then, let us suppose that the fictionalist's proposed attitude to the mathematical posits of our theories is at least possible, that is, that one can if one chooses *merely* make-believe that there are such objects for the purpose of building tractable representations of the non-mathematical objects we do believe to exist. And, if only for the sake of argument, let us likewise suppose that the realist's and the constructive empiricist's proposed attitudes to our scientific theories are also possible. The question we must now consider is how to choose between these various attitudes to our scientific theories. Which attitude is most reasonable in the light of our scientific practices? It is to this question that we will turn in Chapter 9.

9

Explaining the Success of Mathematics

To the debate between scientific realism and constructive empiricism we have added a third position, mathematical *fictionalism*. Realists hold that we should believe our best scientific theories in their entirety; constructive empiricists hold that we should believe only their observational content; and mathematical fictionalists hold that we should believe only their nominalistic content. I have argued in Chapter 8 that fictionalism is a coherent alternative to scientific realism and constructive empiricism, but we must now consider whether mathematical fictionalism is to be preferred to these other attitudes to our empirical scientific theories.

In this chapter, I will look more closely at the fictionalist's understanding of the role of mathematics in empirical science in order to make a case for the reasonableness of the fictionalist's attitude. In particular, I will consider how a fictionalist can account for important aspects of our successful scientific practices, and I will argue that fictionalism does better than constructive empiricism, and at least as well as realism, in accounting for those practices. I will also consider how the anti-realist version of fictionalism presented here deals with some of the central problems we saw for Hartry Field's scientific realist version of the view, and in particular how our fictionalism can deal with uses of mathematics in phase space theories. Through this discussion, I hope to respond to Putnam's (1975: 73) charge that scientific realism 'is the only philosophy that doesn't make the success of science a miracle'. If we can account for the successes of our scientific theories (in particular in allowing us to predict and explain phenomena) from a fictionalist perspective, then we will find ourselves with a viable alternative to realism. But if realism and fictionalism can both provide equally plausible explanations of our theoretical successes, Ockham's razor would counsel adopting the fictionalist alternative.

Before embarking on providing a fictionalist understanding of the success of science, though, it is worth considering a worry about the fictionalist's argumentative strategy. Is it really appropriate for a fictionalist, who may reject the general (inductive) validity of inference to the best explanation, to defend fictionalism on the grounds of its ability to explain the success of our scientific practices?

9.1. Fictionalism and Inference to the Best Explanation

In this book, I have been arguing that the question of which, amongst our theoretical utterances, we have reason to believe in the light of our successful scientific theorizing should be answered, in the context of our 'naturalistic' project, by looking to our best reflective understanding of our successful scientific practices. And many involved in the debate over scientific realism agree. As we have seen, in presenting his 'no miracles' argument for scientific realism Hilary Putnam clearly thinks that it is reflection on our successful scientific practices that establishes realism as the only satisfactory explanation of those theoretical successes. And, despite expressing some reservations about the demand for explanations, Bas van Fraassen (1980: 73) also, ultimately, rests his defence of constructive empiricism on a reflective understanding of scientific practice, claiming that there is a 'positive argument for constructive empiricism—it makes better sense of science, and of scientific activity, than realism does and does so without inflationary metaphysics'. So on either side of the dispute, both Putnam and van Fraassen appear to be accepting our own naturalistic commitment to decide which amongst our theoretical utterances we have reason to believe on the basis of our best reflective understanding of our successful scientific practices. In entering this dispute, my own argument will be that both Putnam and van Fraassen are mistaken. For, while Putnam is right that realism makes better sense of science, and scientific activity, than does constructive empiricism, I will argue that realism is not the *only* view of science that does not make the success of science a miracle.

But, despite this apparent agreement over the *nature* of the dispute between realists, fictionalists, and constructive empiricists, one might worry about the ability of constructive empiricists and fictionalists to accept the terms of this dispute. For, as we have presented it, the argument appears to concern the question of how best to explain our successful scientific practices (from a realist, fictionalist, or constructive empiricist perspective). And, in claiming that, since realism (or fictionalism, or constructive empiricism) makes the best sense of scientific activity, we ought to be realists (or fictionalists, or constructive empiricists), it looks as though each party in the debate is relying on an inference to the best explanation. Yet the (inductive) validity of such inferences is, surely, precisely what is at issue, at least between constructive empiricism and realism. The constructive empiricist thinks that good theoretical explanations need not also be true. And likewise, if mathematical hypotheses occur in the context of our best theoretical explanations of non-mathematical phenomena (as, I will suggest in sect. 9.3, they sometimes do), the mathematical fictionalist will also have to argue that such explanations can be good without also being true.

Arthur Fine (1984) has used this observation to argue that the realist's 'no miracles' argument against constructive empiricism is question-begging, for even if realism *does* provide the best explanation of the success of science, this will give us no reason to believe that realism is *true*, unless we already accept inference to the best explanation as an inductively valid rule of inference. For, as Fine (ibid.: 86) points out, in adjudicating between realist and anti-realist views of science, 'one must not beg the question as to the significance of explanatory hypotheses by assuming that they carry truth as well as explanatory efficacy'. If good explanations do not need to be true, then the fact that the realist has a good (perhaps even the best) explanation of the success of science need not move the anti-realist who is already, after all, happy to live with the phenomena of good, but false, explanations.

But in so far as constructive empiricists and fictionalists wish to *defend* their respective attitudes to our theoretical utterances, they should take no comfort in Fine's objection to the realist's own defence of realism. For, if our aim is to defend one such attitude as a plausible alternative to realism, then Fine's objection raises a dilemma as regards our ability to provide such a defence. On the one hand, if we *do* try to defend fictionalism (or constructive empiricism) on the grounds that it provides at least as good an explanation of our theoretical successes as does realism, then it looks as if we are conceding the rationality of inference to the best explanation. But if, as the fictionalist and constructive empiricist must claim, it is not always reasonable to infer the truth of the best explanation in the context of our ordinary scientific theorizing, then neither should it be considered a reasonable rule of inference in the context of providing a reflective understanding of that theorizing. At least in so far as we accept the naturalistic commitment to take our cue, in our reflections *on* science, from science itself, then our standards of rational inference in the context of our reflective, philosophical theorizing *about* science should not be substantially different from the standards we take to be at work in the context of our ordinary scientific theorizing. So accepting the rationality of inference to the best explanation in the 'global' case would imply that we ought to accept its rationality in 'local' cases too, thus undermining the claim, apparently essential to fictionalism and constructive empiricism, that it might be rational to withhold belief from some of our best explanations.

If, on the other hand, we avoid making 'global' use of inference to the best explanation, to conclude, from the premise 'fictionalism (or constructive empiricism) best explains our successful scientific practices', that we ought to be fictionalists (or constructive empiricists), then it is hard to see how we *could* defend our own preferred attitude to science. Certainly van Fraassen's own professed reason for adopting constructive empiricism is that he thinks that it makes good sense of our scientific practices. And, against our backdrop commitment to naturalism, it looks as though we can only defend *fictionalism* on the grounds that our reflection on our scientific practices shows the fictionalist's attitude to be a reasonable one. But even if we *could* find some alternative local inference rule whose validity we did (as fictionalists or constructive empiricists) concede, and which, applied globally (in the context of our reflections of science itself), yielded fictionalism (or constructive empiricism), we might worry that Fine's objection might apply equally well to our justification of fictionalism (or constructive empiricism) in favour of realism by reference to such a rule. For the realist might not accept the validity of our own preferred inference rule, thus holding that our own defence of our preferred alternative to realism likewise begs the question. In such a case, in the absence of any agreed way of proceeding, the debate between realism and fictionalism (or constructive empiricism) would become gridlocked.[1]

Fortunately, though, this stand-off can be avoided, at least to the extent that all parties in the debate (between fictionalism, constructive empiricism, and realism) concede the very minimal naturalistic demand to provide a reflective account of science which respects our ordinary scientific practices as generally a good way of proceeding. For even this very minimal requirement yields a principle to which all parties can agree, *weaker* than the principle according to which we should infer the truth of the best explanation. And this weaker principle can make sense of our viewing the debate between the three views as a debate over whose view of our successful scientific practices best explains those practices, for, even though this principle is weaker than the principle that we should always infer the truth of the best explanation, it will nevertheless have as a consequence that we ought to believe the best available explanation of our successful scientific practices.

To see this weaker principle at work, note, first of all, the grounds on which an anti-realist about science may reject inference to the best explanation. Such a rejection will typically be on the grounds that some explanations can be *good* without also being true. We saw this with Nancy Cartwright's view of explanations of phenomena in terms of ideal models: on such a view, the *value* of an explanation may be due to our model providing a good representation of some aspects of the real objects being modelled, even though some of the assumptions we make about the objects in our model are in fact false of the objects modelled. We extended this account by saying that, if we view talk of ideal models as taking place in the context of a make-believe, then the *pretence* that real objects are like the objects in our model can allow us to provide a good explanation of the phenomena to be explained, even though its literal content (that there are ideal abstract objects that resemble concrete objects in some respects) may be false. And given that we aim similarly to view the value of positing mathematical objects in the context of our scientific theorizing as resulting from the means by which the *pretence* that there are such objects allows us to represent how things are with non-mathematical objects, then we will likewise hope to show that the explanatory value of our *explanations*

---

[1] Leading, perhaps, to a retreat to Fine's own, quietist, 'The natural ontological attitude'.

that posit mathematical objects can be down to their providing good representations of the non-mathematical objects, without also being true. (I will elaborate on this view in sect. 9.3.)

Although van Fraassen's own rejection of inference to the best explanation is based on different considerations, he also wishes to show that we need not infer the truth of the best explanation because explanations can be good without also being true. In van Fraassen's case, this is argued for on the grounds that the explanatoriness of a theory depends only on some relation holding between that theory and the fact it explains, and not on whether the theory is actually true: 'to say that a theory explains some fact or other, is to assert a relationship between this theory and that fact, which is independent of the question whether the real world, as a whole fits that theory' (van Fraassen 1980: 98). So in this case, van Fraassen (1980: 109) thinks, one can accept an explanation *as explanatory* without believing that explanation to be true: 'To have an explanation of a fact is to have (accepted) a theory which is acceptable, and which explains that fact.'

Regardless of whether van Fraassen is right about this, the point to notice is that neither Cartwright nor van Fraassen wishes to *deny* that the kinds of considerations we usually give as explanations really are *explanatory*. Indeed, both see it as important to account for why it is that these considerations are rightly viewed as explanatory, *even if we have no reason to believe those considerations to be true*. We can see this view as arising out of a broadly naturalistic commitment to account for science *as it is*, for on the basis of such a commitment, we ought in general to be able to accept the explanations given by scientists of phenomena as genuinely explanatory. One principle that anyone with a minimal naturalistic respect for science should be able to agree with, then, is that one's own view of science should be able to account for the *explanatoriness* of the kinds of consideration that are standardly viewed to be explanatory. Or, in other words, that putative explanations should still be accessible as genuine *explanations*, from the perspective of one's preferred view of science.

When presented, then, with a putative explanation of a phenomenon, that is widely acknowledged to be good (ideally, the best available), an anti-realist who adopts such a principle need not infer the *truth* of the explanation in question, *so long as she can show why, on her view of science, the explanation is nevertheless a good one*—why, that is, the explanation remains explanatory against the backdrop of her preferred view of science. For example, van Fraassen will insist (and Cartwright and I will deny) that explanations of observable phenomena in terms of unobservable causes are still *accessible* to the constructive empiricist, since on van Fraassen's view of explanation, what it is to *have* an explanation is to have accepted an empirically adequate theory that explains the phenomenon in question.[2] And, in general, any anti-realist who rejects inference to the best explanation on the grounds that we can accept explanations as genuinely *explanatory* without believing them to be true is likewise acknowledging the need to preserve those explanations taken to be good. I suggest, then, that we can view such anti-realists as adopting a principle of 'accessibility of the best explanation': If phenomenon *P* is acknowledged to be best explained by the explanans 'because *E*', then such anti-realists are committed to showing that such an explanation is still explanatory—that is, is still accessible—from the perspective of their anti-realism.

If we adopt this principle (as naturalists who are committed to preserving the explanations standardly given in natural science surely must), then the realist's explanatory argument for realism is (inductively) valid, if not sound. For, let us suppose (for the sake of argument) that the realist is *right* that realism provides the best explanation of various aspects of our scientific practices (perhaps, for example, as an explanation of our predictive successes, or of the success of aspects of our scientific methodology in yielding empirically adequate theories). If, as anti-realists, we acknowledge that realism *does* have the best explanation here, then we are required by the principle of accessibility to show that the *explanatoriness* of the realist's hypothesis is preserved from the perspective of our own anti-realism. We need not be moved to the *truth* of the realist's explanation of the success of science by the fact that it is acknowledged to be the best explanation available, but we must at the very least show why the realist's explanation can still be viewed as genuinely *explanatory* from the perspective of our own preferred anti-realist perspective.

---

[2] In rejecting van Fraassen's claim to preserve the explanatoriness of our theories, we will wish to deny that van Fraassen has things right about what is required in order for us to have an explanation of a phenomenon. Our naturalist commitment to account for actual scientific practices should help to make this case without begging the question: for example, we can consider whether it would be reasonable to view a causal explanation to be explanatory even when we *know* that the causal story we tell is false.

But how can this be? If, for example, we are constructive empiricists, we might wish to locate the explanatoriness of the realist's hypothesis in the fact that that hypothesis is empirically adequate. But the realist's hypothesis is just that our scientific theories are true. If the explanatoriness of this hypothesis is down to the fact that *this* hypothesis is empirically adequate, then this must be because the empirical adequacy of science is *already*, by itself, enough to explain its success (something that the constructive empiricist must show). So the only response that the constructive empiricist who accepts the principle of accessibility of explanations can give to the realist is to show that realism is not in fact the best explanation of the success of science, and that the hypothesis that our theories are empirically adequate, rather than that they are true, is enough to explain whatever phenomena that the hypothesis that our theories are true purports to explain. Similarly, if we turn to mathematical fictionalism, the requirement that explanations be accessible means that the fictionalist is required to show that if we weaken the hypothesis of realism to the hypothesis that our theories are merely nominalistically adequate, we are still able to explain the aspects of scientific practice that realism claims to explain. So the fictionalist must likewise show that realism does not in fact provide the best explanation of the success of science, but rather, that any putative realist explanation of the success of science can be matched by a fictionalist explanation that assumes only that our scientific theories are nominalistically adequate.

Even if we reject the inductive validity of inference to the best explanation, then, in defending fictionalism we are still required, by the principle of *accessibility* of explanations, to show, for any explanation the realist can give of the phenomena of our successful scientific practices, that the fictionalist has (at the very least) an equally good explanation available. For otherwise, there will be an explanation of our theoretical successes that is acknowledged to be a good one, and that is not accessible to fictionalists. So we are right to try to defend fictionalism (and reject constructive empiricism) by showing that fictionalism allows for (at least) as good an explanation of our successful scientific practices as does realism (whereas constructive empiricism fails to account for the success of these practices). Let us consider, then, how fictionalism fares in accounting for the predictive and explanatory successes of our scientific theories.

9.2. Is the Predictive Success of Fictionalist Science a Miracle?

One crucial aspect of scientific practice is our ability to make predictions based on our scientific theories. If one's view of one's theoretical hypotheses made it implausible that such hypotheses should yield good predictions, then one would not, in good faith, be able to rely on those theories in guiding one's expectations. The past predictive success of our scientific theories, and our ready reliance on those theories in making future predictions, thus provide a challenge to those who adopt an attitude to those theories that falls short of belief. Why, it will be asked, should someone who doesn't believe that a given theory is true (or at least approximately true) expect that theory to be predictively successful in the future? And how can someone who doesn't believe a theory that is known to have had past predictive successes *explain* why that theory has been so successful? These questions are really two sides of the same coin, and form the basis for the 'no miracles' argument in favour of scientific realism.

According to the 'no miracles' argument, the predictive successes of our scientific theories should come as no surprise to scientific realists: for, if our theories are true, their consequences, and hence their predictions concerning observable phenomena, will also be true. By contrast, anti-realists will have some work to do if they are to account for the predictive successes of our scientific theories. Maybe there is room for some anti-realists to reject the need for an *explanation* of past theoretical successes. But at the very least, advocates of anti-realist attitudes to science will need to account for their reliance on our current theories in making future predictions that they expect to turn out to be true. And if they do not *believe* those theories, then what considerations can they utilize to account for their expectation that their theories will be predictively successful? The realist suggests that no such considerations can do the job: that, if one denies the truth or approximate truth of our scientific theories, then their success in predictions is nothing short of a miracle.

The most well-known presentation of the 'no miracles' argument for realism is Putnam's (1975: 73), where he boldly makes the claim that it is *only* on the assumption that 'terms in mature scientific theories typically refer . . . that the theories accepted in a mature science are typically approximately true, that the same term can refer to the same thing even when it occurs in different theories' that we can provide a scientifically acceptable explanation of the success of our scientific theories.[3] But for a bare-bones reconstruction of the argument, consider the following (owed to James R. Brown 1982: 232–3)

1. Conclusion P can be deduced from theory T.
2. P is observed to be the case.
3. If T is true then the argument for P is *sound* and P had to be true.
4. If T is false then the argument for P is *merely valid* and the probability of P being true is very small (i.e., it would be very surprising if P were true, a miracle.)

∴. The argument for P was probably sound.
∴. T is probably true (i.e., all of T's statements, including ones about theoretical entities, are probably true).

The weak premise here is clearly premise 4. To challenge the realist's argument, then, all we need to show is that, given the nature of theory T, the probability of deducing a true observable consequence from T is not nearly as small as the realist suggests.

So long as we are allowed to make some assumptions about T, then premise 4 of the argument as Brown presents it is easily defeated, for there are many putative facts about a theory T, aside from its truth, that would make the probability of deducing true observable consequences from that theory high. In the context of our mathematically stated scientific theories, for example, we saw in Chapter 3 that Field's nominalization programme is intended to answer the question of why we should expect such theories to yield true non-mathematical predictions if their mathematical assumptions are not themselves true. Recall that for such a theory, T, Field's project is to find an alternative, non-mathematical theory T', such that T' expresses in non-mathematical terms the true nominalistic content of the mathematically

---

[3] See sect. 6.3 for the rest of Putnam's argument. While this is an oft-quoted passage of Putnam's, it is not often remarked upon that the argument occurs in the context of a discussion of mathematical realism (in Putnam's paper, 'What is mathematical truth?'). In fact, Putnam (1975: 73) continues to assert that 'I believe that the positive argument for realism has an analogue in the case of mathematics. Here too, I believe, realism is the only philosophy that doesn't make the success of science a *miracle*.' It is, then, perhaps surprising that other presentations of the 'no miracles' argument have tended to ignore its implications concerning mathematical realism. Especially surprising given that, as I will argue, it is precisely these implications that defeat the argument.

expressed theory T, and such that T is a conservative extension of T'. In this case, the empirical success of T piggy-backs on the truth of T'. For since (on the assumption of conservativeness), all T's nominalistically acceptable consequences are also consequences of T', then if T' is true, so too will be all T's nominalistically acceptable consequences (and so, in particular, T's *observable* consequences will be true). So the probability of deducing true observable consequences from T will be high, in spite of its supposed falsity, and hence (if T *is* a conservative extension of a true theory T'), the empirical success of T will be no miracle.

Field's project thus provides one answer to the 'no miracles' argument, on the assumption that we *can* find true (or at least approximately true) nominalistically expressible versions of the theories we usually rely on in making predictions. If we had reason to believe that T was indeed a conservative extension of a *true* theory T', then we would *expect* T to have true observable consequences even if we did not believe T to be true. But this is by no means the only way of defeating the realist's premise 4. There are other properties a theory could have, aside from being a conservative extension of a true theory, that would make its predictive success unsurprising.

Speaking for now in inflationary terms,[4] the scientific realist cites 'truth' as a property a theory can have that will explain its successful predictions. But where the realist talks of truth, the constructive empiricist will talk of empirical adequacy, and the fictionalist of nominalistic adequacy. And provided that a theory *is* empirically adequate, it is *guaranteed* to yield true observable consequences (since we have defined a theory to be empirically adequate if its observational *content* is true, and have argued that the observable consequences of a theory form a part of its observational content). So premise 4 is easily defeated by the constructive empiricist who claims that we have reason to believe that our theories are empirically adequate. Similarly, provided that a theory is nominalistically adequate, it is guaranteed to yield true non-mathematical (and, therefore, true observable) consequences (since we have defined a theory to be nominalistically adequate if its nominalistic content is true, and have argued that the nominalistically acceptable consequences of a theory form a part of its nominalistic content), also defeating premise 4. So just as a realist who

---

[4] But see sect. 8.1.2 for the deflationary alternative.

believes herself to be in possession of a *true* theory can expect her theory to yield successful predictions, so can a constructive empiricist who believes herself to be in possession of an *empirically adequate* theory, or a fictionalist who believes herself to be in possession of a *nominalistically adequate* theory. If the realist can cite her belief in the truth of a theory as explanatory of its success, surely the constructive empiricist and the fictionalist can cite their belief that the theory has one of these alternative virtues (of empirical adequacy and nominalistic adequacy respectively) as equally explanatory of its success?

There seems to be something wrong here in this quick route to an explanation of the predictive successes of our theories. Indeed, once we deflate the grand talk of 'empirical adequacy' and 'nominalistic adequacy' and speak again at the ground level, such 'explanations' seem decidedly circular. For what is the content of the constructive empiricist's belief that her theory is empirically adequate? It is just a belief in the observable content of of the theory, where this includes the theory's observational consequences. But it is precisely her entitlement to such a belief that the realist challenges the constructive empiricist to defend: why, it is asked, should the constructive empiricist believe the observable consequences of her theory if she does not believe the theory itself? And for the constructive empiricist to answer that she believes those consequences because she believes the theory to be empirically adequate says little more than simply asserting that she believes those consequences because she believes those consequences. Similarly for the mathematical fictionalist, who cites her belief in the nominalistic adequacy of her theory as explanation of her belief in its observable consequences. For if she believes all non-mathematical consequences of her theory, then a fortiori she will believe all its observable consequences, so claiming that she believes the observable consequences of her theory because she believes the theory's nominalistic consequences does not answer the challenge to show that she is *entitled* to believe just those consequences.

In fact, the blatant circularity in these 'explanations' of empirical success infects to some degree the realist's proposed explanation as well. For, setting aside inflationary talk of 'truth' as a grand property of theories, all that the realist is citing in defending her belief in the observable consequences of T is her belief in T itself. And if the constructive empiricist's justification of her belief in the observable consequences of T in terms of her belief in the observable consequences of T is circular, then we may well wonder what the realist achieves by adding to this conviction her belief in the rest of T as well. The predictive success of true theories, empirically adequate theories, and nominalistically adequate theories are all equally likely (in fact, all equally certain, given our understanding of these terms). Certainly, if we find ourselves in possession of a true, empirically adequate, or nominalistically adequate theory, then there is nothing in the least miraculous about the fact that such a theory yields true predictions. So if there is something wrong with the constructive empiricist (or the mathematical fictionalist) citing her belief in the empirical adequacy (or nominalistic adequacy) of her theory in response to the 'no miracles' argument, then there should be something wrong with the realist's claim that *she* has no reason to find the empirical success of her theory miraculous since she believes her theory to be *true*.

Nevertheless, there is surely something right about the realist's insistence that she has reason to expect her theory to be successful while the constructive empiricist who disbelieves the theory's assertions concerning unobservables does not. Precisely what the realist's argument has going for it can be seen when we contrast Field's nominalization project to the constructive empiricist's approach. Field does not just assert his belief in the non-mathematical consequences of T but, rather, explains what it is *about that theory* T that makes his belief in its non-mathematical consequences reasonable. That is, he asserts that it is because we have reason to believe T', the nominalized version of T, that we have reason to believe T to be (in our, not Field's, terminology) nominalistically adequate. In contrast, the constructive empiricist who *merely* asserts T's empirical adequacy, and the fictionalist who *merely* asserts T's nominalistic adequacy in response to the 'no miracles' argument has, in doing so, provided no account of *why* we should believe that T is empirically (or nominalistically) adequate. In the light of this comparison, the realist's challenge takes on a new bite: the constructive empiricist (or fictionalist) believes T to be empirically adequate (nominalistically adequate). But what, according to such a theorist, is there about that theory T that could give us reason to expect it to be merely empirically (or nominalistically) adequate, without also being true?

The real challenge is not, then, to explain why someone who is already a constructive empiricist (or a fictionalist) can expect her theory to have true observable consequences. Simply adopting a belief in a theory's empirical adequacy or nominalistic adequacy will be enough to allow one to form such expectations, just as adopting a belief in a theory's truth will allow one to expect its empirical successes. Rather, the challenge is to defend the initial adoption of such a belief, to explain *what it is about the kind of theory we have* that should lead us to expect it to be empirically adequate. The realist's challenge to the constructive empiricist is, then, just this: for a theory of the kind we have (which, for example, posits unobservable causes of observable phenomena) to be empirically adequate *without also being true* would surely be miraculous. For what mechanism could account for the fact that the observable phenomena behave just as the theory says they will, except that they are indeed causally interacting with unobservables in the way the theory supposes? This is the form of the 'no miracles' argument that stresses the *cosmic coincidence* that the constructive empiricist must hypothesize to defend her belief in the empirical adequacy of our ordinary scientific theories. Thus, J. J. C. Smart (1963: 39) asks,

Is it not odd that the phenomena of the world should be such as to make a purely instrumental theory true? On the other hand, if we interpret a theory in a realist way, then we have no need of such a cosmic coincidence: it is not surprising that galvanometers and cloud chambers behave in the sort of way they do, for if there really are electrons, etc., this is just what we should expect. A lot of surprising facts no longer seem surprising.

The question we need to ask, then, is whether it is reasonable to expect *the kinds of theory that we have* to be nominalistically adequate (or empirically adequate), and therefore to have true observable consequences, if we do not also assume that they have things right about the mathematical (or unobservable) objects they posit. And here, I think, there are some important disanalogies between the fictionalist's and the constructive empiricist's hypotheses, which show that the former is more reasonable than the latter. These disanalogies help to show that, unlike the constructive empiricist, the fictionalist need not posit any cosmic coincidence in order to defend *her* belief in the nominalistic adequacy of our ordinary scientific theories.

9.2.1. First Disanalogy: A Precedent

The fictionalist and the constructive empiricist alike wish to hold that it would not be unreasonable to expect the kinds of theory we have to have true observable consequences, even if we do not think that their assumptions about mathematical/unobservable objects respectively are themselves true. A first disanalogy comes from considering *why* we might think that the predictive success of the kinds of theory we have is not down to their truth. Our empirical theories predict that certain regularities should hold between observable phenomena. In particular, they predict that the observable phenomena should behave *as if* our theories about the relations between observable and unobservable (mathematical and physical) objects are true. By and large, our theories are successful in these predictions. Why, we might ask, should this be? Here, in the case of at least some of our empirical theories, there is a disanalogy between the responses that the fictionalist and the constructive empiricist can give to this question. For, in at least some cases, the fictionalist has, whereas the constructive empiricist lacks, an explanation of *why* they should expect the regularities we observe to be *as if* a given empirical theory is true.

Constructive empiricists think that it can be reasonable to expect that the regularities that hold between observable objects should be just those that would be predicted by our theories concerning unobservable physical objects, *even if we suppose that our theories have things completely wrong about the relations they suppose to hold between their observable and unobservable posits.* And one way they might try to convince *realists* about unobservable physical objects that this could be so is to note that there are cases *that the realist will acknowledge* where the agreement of a given theory with observable regularities is not, by the realist's own lights, a result of its being correct in its 'behind the scenes' story about the regularities governing the unobservable physical objects it posits. There is certainly some precedent for this, since we know of cases of theories that were predictively successful up to a point, even though it is now acknowledged that they were mistaken about some of the unobservable objects they posited (phlogiston; the ether). In the case of the most sophisticated version of the ether theory (which posited the Lorentz contraction to explain the undetectability of the ether wind), for example, the realist can *explain* why the observable regularities accorded with the predictions of that theory, even though the theory is now thought to be mistaken about the existence of the ether. The fact that the Lorentz contraction is also a consequence of the special theory of relativity means that, if we suppose that *that* theory has got things right about the true nature of light and the lack of a need for an 'ether' for light waves to propagate in, then the realist can explain why the observable phenomena behaved as if our ether theory was true. In short, the realist's alternative story about the unobservable regularities that hold 'behind the scenes' allows her to explain why we should expect many observable regularities to be consistent with the predictions of the ether theory, even though the ether theory is not itself thought to be true.

A constructive empiricist may, then, challenge a realist who acknowledges that the predictive success of our ether theory was not down to the existence of the ether, to say why she should think that the predictive success of our *electron* theory (for example) is not likewise down to something other than the existence of electrons. After all, even from the *realist's* perspective, the predictive success of our *past* theories concerning unobservable physical objects has not always been down to the existence of the unobservable objects posited. Why, the challenge goes, should we think that we are in any different position now as regards electrons?

The trouble with this appeal to precedent is that the explanation that the *realist* can give of why our past theories might have been predictively successful, although wrong in their fundamental ontological claims, is not available to the constructive empiricist. For, unlike the realist, the constructive empiricist does not believe that our current theories have things (approximately) right about the 'behind the scenes' regularities they posit to hold between the unobservable physical objects they posit. But it is just these 'behind the scenes' regularities that are used (by the realist) to explain why the observable regularities might in some cases (such as the case of the ether theory) be expected to accord with the predictions of a theory that is held to be false. The best, then, that the constructive empiricist can do to explain why the observable regularities are as our theory would predict them to be (in the case of the ether theory *or* of our theory of electrons) is to say that the observable regularities might *coincidentally* accord with the predictions of our theory about unobservables, even though the *real reason* that the observable regularities are the way they are is because of some more fundamental ('behind the scenes') regularities that hold between unobservables (we know not what).

But this, the realist will say, just shows why it is reasonable (given our current state of knowledge) to believe that our current theories have things right about the regularities they claim to hold between the unobservable objects they posit, even though we acknowledge that past theories have been predictively successful while having things wrong about the unobservable regularities they posit. For, believing our current theories to have things (approximately) right about the unobservable regularities they posit enables us to explain not only why the observable regularities accord (to the extent that they do) with the predictions of *those* theories, but also why the observable regularities accorded to the extent that they did with the predictions of theories we now believe to be false. On the other hand, if we do not believe our current theories to have things approximately right about the unobservable regularities they posit, then the best explanation we have of the agreement of those theories *or* of past theories with observation is just the rather unsatisfactory claim that this agreement is coincidental.[5] Since we should prefer an account that *explains* the agreement of theory with prediction to an account that can only view this agreement as coincidental, we should prefer realism to constructive empiricism.

Compare, now, the case of predictively successful mathematically stated theories, which posit the existence of mathematical objects that enter into relations (albeit not causal relations) with non-mathematical objects. The mathematical fictionalist wishes to suggest that the predictive success of these theories might be down to some other reason than that these theories have things right about the relations they posit to hold between mathematical and non-mathematical objects. In particular, the fictionalist claims that the regularities that actually hold between non-mathematical objects might reasonably be expected to agree with the predictions of our mathematically stated empirical theories *even if it is supposed that those theories have things completely wrong about the relations they posit to hold between the mathematical and non-mathematical objects they posit.* After all, according to the fictionalist

---

[5] Van Fraassen (1980: 23–5) himself acknowledges this situation, but suggests that, since we cannot expect science to eliminate *all* unexplained regularities (some of the regularities that our theories suppose to hold between unobservable physical objects will not be explicable in terms of some further 'behind the scenes' story), the fact that the constructive empiricist has to posit *some* unexplained regularities holding between observable objects should not count against the rationality of constructive empiricism. Against this, though, it should be noted that even the constructive empiricist will think that the observable regularities are not fundamental: even the constructive empiricist thinks that *these* regularities hold just *because* some further 'behind the scenes' regularities (we know not what) hold. So there is a disanalogy between the more fundamental regularities posited by our theories and the surface regularities they posit, in that even the constructive empiricist thinks that the surface (observable) regularities are the result of some more fundamental regularities, although they do not think that we are able to uncover what these regularities are. The realist may, then, hold that although we need not demand explanations of *all* regularities posited by our theories, we ought to look for explanations of those regularities we do not believe to be fundamental.

there may, for all we can know, be *no* mathematical objects, in which case our mathematically stated empirical theories are wildly mistaken about the relations between their mathematical and non-mathematical posits, since no such relations exist. In defending the fictionalist's position, once again we might look for a precedent, in order to shake the realist's conviction that the predictive success of our mathematically stated empirical theories should always be thought of as being due to their getting things right about the relations they posit to hold between mathematical and non-mathematical objects.

The fictionalist will wish, then, to find some cases where we know that the predictive successes of our mathematically stated empirical theories can be explained *without* supposing that the they are actually right about the relations they posit to hold between mathematical and non-mathematical objects. And there are indeed some cases where the predictive success of mathematically stated empirical assumptions can be explained without supposing that the mathematical objects they posit exist and are related to non-mathematical objects in the way that our theories state them to be. For, although we may be sceptical about the prospects of providing Field-style nominalizations across the board, to the extent that Hartry Field *has* provided nominalistically acceptable alternatives to *some* of our empirical theories, we are able to explain the predictive success of the mathematical versions of those theories by showing that they respect the non-mathematical relations that our nominalistically acceptable theories claim to hold between their non-mathematical objects. So (the fictionalist will claim), in such cases our best explanation of the agreement of non-mathematical regularities with the predictions of our mathematically stated empirical theory is not that our mathematical theory is *true*, but rather, that its predictions accord with the predictions of a more fundamental non-mathematical theory. Fundamentally, then, in such cases it is the regularities that hold between *non-mathematical* objects that explain why the observable regularities are *as if* our mathematically stated empirical theory is true.

Now, although (we are supposing) the fictionalist does not generally have alternative theoretical accounts of the fundamental non-mathematical relations holding between the non-mathematical objects posited by our theories, which could be used to explain why *all* our ordinary mathematically stated empirical theories are predictively successful, the existence of *some* such explanations of the success of our mathematically stated empirical theories provides room for a challenge to the mathematical realist. For, given that our best explanation of why our empirical observations agree (to the extent that they do) with the predictions of (for example) Newtonian gravitational theory is not that that theory is *true* in its mathematical portions, but rather, that that theory respects the fundamental regularities that (according to an alternative, non-mathematical theory) hold between its non-mathematical objects, we may challenge the realist to say why we should not believe the same of our other mathematically stated empirical theories. That is, although in some of these cases we lack a non-mathematical account of the fundamental regularities holding between their non-mathematical objects, which would explain why the observed regularities agree with the predictions of our mathematically stated empirical theories, why should we not think that the real reason for the success of our mathematically stated empirical theories is just that there are fundamental regularities holding between non-mathematical objects that are preserved in our mathematical presentations? Or, in other words, why should we not think that the real reason for the success of our mathematically stated empirical theories is just that they are correct in their nominalistic content (even if we cannot, without the help of those theories, fully characterize that content)?

In some cases at least, then, the fictionalist has what the constructive empiricist lacks: a literally believed explanation of the accordance of observable regularities with the predictions of a given empirical theory which does not put this accordance down to a lucky *coincidence*, but rather, explains why these observable regularities are the way our theory predicts them to be, by positing more fundamental regularities to hold. For, where we *can* provide a nominalistically acceptable alternative to a given mathematically stated scientific theory, this alternative theory will allow us to say explicitly just what it is about the non-mathematical world that makes our use of the mathematically stated theory appropriate. And given that such an explanation does not require that the mathematical objects posited by our theory exist, but only that the non-mathematical relations that hold between the theory's non-mathematical posits are respected by our mathematically stated empirical theory, the fictionalist will wish to suggest that, even in the absence of such explicit explanations across the board, nevertheless, we have reason to think that the success of other uses of mathematics is likewise due to their correct nominalistic content, rather than their truth. The precedent of explicit, Field-style explanations of the successful application of *some* of our mathematically stated scientific theories suggests that the reason that our mathematically stated empirical theories are successful might in general be likewise down to the fact that they respect fundamental regularities that genuinely hold between their non-mathematical objects, and not a result of the truth of their mathematical assumptions.

9.2.2. Second Disanalogy: Fundamental Explanatory Facts

But although the fictionalist might in some cases be able to provide a non-mathematical account of the fundamental relations holding between the non-mathematical objects posited by our theories, which explains why the mathematically stated versions of those theories should be predictively successful, the fact remains that, unless Field's nominalization project can be completed, we will lack such explanations in general. Perhaps, then, the realist's requirement to avoid explanatory coincidences will apply against the fictionalist after all. Recall the difference between the realist's attitude to the ether theory and our current theory of electrons. The realist says that we need not believe in the ether, because we have an explanation of why the observable phenomena agree (to the extent that they do) with our ether theory, that does not assume the existence of the ether. On the other hand, *if we do not assume that there are electrons*, the only explanation we have of the agreement of observation with our electron theory must put that agreement down to coincidence. Since we should try to explain at least those regularities that are not taken to be fundamental wherever possible, and since the existence of objects satisfying our theory of electrons would explain the agreement of observation with theory, we ought to believe in electrons.

Similarly, then, the realist might say, since we have an explanation of *why* the observable regularities conform (to the extent that they do) with our Newtonian gravitational theory that does not assume that the mathematical objects posited by that theory exist, the requirement that we provide explanations wherever possible of regularities that are not taken to be fundamental does not, in *this* case, give us reason to believe in the mathematical objects posited by our Newtonian gravitational theory. On the other hand, though, for a mathematically stated empirical theory such as our theory of quantum mechanics, where we do not have an underlying *non-mathematical* theory of non-mathematical objects that can be used to explain why it is that the observable regularities are as that theory predicts them to be, it appears that our *only* available explanation of why the observable regularities accord with the theory is just that our theory is *true*. It looks, then, as if we are faced with a stark choice, between positing a *coincidence* to account for the agreement between theory and observation, or supposing that the agreement is a result of the truth of our background theory.

In response to this objection, the fictionalist may question whether the realist's own proposed explanation of the predictive success of a mathematically stated empirical theory in terms of its truth really *explains* why it is that the observable regularities accord with the predictions of that theory. Certainly, if we have reason to believe that such a theory is true, then we will have reason to expect its predictions to be borne out (just as, if we have reason to believe that such a theory is nominalistically adequate, or empirically adequate, we will have reason to expect its predictions to be borne out). But can the realist claim that it is *because* such a theory is true that it is predictively successful? Such a theory will propose various relations to hold between mathematical and non-mathematical objects, on the basis of which conclusions can be drawn about the behaviour of its non-mathematical objects. Do we have reason to think that it is *because* the proposed relations *do* in fact hold between the theory's mathematical and non-mathematical posits that the non-mathematical objects the theory posits behave in the way they do?

It is not at all clear that we should generally be able to explain the behaviour of non-mathematical objects as resulting from their relations to mathematical objects in this way.[6] For why, we might ask, should the behaviour of *non-mathematical* objects be governed by (acausal) relations that hold between those objects and causally isolated mathematical objects? Certainly, if there are all the mathematical objects supposed to exist by our set theory with non-mathematical urelements, then facts about *non-mathematical* objects will make it the case that certain *mathematical* objects exist and are related to each other in various ways. But it would surely get things the wrong way around to suppose that it is *because* there is an

---

[6] This is not to say that mathematical *posits* are not present in our best formulations of some genuine explanations of empirical phenomena—as we will see in sect. 9.3.

isomorphism between the set of fingers on my left hand and the set of fingers on my right that I can match up my fingers one to one. If (with the scientific realist) we think that we are in possession of a *true* theory of the relations between mathematical and non-mathematical objects, then we can certainly expect this theory to agree with observation. But, if we want an *explanation* of why such a theory agrees with observation, it looks as though we will need an explanation of *why* the non-mathematical objects are such as to make *that* theory true.

A second disanalogy with the realist's case against constructive empiricism, then, is that while it looks as though any explanation a *realist* might wish to give of the agreement of observable regularities with the predictions of a given theory would probably appeal to more fundamental relations holding between unobservable physical objects, it is not likewise the case that the kinds of explanation the realist will wish to give of the agreement of observable regularities with the predictions of such a theory would similarly appeal to more fundamental relations holding between its mathematical objects. As we noted in the previous subsection, in cases where we *do* offer explanations of the agreement of observation with the predictions of a mathematically stated empirical theory, these explanations do *not* posit the relations that theory supposes to hold between its mathematical and non-mathematical posits as fundamental, but, rather, suggests that our theory that supposes that such relations hold is successful because it respects some more fundamental relations between non-mathematical objects that do indeed obtain. And when we have *no* such non-mathematical explanation of the agreement of observations with the predictions of a mathematically stated empirical theory, *explaining* this agreement in terms of its correctness in its claims about the relations between mathematical and non-mathematical objects seems out of the question, for the hypothesis that a theory of that sort should be *true* is in as least as much need of explanation as the hypothesis that it should reliably yield true predictions.

9.2.3. Third Disanalogy: Theory Construction

At the start of the previous subsection we presented two options for an account of why it is that the mathematically stated empirical theories we have could be predictively successful, to be used in cases where we do not have non-mathematical alternatives to the mathematical theories we make use of. In such cases, it was suggested that *either* we should view the predictive success of such theories as resulting from their truth, *or* alternatively, we should account for this success as a happy coincidence. We have now suggested that the first explanatory option is not available, even to *realists*, since, even if we do believe in mathematical objects, the fact that the kinds of theory we have of the relations between mathematical and non-mathematical objects could be *true* is in as much need of explanation as the fact that such theories could have true empirical predictions. Since we do not think that the non-mathematical objects posited by our theories are the way they are *because* of their relations to the various mathematical objects our theories posit to exist, but rather, that the relations our theories suppose to hold between their mathematical and non-mathematical objects hold (if they do) *because* of the way things are with non-mathematical objects, even *realists* will need to answer the question of what it is about *non-mathematical* objects that ensures that our theories that concern the relations of these objects to mathematical objects are good ones. So (even on the realist's hypothesis, according to which there are all the mathematical objects required to exist for our mathematically stated empirical theories to be true), although the assumption that our mathematically stated empirical theories are true allows us to predict that they will be empirically successful, the fact that they are true (if it is a fact) cannot be the *reason* why they are successful.

Does this mean that realists and fictionalists alike lack *any* kind of explanation of the predictive success of our mathematically stated scientific theories, such that they can only put this success down to a cosmic coincidence? I do not think so. For the fictionalist at least will wish to say that such theories are predictively successful because their claims about the relations that hold between the mathematical and non-mathematical objects they posit are indeed *fictional'* on the supposition that non-mathematical objects can be collected into sets satisfying the axioms of our preferred version of set theory with non-mathematical urelements. If these claims *are* fictional under this supposition, then they will respect whatever fundamental relations in fact obtain between their non-mathematical objects. So if we wish to explain the success of our mathematically stated empirical theories by saying that they preserve the fundamental *non-mathematical* relations that in fact hold between their non-mathematical objects, we can give such an explanation even if we lack a non-mathematical story of those non-mathematical relations. Our explanation can just be that those theories are successful because they are fictional (and thus because their nominalistic content is true).[7]

Is this not just the same as the constructive empiricist citing her belief in the empirical adequacy of our theories to explain their success? Not at all, and here we have one final disanalogy between our version of fictionalism and constructive empiricism. While the constructive empiricist has no account of why the kinds of theory we find ourselves with could be expected to be empirically adequate without also being true, the fictionalist has an account of the nature of scientific theorizing, and of theory construction, according to which we should *expect* that, over time, we would develop nominalistically adequate theories. For, unlike the constructive empiricist, who thinks that the hypotheses of our empirical theories concerning unobservables might be mere fictions but has no account of how such fictions are to be generated (or of why it is that adopting such fictional representations might be expected to be useful), our mathematical fictionalist has been able to identify (in the axioms of set theory with urelements) generative hypotheses of a fiction, and to show how adopting such hypotheses might turn out to be useful in representing how things are taken to be with non-mathematical objects. Furthermore, the fictionalist has suggested that our scientific practice of theory construction involves the generation of (indirectly expressed) hypotheses concerning what is fictional in this game. So, to the extent that we test and refine our theoretical assumptions, we can be thought of as indirectly testing and refining our account of what's fictional against the supposition of the axioms of set theory with non-mathematical urelements (a backdrop supposition that, it should be noted, *by itself* places no restrictions on non-mathematical urelements, so cannot itself be tested against experience).[8] The reason, then,

---

[7] Note that if fictionalists can give such an explanation of the success of our mathematical theories, realists can too.

[8] Is it safe to assume this much (i.e. that set theory with non-mathematical objects as urelements is entirely neutral about the question of what non-mathematical objects there are and what they are like)? What about Melia's discussion (considered in Ch. 8) of the added *regions* implied to exist when we add set theory with non-mathematical urelements to our theory of mereology? Does this not show that the generative assumption that whatever non-mathematical objects there are can be collected into sets places restrictions on what non-mathematical objects there are, since, by allowing for the existence of arbitrary sets of non-mathematical atoms, it also allows for the existence of arbitrary mereological sums of non-mathematical atoms? No, for it is not the generative assumption of the axioms of set theory with urelements that implies the existence of such regions, but rather, these axioms *taken together with the assumption that*, for every set-theoretically defined predicate ϕ, there is a region containing all the non-mathematical objects that satisfy ϕs. If we do not think that there are such regions, we should not

that the *fictionalist* has for believing the theories we have to be genuinely fictional (and therefore good representations of their non-mathematical objects) is just that our empirical methods of testing are set up to test the fictionality of our empirical hypotheses, such that, if these hypotheses fail, then we will formulate alternative accounts of what is fictional in our make-believe.

9.3. Can Fictionalism Account for the Explanatory Power of Our Mathematical Hypotheses?

In the previous section, I argued that the truth of our theoretical claims about the relations between mathematical and non-mathematical objects cannot be what ultimately accounts for the predictive successes of our theories, since the reason non-mathematical objects are the way they are cannot be because of the relations that hold between those objects and mathematical objects. Rather, I have suggested, the order of explanation should be the other way round: even if we suppose that there *are* all the mathematical objects supposed to exist by our set theory with non-mathematical urelements, then the reason some of those mathematical objects are the way *they* are (for example, the reason that certain sets of non-mathematical urelements exist) is surely a result of how things are with the non-mathematical objects. So, even the platonist, who believes that non-mathematical objects *do* indeed form the basic members of sets satisfying the axioms of our favoured set theory with urelements, will have to concede that it is *how things are with the non-mathematical objects* that ultimately explains why it is that, if two theories agree on the axioms of our set theory with urelements, one collection of theoretical claims about the relations between mathematical and non-mathematical objects, rather than another, might be true.[9]

---

hypothesize this additional assumption to be *fictional*. Our set theory with urelements just provides a background framework against which such hypotheses can be considered.

[9] Incidentally, it is interesting to note here that the fact that applications of mathematics require us to have theories that relate mathematical to non-mathematical objects (such as set theory with non-mathematical objects with urelements) means that realists cannot maintain that *all* mathematical objects are necessarily existent. For, although *some* mathematical objects will, on the realists' hypothesis, exist in all possible worlds (the *pure* sets will), if we allow contingently existing objects to be the

But hold on a minute! Does this mean that we cannot appeal to any (purported) facts about mathematical objects in our explanations of non-mathematical phenomena? And if so, wouldn't this violate our naturalistic commitment to preserve the explanations standardly viewed as explanatory by scientists? For surely there *are* cases where we do appeal to theoretical hypotheses concerning mathematical objects and the relations that hold between mathematical and non-mathematical objects in our explanations of non-mathematical phenomena? Thus, we might explain why we can't share ten sweets evenly between three people by pointing to the mathematical fact that 3 is not a factor of 10; we might explain why we cannot, with ruler and compasses alone, construct a square with the same area as a given circle by pointing to the mathematical fact that π is transcendental; and so on. And, at least prima facie, all of these are *good* explanations of the phenomena to be explained. So if the fictionalist cannot view such explanations as genuinely *explanatory*, then it looks like fictionalism will fall foul of our naturalistic commitment to account for our ordinary scientific practices (including our ordinary *explanatory* practices) as rational.

One response to this worry would be to deny that any of these purported explanations of non-mathematical phenomena which appeal, in their explanans, to mathematical objects and their properties are genuine explanations. We might, for example, follow Field in suggesting that such apparent mathematical explanations of non-mathematical phenomena are just place holders for the more fundamental *non-mathematical* explanations that can be provided from the perspective of our alternative, nominalistically statable mathematical theories. This, however, will not be the route I wish to take, not least because I have already suggested (in Ch. 5), that part of the *value* of introducing theoretical fictions might be that they allow for tractable explanations of real phenomena.[10] A literally believed description of non-mathematical objects and their relations might simply obscure aspects of their behaviour that are best represented by imagining them to be related in certain ways to mathematical objects. So, for example, although

members of sets (as we surely must if we wish to apply mathematics), then what impure sets there are will vary between worlds.

[10] Thus, for example, we suggested that viewing various real fluids as all similar, in certain respects, to the continuous ideal fluids of fictional models may allow us to explain similarities in their behaviour in spite of their differences at the molecular level. The *explanation* of fluid behaviour in that case was a good one to the extent that the *pretence* that there are continuous ideal fluids resembling real fluids in certain respects was itself a good one.

we *can* find a nominalistically stated alternative to the mathematically stated explanation of our inability to share ten sweets evenly between three people,[11] our *best* (graspable; tractable) explanation of this fact might well be the one that is expressed in mathematical terms. Furthermore, given that we are supposing that the hypothesis that there are mathematical objects satisfying the axioms of set theory with non-mathematical objects as urelements might provide us with an *indispensable* way of representing how things are taken to be with non-mathematical objects, there might well be cases of mathematical explanations of non-mathematical phenomena where we have no alternative non-mathematical account available which could even count as a *candidate* explanation of the phenomena in question.

Rather than try to avoid giving mathematical explanations of non-mathematical phenomena, then, I propose to embrace such explanations as sometimes genuinely *explanatory*. But how can this be squared with my claim that it is not *because* of their relations to mathematical objects that non-mathematical objects are the way they are? The key to reconciling these two claims (that there can be genuine mathematical explanations of non-mathematical phenomena and yet that it is not *because* of the relations between non-mathematical and mathematical objects that the non-mathematical phenomena are the way they are) is to consider what it is that makes mathematical explanations of non-mathematical phenomena explanatory. For, if such explanations can be *explanatory* without also being *true*, then although these explanations posit relations between mathematical and non-mathematical objects in their explanans, it may not be the *truth* of these hypotheses that is doing the explanatory work. And in this case, even though our explanations of non-mathematical phenomena in mathematical terms appear to appeal to facts about mathematical objects and the relations that hold between mathematical and non-mathematical objects, it is perhaps plausible that it is not the existence of such facts about mathematical objects and their relations with non-mathematical objects that is doing the explanatory work.

I have been suggesting that the value of including mathematically stated hypotheses in our empirical theories might not be because these hypotheses are *true*, but might instead be because, in the context of the *pretence* that there

---

[11] For, we can simply list all the alternative ways of sharing out the sweets, showing that in each case either one sweet will remain or one person will have more than another.

are sets satisfying the axioms of our favoured set theory with urelements, such hypotheses can be used indirectly to represent non-mathematical objects as being they way they would have to be in order to make our utterances *fictional*. Can the same be said in the special case of theoretical explanations? That is, could it be that the *reason* that a given mathematical explanation of a non-mathematical phenomenon is a good one is not that the mathematical utterances that make up its explanans are *true*, but rather that they are *fictional* in our make-believe of set theory with non-mathematical objects as urelements? I would like to suggest that it could be. Just as the explanatory value of appeals to ideal objects in ideal models is plausibly not a result of the *existence* of such objects, but is rather a result of the aptness of the *pretence* that such objects resemble really existing objects in certain respects, so, I will claim, the explanatory value of appeals to mathematical objects is plausibly not a result of the *existence* of such objects, but rather a result of the aptness of the *pretence* that such objects are related to non-mathematical objects in the ways our 'explanations' suppose.

To make this case, it will be useful to consider an example of a mathematical explanation of a non-mathematical phenomenon that has been held to show that, if we do not believe in the mathematical objects posited by our empirical theories, we suffer a loss of explanatory power. Several such examples have been suggested by Mark Colyvan and Alan Baker (see Colyvan 2001: 45–53, 2002, 2007; Baker 2005), in response to anti-realists about mathematics, such as myself and Melia, who have suggested that the value of positing mathematical hypotheses is *just* to provide us with a means to *represent* how things are with non-mathematical objects. Melia makes the supposed contrast between mathematical and non-mathematical posits clear when he claims that, while electrons and quarks play a role in *explaining* observable phenomena, 'nobody thinks that the numbers explain why certain bodies stand in the distance relations they do'. Rather, Melia (1998: 70–1) asserts, the utility of positing mathematical objects is just that 'the mathematics is used simply in order to make more things sayable about concrete objects. And it scarcely seems like a good reason to accept objects into our ontology simply because quantifying over such objects allows us to express more things.'

By finding examples of mathematical *explanations* of non-mathematical phenomena, Colyvan and Baker have hoped to show that mathematics is being used as more than a tool for *representing* how things are with non-mathematical objects. As Colyvan (2007) puts it, 'mathematics may contribute directly to explanations in science. If this is right, then mathematics is more than a *mere* representational tool.' When, for example, we account for the impossibility of circle-squaring by noting that π is transcendental, it seems that the mathematics, Colyvan (ibid.) suggests, 'is not only modelling, but also *explaining* the impossibility of certain physical activities.' My proposed response to such examples, then, is to claim that *even though* we posit mathematical objects in the context of our best explanations of empirical phenomena, the role that mathematical posits play in these explanations is just the same as the role they play in any theoretical representations of empirical phenomena. That is, what makes the mathematical explanations *good* explanations is not that their mathematical hypotheses are true of a realm of really existing mathematical objects, but rather, that they allow for good *representations* of the non-mathematical objects they model.

Consider, then, Alan Baker's favoured example of a mathematical explanation of a non-mathematical phenomenon.[12] Baker (2005) takes the example of periodical *Magicicada* cicadas. These North American insects appear cyclically, every thirteen or seventeen years (depending on the geographical area). Why, one might ask, periods of these lengths? Part of the explanation is the impact of environmental conditions on gestation period: the insect pupae are buried underground and will take longer to develop in the colder northern climates than in warmer southern states. This explains the differing lengths, and why the gestation period is relatively long. But it does not explain why the periods are the precise lengths they are. As Baker points out, part of the explanation evolutionary biologists give for this fact is that the cicadas have evolved to avoid overlapping with *other* periodical creatures. And it follows from some simple mathematical results that prime periods will minimize overlaps with nearby periods. So it looks as if a fact about prime numbers is used here to explain why it is advantageous for the cicadas to have the period lengths they have.

If we wish to account for the explanatoriness of this explanation from a fictionalist perspective, then, we will need to show that this explanation

---

[12] Although Baker is a mathematical realist, who thinks that there are genuine mathematical explanations of non-mathematical phenomena, he has some worries about some of Colyvan's examples of such explanations (both concerning whether they are really *mathematical*, and whether they are really *explanatory* of phenomena that had independently been observed to exist). Given these worries, it is worth focusing on Baker's example as the best that the realist has come up with.

is still explanatory even if we view its explanans as *merely* fictional in the game of set theory with non-mathematical urelements. In order to see how this could be, we will need to fill out some more details of the form of the proposed explanation. First of all, we can note that in the context of the generative hypothesis of set theory with urelements, we can define a natural number system as any ordered triple $\langle \mathbb{N}, 0, S \rangle$, where $\mathbb{N}$ is a set, $0 \in \mathbb{N}$; $S : \mathbb{N} \to \mathbb{N}$, satisfying the Dedekind–Peano axioms. Definitions of the individual numbers, addition and multiplication, primeness, and so on can be given relative to any natural number system. And in the light of these definitions, any *theorems* about prime numbers, for example, will apply to the primes of any natural number system. In particular, the relevant theorems for the explanation of the primeness of period lengths, Baker's

> Lemma 1: the lowest common multiple of m and n is maximal if and only if m and n are coprime.

and

> Lemma 2: a number, m, is coprime with each number $n > 2m$, $n \neq m$ if and only if m is prime.

which together imply that, for a given prime p, and for any pair of numbers m and n both less than p, the lcm of p and m is greater than the lcm of n and m, can be proved to hold of any natural number system.

How, then, are these lemmas used to draw conclusions about the appearance of cicadas? Well, the theorem is applied to the *years* in which cicadas appear, with years being *numbered*, starting from some arbitrarily chosen starting point (a year in which cicadas appear). A fictionalist about *mathematical* objects can happily be realist about time and periods of time, so 'years' as periods of time can be accepted into our ontology. Note also that there is nothing to stop the fictionalist about mathematical objects believing in temporal succession, such that years can be related by a relation 'immediately follows', which is such that for any year a, there is a unique year 'the year after a', which immediately follows a.[13] Now,

---

[13] At least, this will be so unless a is somehow at the end of time, or at the end of earth time if we are defining years as calendar years—this case requires a slight modification, but nothing too problematic.

we can pick one such year a, in the evolutionary history of cicadas, in which cicadas and some other periodical creatures all appear. Then this will be followed by years 'the year after a', 'the year after the year after a', 'the year after the year after the year after a', . . . , for very many (if not infinitely many) iterations of the operator 'the year after'. On our assumption that whatever non-mathematical objects we accept there to be can be collected into *sets*, there will be a set A containing all of these years and nothing else. Now either (it is fictional that) this set is finite or it is infinite, depending on whether (in fact) the sequence of years goes on for ever. Suppose for simplicity that A is infinite.[14] Then consider the set-theoretic relation R defined on $A \times A$ by $\langle x, y \rangle \in R$ iff y immediately follows x. Since we have said that the relation that holds between years y and x iff y immediately follows x picks out a unique y for any x, our set-theoretic relation R will be a *function* from $A \rightarrow A$, which can be written $Rx = y$. Furthermore, since we know that, if it is both the case that y immediately follows x and y immediately follows z, then $x = z$, this function will be 1–1. And finally, since all the years in the set A are either a or the year after the year after . . . the year after a, for finitely many iterations of the operator 'the year after', this function will be *onto* the set $A - \{a\}$. In short, the set $\langle A, a, R \rangle$ will be a natural number system. So theorems about natural number systems will apply to this set.[15]

   The set-theoretic setting then allows us to represent, mathematically, facts about the appearance of cicadas and other periodical creatures. For we can now label the successive years $0, 1, 2, \ldots$, such that, if some cicadas appear in year 0 and then next in year c, the fact that these are periodical creatures can be represented in the set-theoretic setting by saying that they appear in all and only the years cn for $n \in \mathbb{N}$.[16] Furthermore, if another periodical creature appears in year 0 and again in year d, these can be

<hr>

[14] The finite case is more complicated, but not significantly different—see n. 15

[15] Suppose, on the other hand, that A is finite. Then there is some final year 'the year after the year after . . . the year after a'. Pick any natural number system $\langle \mathbb{N}, 0, S \rangle$, where $\mathbb{N} \cap A = \emptyset$, and define R on $(A \cup \mathbb{N}) \times (A \cup \mathbb{N})$ by xRy iff (a) $x, y \in A$ and y immediately follows x; or (b) $x, y, \in \mathbb{N}$, and $Sx = y$; or (c) $x \in A$ and $\neg \exists z(z$ immediately follows $x)$, and $y = 0$. Then $\langle (A \cup \mathbb{N}), a, R \rangle$ will be a natural number system, with A an initial segment of this natural number system.

[16] Of course, this is an idealization: the cicadas won't go on appearing *forever*, but this (inessential) simplifying idealization won't get us into any trouble. If we wished to be more realistic, we could put some upper bound b on the years in which cicadas appear, such that we only hypothesize that they appear in every year cn where $cn < b$.

represented as appearing in years dn for $n \in \mathbb{N}$. Suppose (as the evolutionary biologists do) that there are many periodical creatures of differing length period all appearing in our chosen year 0,[17] and suppose further (as is also hypothesized by evolutionary biologists) that cicadas do badly in years where they overlap with other periodical creatures. Then over time the cicadas that overlap least with other periodical creatures will stand most chance of surviving. But since a creature with period c will overlap with a creature with period d in years cn after year 0 where $cn = dm$ for some m, the cicadas with periods that maximize their lowest common multiple with the periods of other periodic creatures will suffer fewest overlaps. In particular, then, Baker's two lemmas apply to show that creatures with prime number periods will do best.

What is it that makes this a *good* explanation? That the succession of years starting from a and related by the relation 'x immediately follows y' *does* form a set that satisfies the Dedekind–Peano axioms (with a suitably defined set-theoretic relation R and with a playing the role of 0)? Or only that these years and this relation are such as to make it *fictional*, against the backdrop generative hypotheses of set theory with non-mathematical urelements, that the *set* of years together with suitably defined R and 0 satisfy the axioms? The fictionalist will say only the latter: it is only because our *modelling* of the succession of years as a set with a set-theoretic relation satisfying the Dedekind–Peano axioms is an *apt* one, only because it *respects* facts about the years and their succession, that our explanation of the behaviour of cicadas in terms of facts about prime numbers is a good one. It is because the structure of the sequence of years *is respected* in the set-theoretic setting, and in particular because the years in which cicadas appear *are mirrored* by years labelled (in this setting) by cn, that our mathematical argument about what facts *about c* make for an advantageous length period is a good one. A fictionalist, then, will claim that, although we appeal to mathematical objects (sets; set-theoretically defined relations; natural number systems as kinds of sets) in our *explanation* of the behaviour of the cicadas, it is just that our mathematical model is a *good* one, just that it respects fundamental facts about the succession of years and about the cicadas, that it allows for a good explanation of cicada behaviour. *Facts* about various sets and natural number systems need not come into it:

---

[17] This year is thus some hypothesized point in the early history of the cicadas.

the *fictionality* of our mathematical representation of the non-mathematical phenomena will suffice for our mathematical explanation to be explanatory.

9.4. Fictionalism and Phase Space Theories

Our anti-realist version of fictionalism can, then, account for the predictive and explanatory successes of our mathematically stated scientific theories. I have argued that the nature of scientific theorizing gives us reason to expect the kinds of theories we have to be nominalistically adequate, since the fictionality of our theoretical hypotheses, in the context of the generative assumptions of set theory with non-mathematical urelements, is constantly put to the test in the context of our scientific theorizing. And I have argued that the explanatoriness of our explanations given in mathematical terms is preserved if we simply adopt the hypothesis that those explanations are nominalistically adequate, and not that they are true. In providing an account of the successes of our scientific theories, fictionalism has an advantage over constructive empiricism, which lacks an explanation of why the kinds of theories we have developed should be expected to be empirically adequate if they are not correct in their picture of their unobservable physical posits, and which lacks a compelling account of why *causal* explanations can be preserved as genuinely *explanatory* if we do not believe in the causal processes posited. Mathematical fictionalism therefore emerges as a more plausible alternative to realism as an account of the success of empirical science.

My final concern in this chapter, however, is with some issues specific to mathematical fictionalism, which may undermine the fictionalist's claim to be able to account for our successful scientific practices. In particular, can the anti-realist version of fictionalism I have been developing deal with the problems we found with Field's scientific realist version of the view?

The main difficulty we found with Field's version of fictionalism was that Field was committed to finding literally believed 'underlying' empirical theories that our mathematically stated theories conservatively extend. As we saw in sect. 3.3, this presents something of a problem for nominalizing our *current* theories, since these theories appear to make stronger assumptions about space and time than scientists take to be warranted (for example, by modelling space-time as continuous), and indeed to make literally false assumptions for the purpose of simplification (for example, by using continuous functions to model properties such as temperature). We allowed Field (with Quine) the option of viewing our best current theories as imperfect approximations of some final, perfectly literal theory (with Field betting that, once merely convenient idealizations were ironed out, the final theory could be nominalized, and Quine betting that it couldn't), but even with this concession,[18] Field's commitment to finding literally true underlying theories remained problematic when one considered the prevalence of phase space theories in contemporary science. For, the fundamental non-mathematical subject matter of these theories appeared to consist of *possibilia*, or other objects (such as propositions) equally problematic for anyone attracted to nominalism.

In presenting my own version of fictionalism, I have at various points simplified matters by assuming (as Field does) that in presenting our scientific theories against the backdrop of set theory with urelements, we are using our mathematical posits to build fictional models of a literally believed content. In fact, however, our discussion of models and idealizations in science shows that things are much more complicated than this. Having recognized the ubiquity of models and idealizations in scientific theorizing, it should be clear that our mathematically stated hypotheses are themselves most often applied, not directly to actual objects, but indirectly to the ideal objects of ideal models (e.g. truly continuous fluids in truly continuous space-time), which are then held to resemble the real world in important respects. As Mary S. Morgan and Margaret Morrison (1999) contend, models are needed to act as *mediators* between theory and world (in Cartwright's (1983) terms, our mathematically stated theories are applied to *prepared descriptions* of the phenomena, rather than to the phenomena themselves).

Allowing in this way for *layers* of representatively useful fictions, we avoid the difficulty of having to accept the truth of implausible or unwarranted assumptions concerning the fundamental nature of the actual world. Instead, we can accept that the application of mathematics itself often requires us to make strictly false, or at least unwarranted, idealizing assumptions about the phenomena to which our mathematics is ultimately being applied. In the

---

[18] Which might, at any rate, be over-generous, given the ambitions of Field's nominalization project. For example, if we did not posit that space-time is structured like $\mathbb{R}^4$, it would be very difficult to get anything like the representation theorems Field's programme needs.

case of theories that use continuum mathematics to model space-time, for example, we can view the picture they paint of physical space as continuous as itself a convenient idealization, following physicists in remaining agnostic about the actual fundamental nature of space-time. And in the case of phase space theories, we may similarly wish to view the notion of a phase space, modelled mathematically, as a convenient fiction for representing, for example, fundamentally modal facts about the possible trajectories of real systems of objects. The question of which of our theoretical posits are to be taken to be *merely* ideal, and which correspond to actual objects in the world, will as ever come down to how we can explain the success of our use of those posits in our theorizing. Such explanations are beyond the scope of this book, as our interest is in the mathematical posits of our scientific theories. I will simply note that, by viewing our theories as consisting of layers of representatively useful, and, indeed, sometimes essential fictional models we may accept that the *pretence* that there are possibilia might be representatively essential without concluding that we ought to believe in such objects as possible dynamic states.

The fictionalist hypothesis developed in this book can, then, account for the predictive and explanatory successes of our mathematically stated scientific theories, without following Field in attempting to provide a literally believed, underlying non-mathematical theory of the non-mathematical realm. We have accepted that adopting the pretence that there are mathematical objects may be essential in formulating tractable, explanatory scientific theories, and likewise that further uses of pretence, for example in the form of the ideal objects of ideal models, may be similarly essential. To discover, amongst these layers of idealizations, which objects we are committed to believing in, we must consider how we can explain the success of our theorizing. I have suggested that, while we can explain the success of the mathematical assumptions of our theories from a perspective that does not assume that there are any distinctively mathematical objects, we cannot similarly explain the success of many of our theoretical assumptions concerning unobservable physical objects without assuming that at least some such objects exist (for example, to act as causes in causal explanations). So I conclude that, while scientific realists are right that their view provides a more plausible explanation of the success of science than does constructive empiricism, they are wrong in thinking that realism provides a better explanation of this success than does any anti-realist view of science. Mathematical fictionalism has at least as good an explanation of the success of our mathematically stated scientific theories (and, in providing in some cases intrinsic *non-mathematical* explanations of these successes, arguably does better than does scientific realism in accounting for why our mathematically stated theories should reliably get things right about the non-mathematical world).

10

Conclusion

I have argued that nothing in our best mathematical and scientific practices provides us with reason to believe that there are mathematical objects. In the case of pure mathematics, this was argued directly and briefly: I claimed that we can make sense of our pure mathematical practices on the assumption that our main purpose in developing pure mathematical theories is in uncovering the *consequences* of the assumption that there are objects satisfying various mathematical *concepts*, without concern for whether that assumption is itself true. The main focus of this book, though, has been on the use we make of mathematics in empirical science, and on the question of whether our use of mathematics there provides us reason to believe the mathematical hypotheses that we utilize. My argumentative strategy has been first to question the assumption of confirmational holism, according to which the mere presence of a hypothesis in a successful empirical theory provides us with a reason to believe that hypothesis. I claimed that this holism was not borne out by a naturalistic look at our best scientific practices, where it appears that the question of whether a theoretical hypothesis ought to be considered to be confirmed by our theoretical successes is held to be a rather more complex matter. In particular, given that it is often recognized that literally false hypotheses can lead to tractable theories (even in the case of our *best* empirical theories), the question of whether we have reason to believe a given theoretical hypothesis is closely tied up with the question of whether our best reflective understanding of the contribution of that hypothesis to our theoretical successes requires us to assume that that hypothesis is true.

In the case of mathematics, then, the question of whether mathematical hypotheses are confirmed by their presence in our successful scientific theories should be answered by appeal to an account of how it is that mathematical hypotheses can contribute to our theoretical successes. Here

I argued that a fictionalist account of the role of mathematical hypotheses was possible, which viewed those hypotheses as literally false but useful means of representing how things are taken to be with non-mathematical objects. In particular, if we take the axioms of our favourite version of set theory with urelements to be generative of a make-believe according to which non-mathematical objects can be the members of sets (and therefore can stand in various set-theoretical relations to further sets), we can provide an account of how participating in such a game of make-believe can provide us with a useful means of representing hypotheses concerning non-mathematical objects and their relations. By arguing that our ordinary scientific practices can be accounted for on the basis of this fictionalist view of the role of mathematical hypotheses in our empirical theories, my aim has been to establish that nothing in our reflective understanding of the role mathematically stated hypotheses play in our empirical theories requires us to take those hypotheses to be *true* rather than merely *fictional*.

In this final chapter, I wish just to tie up some loose ends, and to consider some implications of my claim that the success of our empirical theories does not confirm the truth of their mathematically stated hypotheses. In particular, given that I have stressed that my response to the indispensability argument involves rejecting confirmational holism, I would like briefly to consider whether my fictionalist account of the role of mathematics in empirical science is able to respond to an alternative version of the indispensability argument, which does not rely so closely on holism. Having dealt with this question, I will turn to the question of whether, by arguing that nothing in our empirical scientific practices provides us with reason to believe that there *are* any mathematical objects, I am able to establish any more than just *agnosticism* concerning the existence of mathematical objects. Does the plausibility of my fictionalist account of the role of mathematics in empirical science provide any positive reason to deny the existence of mathematical objects, viewing those theoretical hypotheses whose truth would require the existence of such objects as literally *false*? And, finally, I will consider an important sense in which the account I have given of the role of mathematics in empirical science is, while broadly *naturalistic*, nevertheless profoundly un-*Quinean*. For, by viewing the truth of the mathematically stated hypotheses of our scientific theories as *unconfirmed* by their role in those theories, there is a sense in which my own fictionalist view of mathematics preserves something of the intuition that the mathematical framework within which we describe and organize our experience is *analytic*.

10.1. An Alternative Indispensability Argument

The original indispensability argument as presented in Chapter 1 included confirmational holism as a premise. And in arguing against this premise, I hoped to make room for the possibility that the mathematical hypotheses of our scientific theories are not confirmed by our theoretical successes. But Michael D. Resnik has argued that there is a version of the indispensability argument that does not depend on confirmational holism. This *Pragmatic Indispensability Argument* claims that we need to assume the truth of mathematics in doing science *even if* we do not believe that our scientific theories are themselves true. Given that my discussion of the role of mathematics in science has so far been aimed against the confirmational version of the indispensability argument, it is worth considering at this point how the account I have been defending of the applications of mathematics fares as a response to Resnik's alternative argument.

Resnik's (1995: 169–70) Pragmatic Indispensability Argument is:

1) In stating its laws and conducting its derivations science assumes the existence of many mathematical objects and the truth of much mathematics. 2) These assumptions are indispensable to the pursuit of science; moreover, many of the important conclusions drawn from and within science could not be drawn without taking mathematical claims to be true. 3) So we are justified in drawing conclusions from and within science only if we are justified in taking the mathematics used in science to be true.[1]

Resnik's point is that, even if we do not *believe* the hypotheses of our empirical scientific theories, we do believe them to be *meaningful*, and to have genuine *consequences*. Scientific practice surely requires us to believe this much, since in order to discover whether we have reason to believe that a theoretical hypothesis is true, we need to be able to understand that hypothesis and to draw out its empirical consequences. But it is,

---

[1] Actually, this is just Part 1 of Resnik's 'Pragmatic' indispensability argument. Part 2 aims to establish that we are indeed justified in drawing conclusions from and within science. Clearly naturalists must accept Part 2 of the argument.

Resnik thinks, just the existence of the *mathematical* objects that we posit to exist in formulating scientific laws that ensures that those laws are *meaningful*, if not true (hence the importance of the fact, pointed to in premise 1, that the existence of mathematical objects is assumed in stating scientific laws). And it is, Resnik thinks, just the existence of those mathematical objects required by our *derivations* that ensures that we are justified in our claims about the consequences of our scientific theories.

As concerns the first point, that we need to assume the existence of mathematical objects in order to make sense of our empirical hypotheses (even if we do not believe those hypotheses to be true), this point is already present in Putnam's (1975: 74) discussion of scientific laws, when he asks not just how laws such as the law of universal gravitation can be true if there are no mathematical objects, but also, 'how can such a statement have any objective content at all if numbers and "associations" (i.e. functions) are alike mere fictions?' On this point, then, our response to Resnik should just be to reiterate our response to Putnam. We have presented an account of how merely fictional hypotheses can be used to talk about real-worldly *props*, such that the 'objective content' of a hypothesis presented in the context of a fiction is just the content expressed by the claim that the props are such as to make that hypothesis fictional in the game. In the case of mathematical hypotheses, the objective content of a hypothesis presented in the context of the generative assumption that the axioms of set theory with non-mathematical objects as urelements are true, is just that the *non-mathematical* objects are such as to make that hypothesis fictional. So although we may need to use mathematical hypotheses to formulate any of our candidate *empirical* hypotheses, this does not require us to believe that those hypotheses are true.

Resnik's second point concerns the logic of science: his claim is that we are required to assume that there are mathematical objects in our derivations of consequences of (perhaps false) empirical assumptions. In particular, according to Resnik (1995: 172),

we can construe scientists as employing mathematics as their 'underlying logic' to establish claims of the form 'if X is a (possibly idealized) physical situation of type I, then law L holds for X'. These claims are truths of applied mathematics, which can then be deployed to describe features of models that are based upon the physical statements contained in their antecedents.

Regarding this point, we should note that the kinds of 'truths' of applied mathematics that these claims require are just truths of the form $\Box(I \supset L)$, that is, truths concerning the consequences of our theoretical hypotheses. And, as we said in our discussion of uses of mathematics that involved finding (possibly idealized) physical models of mathematical systems, so long as we are confident that our mathematical derivation of L from I does establish that L is a logical consequence of I, these uses of mathematics provide no problems for a fictionalist view of mathematics. For the statement of the logical implication, $\Box(I \supset L)$, does not posit any specifically mathematical objects, and neither does the application of that implication to a (possibly idealized) physical situation X.

Indeed, Resnik recognizes this point, noting that we might account for such applications of mathematics in empirical arguments as on a par with arguments by analogy. Thus, Resnik (ibid.: 173) acknowledges,

We might reduce some of our mathematical assumptions by extending Nancy Cartwright's approach to science and take mathematical models as stories and scientific prediction and explanation as inference by analogy. You need not believe that *The Simpsons* is true to follow an explanation that goes 'the dog my daughter left with us is driving us crazy; he is just like the dog on *The Simpsons*'.

But this, Resnik thinks, does not completely avoid the problem that we have to assume the existence of at least some mathematical objects in accounting for such uses of mathematics in drawing out empirical predictions. For, in order for this account to work, we will need to assume that the hypotheses of our fictional theories are *consistent*, and to draw conclusions about the consequences of these hypotheses. And, Resnik (ibid.) claims, 'Stating and proving that various stories have these properties will require a background mathematics.' Thus, if by the consistency of a mathematical theory we mean that our mathematical assumptions have a model, the claim that our fictional hypotheses are consistent will amount to a claim about the existence of sets. Alternatively, if by consistency we mean that there is no derivation of a contradiction from our theoretical assumptions, the claim that our fictional hypotheses are consistent will amount to a claim about (presumably abstract) derivations. And either way, the *arguments* we give to establish the consistency of our fictional hypotheses will themselves be largely mathematical, and hence will assume the existence of some mathematical objects.

At the root of this part of Resnik's pragmatic indispensability argument is, then, the argument we considered in sect. 4.3.3, from the indispensability of mathematical assumptions in metalogue to the truth of those assumptions. So in responding to this point, we can simply reiterate the counterargument we made there (which was taken from Hartry Field's (1984) nominalistic account of logical knowledge). First of all, I argued that mathematics is dispensable to the *statement* of hypotheses concerning logical consistency (and the various other logical properties that are definable in terms of logical consistency). For rather than *define* consistency in terms of models and derivations, we should allow that there are primitive modal truths, and therefore accept into our language a primitive modal sentential operator '$\Diamond$' to express these truths (where '$\Diamond P$' is read as 'it is logically consistent that P'). Our reasonable use of various mathematical theories in justifying our claims concerning the applicability of this operator can then be shown to require only the assumption that those theories are themselves consistent, not that they are true. Of course, the acceptance of primitive modal facts will be baulked at by some nominalists. But it strikes me, as it does Field, that we have more reason to believe that our experience of the world (in conjunction with our grasp, through its inferential role, of the meaning of the '$\Diamond$' operator) can give us some knowledge of what is logically consistent, than we have to believe that that experience gives us knowledge of the existence of abstract mathematical objects. After all, our experience gives us knowledge of truths, and it is part of the meaning of logical consistency that, if it is true that P, it is also logically consistent that P.

10.2. Anti-Platonism or Agnosticism?

I have presented a view of the mathematically stated hypotheses of our empirical theories that sees these hypotheses as representatively useful fictions. And I have argued that such a view can make sense of our ordinary scientific practices, such that it would not be unreasonable for one who adopts the fictionalist's proposed attitude to our mathematically stated scientific theories, believing just that they are correct in their representation of their non-mathematical objects and not that they are true, to remain an immersed participant in our ordinary scientific activity. Thus, for example,

I argued that viewing our mathematically stated empirical hypotheses as representatively useful fictions does not detract from the reasonableness of our expectation that the mathematically stated theories that we have will yield true predictions. And viewing our mathematically stated empirical hypotheses as representatively useful fictions does not detract from our ability to appeal to those hypotheses in our explanations of empirical phenomena. In short, a reflective understanding of the role of mathematics in our scientific practices does not rule out the possibility that our fictionalist hypothesis is correct, and that, therefore, it is not *true* that (for example) there is a real number M_a which represents the mass of an object a as a multiple of some unit mass, but merely *fictional* in the context of a make-believe that this is so.

In rejecting confirmational holism, I argued that we should look instead to our best reflective understanding of the role of various theoretical posits in our scientific theories in order to discover whether the existence of the objects posited is confirmed by our theoretical successes. I argued that a reflective understanding of the role of our mathematical posits does not rule out our viewing these as merely representatively useful fictions. If this is correct, then we have shown, as against the claims of defenders of the indispensability argument, that a broadly naturalistic or non-sceptical approach to empirical science does not *require* us to be realists. But what I have not, so far, argued is that our reflective understanding of the role of mathematical hypotheses in our theories *rules out* taking a realist attitude to those hypotheses, and viewing them as assertions of truths about the relations between really existing mathematical and non-mathematical objects. And if mathematical platonism is not ruled out by our understanding of the role of mathematics in empirical science, then it looks as though the most we can conclude is that adopting a broadly naturalistic approach to ontological questions requires us to be *agnostic* about the question of whether there are any mathematical objects.

In so far as my interest has been in rejecting the claim that a naturalistic approach to science requires us to be platonists, it would perhaps be reasonable to stop there. But in fact I think that we can go further than this, and hold that, if we can account for our successful scientific practices *without* assuming that our mathematically stated empirical theories assert truths about mathematical objects, then this provides us with a positive reason to *reject* the claim that there are any mathematical objects. For, although we cannot conclusively *prove* that there are no mathematical objects, and although our uses of mathematics are *consistent* with the possibility that there are mathematical objects satisfying the existentially quantified claims of our mathematically stated empirical theories, adopting our ordinary scientific standards of inquiry surely requires us to adopt the principle of Ockham's razor, according to which we ought not to multiply entities beyond necessity. Thus I feel justified in following Field (1989: 45) in moving beyond mere agnosticism and concluding that we are justified in denying the existence of mathematical objects:

> Admittedly, we can't have *direct evidence* against mathematical entities. We also can't have direct evidence against the hypothesis that there are little green people living inside electrons and that are in principle undiscoverable to human beings; but it seems to me undue epistemological caution to maintain agnosticism rather than flat out disbelief about such an idle hypothesis. I think that platonism has seemed a plausible position because it has been assumed that the existence of mathematical entities is *not* an idle hypothesis. But if it can be shown that the hypothesis is dispensable without loss (in explanations, in descriptions of our observations, in accounts of metalogic, and so on), then I think it natural to go beyond agnosticism and assert that mathematical entities do not exist.

Thus, I conclude, adopting a naturalistic trust of our ordinary scientific methods of confirmation requires us to reject the existence of mathematical objects.[2]

10.3. Reviving a Dogma

A final consequence of my argument that I would like to draw out is the extent to which, despite my Quinean starting points, the conclusion we have come to is profoundly *un*-Quinean. For, my argument

---

[2] Those familiar with Mark Balaguer's (1998) discussion of platonism and anti-platonism in mathematics will perhaps find this conclusion rather hasty. Balaguer argues against the use of Ockham's razor in deciding between platonism and fictionalism, since he argues that Ockham's razor can only be applied to decide between alternative explanations of a shared core of facts. And since fictionalists and platonists disagree about the very facts that need explaining (since they disagree about whether the mathematically stated hypotheses of our scientific theories state facts) they lack the shared agreement that would allow for the application of Ockham's razor. But since the facts *I* have been suggesting that fictionalism provides the means to explain are not the disputed facts concerning whether there are mathematical objects, but rather, facts about our successful scientific practices (for example, facts such as 'Supposing that *P* has led to the successful prediction *Q*'), I think that I am safe in assuming that fictionalism and platonism can be compared as competing explanations of this common core of facts.

against confirmational holism has ultimately involved reviving a distinction between *merely* practical, and genuinely *evidential* reasons to speak as if S is true. So while I accept Quine's view that it is theories as a whole that face the tribunal of sense experience, I do not accept that it is the *truth* of these theories as a whole that is confirmed by their success when put to the test, but rather, that in the case of our mathematically stated empirical hypotheses, it is their status as *fictional* in the context of a make-believe that is tested. But the claim that what is confirmed when we make use of mathematically stated empirical hypotheses is just the *fictionality* of those hypotheses (in the context of the 'make-believe' generated by the axioms of set theory with non-mathematical objects as urelements) brings us very close to a revival of a notion of truth *by convention*. For viewing the axioms of our set theory as *generative* of a make-believe, such that those axioms are themselves not subject to revision (except to the extent that we decide an alternative make-believe would be more fruitful) is surely very close to a restoration of the idea that those axioms are to be viewed as true by fiat. Should we conclude, then, that this book amounts to a revival of the claim that the axioms of our mathematical theories are *analytic*, or true *by definition*?

   In a sense, this is what I have been arguing, except with the important caveat that I do not think that we can *define* objects into being. Mathematical hypotheses, on my view, are best thought of not as truths by convention (for they do not have the status of *truths*), but rather, as conventionally adopted useful fictions. But it is certainly the case that the motivating force behind my response to Quine has all along been the thought that there is something wrong with his claim that the mathematical hypotheses of our scientific theories are in the same boat, confirmationally speaking, as the rest. And so the restoration of a special place for mathematics in empirical science is something I am happy to defend, even though I would baulk at putting this special status down to the *analyticity* of mathematics, since I am enough of an empiricist to think that if we do not have empirical evidence for the *truth* of mathematical claims, then we cannot claim to have evidence for their *analyticity* (or truth by definition) either.[3]

---

[3] In fact, in her recent study of conventionalism, Yemima Ben-Menahem (2006) argues that the label 'truth by convention' is a misnomer, and that conventionalists such as Carnap actually sought to expose apparent necessary truths as mere conventions. If this is right, then the view developed here appears quite close to the Carnapian view of so-called analytic 'truths'.

While we might well, then, find it indispensable in our empirical theorizing to adopt a mathematical framework in order to provide (in Melia's terms) a 'necessary scaffolding' against which our empirical hypotheses can be framed, our indispensable reliance on mathematics in characterizing and defining empirical concepts perhaps tells us more about the requirements of theorizing than the truth of the mathematical hypotheses we assume. But to see that what is practically essential does not always bear much relation to what is true, we need only look to C. S. Peirce's lament: 'I do not admit that indispensability is any ground of belief. It may be indispensable that I should have $500 in the bank—because I have given checks to that amount. But I have never found that the indispensability directly affected my balance, in the least' (CP 2.113, 1901; see Hartshorne and Weiss 1932). We are fortunate, then, that while the falsity of Peirce's indispensable hypothesis leads to financial ruin, the falsity of our own indispensable hypothesis that there are mathematical objects makes no difference to our ability to theorize as we ever have done.

References

Anderson, A. R., Marcus, R. B., and Martin R. M. (eds.) (1974), *The Logical Enterprise*, Yale University Press, New Haven.

Ayer, A. J. (1936), *Language, Truth and Logic*, (1947) 2nd edn., Penguin, London.

Azzouni, J. (1994), *Metaphysical Myths, Mathematical Practice: The Ontology and Epistemology of the Exact Sciences*, Cambridge University Press, Cambridge.

—— (1998), 'On "On what there is" ', *Pacific Philosophical Quarterly* 79: 1–18.

—— (2004), *Deflating Existential Consequence: A Case for Nominalism*, Oxford University Press, Oxford.

Baker, A. (2003), 'Does the existence of mathematical objects make a difference?', *Australasian Journal of Philosophy* 81(2): 246–64.

—— (2005), 'Are there genuine mathematical explanations of physical phenomena?', *Mind* 114: 223–38.

Balaguer, M. (1996), 'Towards a nominalization of quantum mechanics', *Mind* 105(418): 209–26.

—— (1998), *Platonism and Anti-Platonism in Mathematics*, Oxford University Press, Oxford.

—— (2001), 'A theory of mathematical correctness and mathematical truth', *Pacific Philosophical Quarterly* 82: 87–114.

Batchelor, G. K. (1967), *An Introduction to Fluid Dynamics*, Cambridge University Press, Cambridge.

Begg, D. (2003), *Economics*, 7th edn., McGraw-Hill, London.

Ben Menahem, Y. (2006), *Conventionalism*, Cambridge University Press, Cambridge.

Benacerraf, P. (1965), 'What numbers could not be', *Philosophical Review* 74: 47–73.

—— and Putnam, H. (eds.) (1983), *Philosophy of Mathematics: Selected Readings*, 2nd edn., Cambridge University Press, Cambridge.

Black, M. (ed.) (1965), *Frege's Theory of Number*, Cornell University Press, Ithaca, New York.

Boolos, G. (1984), 'To be is to be the value of a variable (or some values of some variables)', *Journal of Philosophy* 81: 430–50.

—— (1997), 'Is Hume's principle analytic?', in Heck (1997), 245–61.

Brown, J. R. (1982), 'The miracle of science', *Philosophical Quarterly* 32: 232–44.

Burgess, J. P. (2004), 'Mathematics and *Bleak House*', *Philosophia Mathematica* 12(1): 18–36.

Burgess, J. P. and Rosen, G. (1997), *A Subject with No Object*, Clarendon Press, Oxford.

Carnap, R. (1950), 'Empiricism, semantics and ontology', *Revue Internationale de Philosophie* 4: 20–40. Rev. and repr. in Carnap (1956), 205–21.

—— (1956), *Meaning and Necessity: A Study in Semantics and Modal Logic*, 2nd edn., University of Chicago Press, Chicago.

Cartwright, N. (1983), *How the Laws of Physics Lie*, Oxford University Press, Oxford.

—— (1999), *The Dappled World*, Cambridge University Press, Cambridge.

Cellucci, C., and Gillies, D. (eds.) (2005), *Mathematical Reasoning and Heuristics*, King's College Publications, London,

Colyvan, M. (2001), *The Indispensability of Mathematics*, Oxford University Press, Oxford.

—— (2002), 'Mathematics and aesthetic considerations in science', *Mind* 111: 69–74.

—— (2007), 'Mathematical recreation versus mathematical knowledge', in Leng et al. (2007), 109–22.

Comte, A. (1953), *The Positivist Philosophy*, John Chapman, London, ii.

Cornwell, S. (1992), 'Counterfactuals and the applications of mathematics', *Philosophical Studies* 66: 73–87.

Davies, P. (1989), *The New Physics*, Cambridge University Press, Cambridge.

Dedekind, R. (1888), 'Was sind und was sollen die Zahlen?' Repr. in Dedekind (1930–2), iii. 335–91.

—— (1901*a*), *Essays on the Theory of Numbers*, Open Court, Chicago.

—— (1901*b*), 'The nature and meaning of numbers', in Dedekind (1901*a*), 29–115; English trans. of Dedekind (1888).

—— (1930–2), *Gesammelte Mathematische Wereke*, Viewag, Braunschweig, i–iii.

Dieterle, J. M. (1999), 'Mathematical, astrological, and theological naturalism', *Philosophia Mathematica* 7: 129–35.

Dummett, M. (1963), 'Realism', in Dummett (1978), 145–65.

—— (1978), *Truth and Other Enigmas*, Harvard University Press, Cambridge, Massachusetts.

Ellis, B. (1990), *Truth and Objectivity*, Basil Blackwell, Oxford.

Feferman, S. (1992), 'Why a little bit goes a long way: logical foundations of scientifically applicable mathematics', *PSA: Proceedings of the Biennial Meeting of the Philosophy of Science Association* 2: 442–55.

Feynman, R. (1965), *The Character of a Physical Law*, Cox & Wyman, London.

Field, H. (1980), *Science Without Numbers: A Defence of Nominalism*, Princeton University Press, Princeton, New Jersey.

—— (1984), 'Is mathematical knowledge just logical knowledge?', *Philosophical Review* 93: 509–52. Repr. with a postscript in Field (1989), 79–124.

—— (1985), 'On conservativeness and incompleteness', *Journal of Philosophy* 81: 239–60. Repr. with a postscript in Field (1989), 125–46.

—— (1989), *Realism, Mathematics, and Modality*, Blackwell, Oxford.

—— (1991), 'Metalogic and modality', *Philosophical Studies* 62: 1–22.

—— (1998), 'Mathematical objectivity and mathematical objects', in MacDonald and Laurence (1998), 387–403.

Fine, A. (1984), 'The natural ontological attitude', in Leplin (1984), 83–7.

Frege, G. (1967), *The Basic Laws of Arithmetic*, University of California Press, Berkeley. Trans. M. Furth.

Fricke, M. (ed.) (1986), *Essays in Honour of Bob Durant*, Otago University Philosophy Department, Dunedin.

Gabriel, G., Hermes, H., Kambartel, F., Thiel, C., and Veraat, A. (eds.) (1980), *Gottlob Frege: Philosophical and Mathematical Correspondence*, University of Chicago Press, Chicago. Abridged from the German edn. by Brian McGuinness.

Giere, R. N. (1988), *Explaining Science*, University of Chicago Press, Chicago.

—— (2004), 'How models are used to represent reality', *Philosophy of Science* 71: 742–52.

Gödel, K. (1947), 'What is Cantor's continuum problem?', *American Mathematical Monthly* 54: 515–25. Rev. and expanded version (1963), repr. in Benacerraf and Putnam (1983), 470–85.

Hacking, I. (1983), *Representing and Intervening*, Cambridge University Press, Cambridge.

Hahn, L. E., and Schilpp, P. A. (eds.) (1986), *The Philosophy of W. V. Quine*, Library of Living Philosophers 18, Open Court Publishing Company, La Salle, Illinois.

Hartshorne, C., and Weiss, P. (eds.) (1932), *The Collected Papers of Charles Sanders Peirce*, Harvard University Press, Cambridge, Massachusetts, i–ii.

Heck, R. J. Jr. (ed.) (1997), *Language, Thought, and Logic: Essays in Honour of Michael Dummett*, Oxford University Press, Oxford.

Hempel, C. G. (1945), 'On the nature of mathematical truth', *American Mathematical Monthly* 52: 543–56. Repr. in Benacerraf and Putnam (1983), 377–93.

Hesse, M. (1963), *Models and Analogies in Science*, Sheed and Ward, London.

Horgan, T. (1987), 'Discussion: science nominalized properly', *Philosophy of Science* 54: 281–2.

Horwich, P. (1991), 'On the nature and norms of theoretical commitment', *Philosophy of Science* 58: 1–14.

Hughes, R. I. G. (1989), *The Structure and Interpretation of Quantum Mechanics*, Harvard University Press, Cambridge, Massachusetts.

Irvine, A. (1990), *Physicalism in Mathematics*, Kluwer, Dordrecht.

Isham, C. (1989), 'Quantum gravity', in Davies (1989), 70–93.

Kalderon, M. E. (ed.) (2005), *Fictionalism in Metaphysics*, Oxford University Press, Oxford.

Kreisel, G. (1967), 'Informal rigour and completeness proofs', in Lakatos (1967), 138–71.

Lakatos, I. (ed.) (1967), *Problems in the Philosophy of Mathematics*, North-Holland, Amsterdam.

Leng, M. (2005a), 'Mathematical explanation', in Cellucci and Gillies (2005), 167–89.

—— (2005b), 'Platonism and anti-platonism: why worry?', *International Studies in the Philosophy of Science* 19(1): 65–84.

—— (2005c), 'Revolutionary fictionalism: a call to arms', *Philosophia Mathematica* 13(3): 277–93.

—— (2007), 'What's there to know? A fictionalist account of mathematical knowledge', in Leng et al. (2007), 84–108.

—— Paseau, A., and Potter, M. (2007), *Mathematical Knowledge*, Oxford University Press, Oxford.

Leplin, J. (ed.) (1984), *Scientific Realism*, University of California Press, Berkeley.

Lewis, D. (1986), *On the Plurality of Worlds*, Blackwell, Oxford.

—— (1991), *Parts of Classes*, Oxford University Press, Oxford.

Lyon, A., and Colyvan, M. (2008), 'The explanatory power of phase spaces', *Philosophia Mathematica* 16(2): 227–43.

MacDonald, C., and Laurence, S. (eds.) (1998), *Contemporary Readings in the Foundations of Metaphysics*, Blackwell, Oxford.

McMullin, E. (1985), 'Galilean idealization', *Studies in the History and Philosophy of Science* 16: 247–73.

Maddy, P. (1990), *Realism in Mathematics*, Clarenden Press, Oxford.

—— (1992), 'Indispensability and practice', *The Journal of Philosophy* 89: 275–89.

—— (1995), 'Naturalism and ontology', *Philosophia Mathematica* 3: 248–70.

—— (1997), *Naturalism in Mathematics*, Clarendon Press, Oxford.

Malament, D. (1982), 'Review of *Science Without Numbers: A Defense of Nominalism*', *Journal of Philosophy* 79: 523–34.

Melia, J. (1995), 'On what there's not', *Analysis* 55: 223–9.

—— (1998), 'Field's programme: some interference', *Analysis* 58: 63–71.

—— (2000), 'Weaseling away the indispensability argument', *Mind* 109: 455–79.

Misak, C. J. (1991), *Truth and the End of Inquiry*, Clarendon Press, Oxford.

Morgan, M. S., and Morrison, M. (1999), *Models as Mediators: Perspectives on Natural and Social Science*, Cambridge University Press, Cambridge.

Musgrave, A. (1986), 'Arithmetical platonism: is Wright wrong or must Field yield?', in Fricke (1986), 90–110.

Parsons, C. (1965), 'Frege's theory of number', in Black (1965), 180–203.

—— (1979–80), 'Mathematical intuition', *Proceedings of the Aristotelian Society* 80: 145–68.

—— (1983*a*), *Mathematics and Philosophy*, Cornell University Press, Ithaca, NY.

—— (1983*b*), 'Quine on the philosophy of mathematics'. First pub. in Parsons (1983*a*), repr. in Hahn and Schilpp (1986), 370–95.

Parsons, T. (1980), *Nonexistent Objects*, Yale University Press, New Haven, Connecticut.

Peressini, A. (1999), 'Confirming mathematical theories: an ontologically agnostic stance', *Synthese* 118: 257–77.

Potter, M. (2007), 'What is the problem of mathematical knowledge?', in Leng et al. (2007), 16–32.

Putnam, H. (1971), *Philosophy of Logic*, Harper & Row, New York. Repr. in Putnam (1979), 323–57.

—— (1975), 'What is mathematical truth?', *Historia Mathematica* 2: 529–43. Repr. in Putnam (1979), 60–78.

—— (1979), *Philosophical Papers, i. Mathematics, Matter and Method*, 2nd edn., Cambridge University Press, Cambridge.

Quine, W. V. (1939), 'A logistical approach to the ontological problem'. Scheduled to be published in the *Journal of Unified Sciences* in 1939, this paper first appeared in Quine (1966), 64–9.

—— (1948), 'On what there is', *Review of Metaphysics* 2. Repr. in Quine (1961), 1–19.

—— (1951), 'Two dogmas of empiricism', *Philosophical Review* 60: 20–43. Rev. and repr. in Quine (1961), 20–46.

—— (1957), 'The scope and language of science', *British Journal for the Philosophy of Science*. Repr. in Quine (1966), 215–32.

—— (1960), *Word and Object*, MIT Press, Cambridge, Massachusetts.

—— (1961), *From a Logical Point of View*, 2nd edn. Harvard University Press, Cambridge, Massachusetts.

—— (1966), *The Ways of Paradox and Other Essays*, Random House, New York.

—— (1969*a*), 'Ontological relativity', in Quine (1969*b*), 26–68.

—— (1969*b*), *Ontological Relativity and Other Essays*, Columbia University Press, New York and London.

—— (1969*c*), 'Speaking of objects', in Quine (1969*b*), 1–25.

—— (1970), *Philosophy of Logic*, 2nd edn. (1986), Harvard University Press, Cambridge, Massachusetts.

—— (1975), 'Five milestones of empiricism'. Repr. in Quine (1981*a*), 67–72.

—— (1978), 'Goodman's Ways of Worldmaking', *New York Review of Books*. Repr. in Quine (1981*a*), 96–9.

—— (1981*a*), *Theories and Things*, Harvard, Cambridge, Massachusetts.

—— (1981*b*), 'Things and their place in theories', in Quine (1981*a*), 1–23.

Quine, W. V. (1986), 'Reply to Charles Parsons', in Hahn and Schilpp (1986), 396–403.

Resnik, M. D. (1995), 'Scientific vs. mathematical realism: the indispensability argument', *Philosophia Mathematica* 3: 166–74.

Rosen, G. (1994), 'What is constructive empiricism?', *Philosophical Studies* 74: 143–78.

—— (1999), 'Review of Penelope Maddy, *Naturalism in Mathematics*', *British Journal for the Philosophy of Science* 50: 467–74.

Rudolph, E., and Stamatescn, I.-O. (eds.) (1994), *Philosophy, Mathematics and Modern Physics*, Springer-Verlag, Berlin.

Russell, B. (1901), 'Recent work on the principles of mathematics', *International Monthly* 4: 83–101.

Scheibe, E. (1994), 'On the mathematical overdetermination of physics', in Rudolph and Stamatescu (1994), 186–99.

Shalkowski, S. (1994), 'The ontological ground of the alethic modality', *Philosophical Review* 103: 669–88.

Shapiro, S. (1983), 'Conservativeness and incompleteness', *Journal of Philosophy* 80(9): 521–31.

—— (1991), *Foundations without Foundationalism*, Oxford University Press, Oxford.

—— (1997), *Philosophy of Mathematics: Structure and Ontology*, Oxford University Press, Oxford.

Sklar, L. (2003), 'Dappled theories in a uniform world', *Philosophy of Science* 70: 424–41.

Smart, J. J. C. (1963), *Philosophy and Scientific Realism*, Routledge & Kegan Paul, London.

Sober, E. (1993), 'Mathematics and indispensability', *Philosophical Review* 102: 35–57.

Urquhart, A. (1990), 'The logic of physical theory', in Irvine (1990), 145–54.

van Fraassen, B. (1974), 'Platonism's Pyrrhic victory', in Anderson, Marcus, and Martin (1974), 39–50.

—— (1980), *The Scientific Image*, Clarendon Press, Oxford.

van Inwagen, P. (1977), 'Creatures of fiction', *American Philosophical Quarterly* 24: 299–308. Repr. in van Inwagen (2001), 37–56.

—— (1998), 'Meta-ontology', *Erkenntnis* 48: 233–50.

—— (2001), *Ontology, Identity, and Modality*, Cambridge University Press, Cambridge.

Vineberg, S. (1996), 'Confirmation and the indispensability of mathematics to science', *Philosophy of Science* 63: S256–S263.

Walton, K. L. (1978), 'Fearing fictions', *Journal of Philosophy* 75(1): 5–27.

—— (1990), *Mimesis as Make-Believe*, Harvard University Press, Cambridge, Massachusetts.

—— (1993), 'Metaphor and prop oriented make-believe', *European Journal of Philosophy* 1: 39–57.

Wright, C. (1983), *Frege's Conception of Numbers as Objects*, Aberdeen University Press, Aberdeen.

—— (1997), 'On the philosophical significance of Frege's theorem', in Heck (1997), 201–44.

Yablo, S. (1998), 'Does ontology rest on a mistake?', *Aristotelian Society, Suppl.* 72: 229–61.

—— (2005), 'The myth of the seven', in Kalderon (2005), 88–115.

Index

Lightning Source UK Ltd.
Milton Keynes UK
UKOW06f0729190315

248135UK00002B/5/P